The Templar
Treasure
at Gisors

The Templar
Treasure
at Gisors

JEAN MARKALE

Inner Traditions
Rochester, Vermont

Inner Traditions International
One Park Street
Rochester, Vermont 05767
www.InnerTraditions.com

Originally published in French under the title *Gisors et L'Énigme des Templiers*
by Éditions Pygmalion/Gérard Watelet, Paris

Library of Congress Cataloging-in-Publication Data

Markale, Jean.
  [Gisors et l'enigme des Templiers. English]
  The Templar treasure at Gisors / Jean Markale.
      p. cm.
  Originally published under title: Gisors et l'enigme des Templiers.
  Paris : Pygmalion/G. Watelet, c1986.
  Includes index.
  ISBN 0-89281-972-3 (pbk.)
  1. Templars—France—Gisors—History. I. Title.
  CR4755.F8 G576 2003
  271'.7913044242—dc21
                            2002154468

Printed and bound in the United States at Lake Book Manufacturing, Inc.

10 9 8 7 6 5 4 3 2 1

Text design by Peri Champine and layout by Priscilla Baker
This book was typeset in Berkeley

Inner Traditions wishes to express its appreciation for assistance given by the government of France through the Ministère de la Culture in the preparation of this translation.

Nous tenons à exprimer nos plus vifs remerciements au gouvernement de la France et
le ministère de la Culture pour leur aide dans la préparation de cette traduction.

Contents

Part 1

The Sites

1

The Shadow of Gisors

FOR AS FAR BACK AS I CAN REMEMBER, no matter what horizon greeted my eyes, I have always felt a strange and somewhat ambiguous connection to Gisors and the Epte Valley, though they are not in my native region and I have no personal ties to them. In fact, it was only when I was twenty years of age that I first visited there. Yet, the land-scape looked familiar to me, like one glimpsed in a childhood dream. It is the kind of countryside that eventually convinces a person he or she once lived there, perhaps even during a previous lifetime. But whatever the truth of the matter, the fact remains that Gisors, the Epte Valley, the whole of Vexin, nourished my imagination.

I have always trusted my instinct, a kind of innate understanding of mine that I unhesitatingly believe to be of Celtic origin. It allows a glimpse of profound realities that are otherwise distorted by the fog of appear-ances. In addition, because I believe in the omnipotence of the mind, I have always felt that my dreams could turn into realities. But for these dreams to be realized, I quickly learned, they must first be embodied and subjected to the play of matter or, in other words, appearance. Due to my rationalist upbringing, I have been loath to believe any proposition, small as it may be, if I have not verified the supports on which it is based.

This tendency is not a denial of the obscure forces of the uncon-scious; to the contrary, it gives them the means they need to act. So I asked myself why and how my mind roamed the large expanses of the Vexin in search of a zone of shadow somewhere along the sinuous course of the Epte or under the extravagant walls of Gisors. The truth is that in looking, we find.

An image emerged from the depths of my memory, an image that was not related to Gisors but to Saint-Clair-sur-Epte. This recollection involved a moronic illustration from a school textbook, a history of France for elementary school students. The picture showed the Norman chief Rollon paying homage to the king of France, Charles III, who was called "the Simple." The caption explained that the proud Norman, who was supposed to kiss the feet of his sovereign, did not want to debase himself by kneeling. So he simply grabbed the king's leg and lifted it to his mouth, thus causing the unfortunate Charles the Simple to tumble from his throne. Oh how the puerile images from our history books have left their mark on our imaginations! To this treatment—or ill treatment—of the Rollon episode is added another: one of an aged Charlemagne sitting in an armchair and sorrowfully looking out his palace window at a horde of frightful Normans in the process of pillaging and burning an abbey. Someday someone should do a rewrite of history based on these kinds of textbook images!

This depiction, however, was the point of departure for my dream of Gisors. You may see that it does not yet include the Templars, but instead, the Normans, who sweep forth from all horizons, preceded by their terrible reputation, which was nothing but a delusion, by the way, the Vikings being no more—or less—rapacious and cruel than the other so-called Christian peoples of that time. In truth, I strongly suspect that the editors of school textbooks from the beginning of the last century cleverly replaced the somewhat worn-out image of the bogeyman—too irrationally suspect—with the much more realistic one of the Men of the North. This, in short, is the earlier version of "the spy who came in from the cold." It clearly articulates that any birth of the personality, whether individual or collective, goes through a period of fearing "the other" or those who come from "the other side."

In this instance, the Epte Valley soon appeared to me as a frontier beyond which still lived the descendants of those dreadful Normans whose ravages I'd heard described. I strongly sensed that there had to be a fundamental difference between the French Vexin and the Norman Vexin and that Normandy was not like the Île-de-France, or even any other part of France. I knew that Normandy had long been English and, because the Normans had conquered England, I wondered if we could consider Normandy the cradle of the future nation of Great Britain.

This idea of a foreign land inside France took root inside me, all the more so because I constantly reminded myself that after having taken part in the conquest of the land of the cursed English, numerous Bretons—my ancestors—had been chased across the Channel from that island of their origin and thus had to settle in Armorica. The Normans subsequently became my allies, and the citadel of Gisors, forty-five miles from Paris, was the first milestone on the route to an imaginary land that I reconstructed following the promptings of my heart and every impulse that might inspire the nostalgic reveries of a young man who considers himself in exile.

Other elements, in particular the literature of the Middle Ages, came to reinforce for me the reality of this frontier. I quickly came to realize that the majority of ancient texts making up what was allegedly French medieval literature had been set down in Anglo-Norman, beginning with the famous *Chanson de Roland*. As for the novels of Britain—the tales from the Arthurian cycle, in other words—excepting those by Chrétien de Troyes, they were the work of Norman clerics whose allegiance was more or less pledged to the Plantagenet Henry II. These include Robert Wace's *Roman de Brut* (meaning the British); Beroul's *Tristan* as well as the work by Thomas of England, *Tristan's Madness*, from the Oxford manuscript; and the *Lais* by Marie de France, who, despite the indication of her name, was Anglo-Norman, probably a half sister of Henry II. To me, who felt more Breton than ever and increasingly proud of Breton traditions, it was obvious that the Normans could only be friends. Hadn't they contributed in striking fashion to the spread of Celtic legends in the world? I clearly owed it to them to take an interest in their history and literature, as well as their Roman and Gothic art.

Alas, I reached this conclusion during the time of the Second World War. Every day I would hear of tons of bombs being spilled from the skies over Norman towns. What would remain after these attacks? How many masterworks would be obliterated in torment? This could not help but increase my empathy for the land where—I knew this for a fact—the soul of the knights of olden days and the glory of the cathedral builders still resonated. On the other side of the Epte, the other side of the "frontier," an entire civilization was in danger of toppling into oblivion.

It was in 1948 that I visited Gisors for the first time. I had been carried out of the Parisian ambience on a train—in fact, on a model already obsolete at that time—winding its way through suburban gardens and emerging, after crossing the Oise River, onto the Vexin tablelands flooded with sunlight and a wind that, in my imagination, was already filled with great gusts from the sea.

Leaving the station, I had the sensation of being truly somewhere else, on the other side of a frontier I had finally managed to cross, despite the fact that the station was located on the left bank of the Epte, which is to say, on the French side. But in front of me was the imposing mass of the château of Gisors. I recalled having read somewhere the odd comment by French king Philip Augustus regarding this fortress. "I would like it if the walls were made of precious stones, that each rock were either gold or silver, on condition that no one knew of it but me." This statement by the young king is obviously a jest and it reveals the extent to which both England and France regarded the château of Gisors as an essential element in their political and military strategies. These words take on a curious resonance, however, when read in light of everything we know concerning the fabulous treasure of the Templars.

But in 1948 I knew nothing about this treasure and had not heard of the excavations undertaken by the castle's guardian. A most unlikely bus, the kind you hardly ever see anymore, carried me through the streets of the town. Traces of the war were still visible. Ruins testified to the 1940 German bombing that had destroyed the center of Gisors; the bare silhouette of the crippled church was painful to see. I had a fleeting vision of that terrible moment when death rained down from the airplanes bearing the black crosses, the sinister Stukas, whose dive-bombing maneuvers made an infernal caterwauling that echoed through the sky, for I too had directly experienced German bombing in 1940. I can easily recall my and my grandmother's wanderings on the roads of Lower Normandy during our headlong and totally inept flight to an inaccessible Brittany. Each time we heard the roar of the Stukas, we quickly dived into the nearest ditch. Their noise forever remains in my memory, like that of machine-gun fire and the sight of the black crosses piercing the wings of those nightmarish birds. It was only much later that I learned that the black crosses were those of the Teutonic Knights, rivals of the Knights Templar who had outlasted them.

During this July of my twentieth year, however, the sun was a beacon of hope and light. I quit the shadows of Gisors to immerse myself in the Norman Vexin, heading in the direction of the Lyon Forest, Bézu-Saint-Éloi, Étrépagny, Doudeauville, and finally Puchay, where people were expecting me. These were sedate landscapes where the harvests to come were beginning to take on the color of the bread baked, in ealier days, in the large ovens found in villages surrounded by tall hedges. In Puchay I saw the wooden porch of a little church whose type was characteristic of the Upper Normandy countryside. (I did not then know that the poet Louis Guillaume—another Breton exile who has since become a friend—resided in the village.) The trace of the Vikings was obvious there, although no one has yet succeeded in truly summoning back the shadow of these sailors from the north. Puchay, located in the middle of a plain now devoted to industrial farming, barely emerges from a sea of green. My first impression of it was that of an enclosed village from which flowers bloomed on all sides through the lattices of gardens and from beneath the walls of the houses.

Soon I found myself in a group of young people in one of those flower-covered houses, this one perpendicular to the street and extended by a garden opening out to the countryside. An old woman whose name I never learned but whom we called "grandmother" officiated in the kitchen, helped by a poor fellow named Jean who served as a jack-of-all-trades. The master of the house was a Franciscan. Father Marie-Bernard was a strange and remarkable man of Breton origin. I knew him by chance from other circumstances, but I never understood exactly what he did or what purpose he had in gathering us together from time to time in various houses in which, by virtue of some mysterious agreement, he held power over people and things. Not that it really mattered. I experienced some intense moments in the midst of this fraternal community that obeyed no rule but that of friendship. In the evening after dinner we gathered to exchange songs, memories, or stories, ranging from the most suggestive to the most serious-minded, before ending with a prayer and psalm in honor of the Virgin.

This is where I first heard mention of Gisors. I was told that not far from the church a Merovingian cemetery had been found containing precious objects. I was assured these objects had not been lost to the world at all. Generations of Gisors' inhabitants, it seemed, had recounted tales about a treasure guarded by the devil. Misfortune to anyone who would dare venture underground with the sole purpose of making off with the cursed treasure! He risked being swallowed forever by the flames of Hell. But there were other, more prosaic individuals who claimed there was no treasure, that beneath the château there was only an enormous gasoline tank that the Germans had built there during the Occupation in hopes that it would be safe from English bombings because the fortress of Gisors is a sacred and historic site to all the citizens of the United Kingdom. The story of the gas tank is authentic, and is one of the reasons a cement paving was laid, by ministerial order, in the courtyard of the château. Regarding anything of value lying beneath the fortress, however, though the name of the Templars was never pronounced, allusions to a treasure buried in the basement recurred constantly, mostly in the form of legend with numerous variations.

As for the underground areas, there was no attempt to keep them a secret. They were everywhere around Gisors. To listen to my friends, the Norman part of the Vexin was nothing but a large Swiss cheese of holes and mysterious corridors. There was no doubt about the actual existence of one between the château of Gisors and the Church of Saint-Gervais-Saint-Protais. It had been seen following the bombardments of the neighborhood in 1940, which revealed a number of previously un-discovered cavities. There was another between the château and the keep of Neaufles-Saint-Martin, which is quite logical because the fortress of Neaufles is much older than that of Gisors. The builders of Gisors came from Neaufles and it would have been surprising if they had not con-trived a connection between the two strong points of the Epte Valley's defense system. In addition, it was alleged there was a large paved un-derground passage (but what was this assertion based on?) that linked Gisors to the Château-sur-Epte, whose ruins facing Saint-Clair-sur-Epte can still be seen, as if they protect the entry to Normandy against those racing toward it on National Highway 14 from the direction of Rouen. The underground passageway that connects Gisors to Andelys, or to Château-Gaillard, to be more precise, could also be included on the list, though this was one I did not consider worthy of note, given the fact that Richard the Lion-Hearted had ordered Château-Gaillard constructed as a counterbalance for the loss of Gisors. But I was ready to accept subterranean chambers beneath the church of Bézu-Saint-Éloi and won-dered at the mysterious meaning of the extremely beautiful Neaufles cross near the passageway on that level.

I also enjoyed hearing about Mortemer. This Cistercian abbey where Henry I of England died of indigestion (ah, the famous Norman gas-tronomy!) was destroyed during the Revolution, but did not lack appeal now that it had been partially restored. Moreover, it did not lack for strange traditions. Inexplicable noises could be heard coming from it on certain evenings. During the First World War, an English driver encoun-tered the ghost of a monk there and gave such a detailed description of the spirit's clothing to the priest of Lyons-la-Forêt that the Father easily recognized it as twelfth-century Cistercian dress. There was also a White Lady who often came to wail under the château's windows on moonless nights, and it was not rare to witness, as it entered the church, a proces-sion of the monks massacred during the Revolution. We believed that if there was only time for an excavation to be undertaken, surely some-thing would be found—if not a treasure, then at least some documents. As you can see, we fantasized about this subject quite a bit.

This was partially because Father Marie-Bernard, who found great amusement in our sometimes ridiculous speculations, poured oil on the fire, if I dare say so, by preparing excellent hot toddies (a blend of water, sugar, and rum, which was then set alight) that increased our enthusiasm. The local boys in our company then talked wildly about what they had heard in the past either from family or friends who shared stories on similar evenings. The idea of secret underground passages, buried treasure that was cursed by the malefic powers that guarded it, and documents capable of upending the world became reality for us. And this was in 1948—in other words, a dozen years before the attention of the public at large was seriously drawn to the Templars' gold in Gisors. Our evenings in Puchay illustrated that at that time there really were questions about a hidden treasure in Gisors and there really were subterranean passages throughout the Vexin.

In this way, a land that had once haunted my imagination, that I knew only through my reading, became more familiar to me. My sojourn in Puchay allowed me to glimpse Gisors not only as the pivotal point of the Norman defense against France, but also as a kind of mysterious pole toward which cold lights converged, like those sometimes seen along the walls of cemeteries.

I once visited Mortemer with my friends and on the way we talked about the ghosts there or, more truthfully, we mocked them. On our return trip, our van broke down. A coincidence? I also visited Bézu-la-Forêt. It was at a time when I was beginning to take a serious interest in etymology and its name intrigued me. It was incontestably Celtic, but was its meaning "the birches," "the tombs" (this was the most likely meaning), or, as derived from the contraction of the ancient *albodunum,* the "white fortress"? Why should there be a "Bézu" in the Aude province—in Razès, to be precise—where the Templars settled under fairly mysterious circumstances?

This name Bézu bothered me even more when I found it repeated in Bézu-Saint-Éloi, right next to Gisors, which in turn shared part of its name with another parish in the region, the charming village of Bézancourt, located in the Lower Seine region (as it was called at that time). We all went there as well, in the same famous van, for the festival of St. Christopher, patron saint of the parish. As part of the festival there was the singing of High Mass, followed by a procession and the traditional benediction of vehicles. We were appointed to be the choir. The Bézancourt priest was a figure of public notoriety, for he and his maid lived openly as husband and wife and had a child together, whom they lovingly raised. The archbishop of Rouen had tried to remove this hardly scrupulous ecclesiastic, but the parishioners, who deeply loved their priest, opposed the archbishop ferociously. His relationship was nothing new, after all. Pope Clement IV, one of the protagonists in the Templar trial, had shamelessly pillaged the church coffers—which is to say, the pockets of the faithful—to subsidize the extravagant expenditures of his mistress, the beautiful Countess de la Marche. Though no one in Clement's time would have dared to speak about it, this priest's liaison was totally out in the open and his parishioners were not the least or last to knowingly provide for the needs of this strange family. During that time, I had not yet heard of Father Béranger Saunière, or even of a certain priest from Urufle who had been the talk of the town during the 1950s for the brutal murder of his pregnant mistress.

In any case, the Bézancourt priest had not found any treasure in any of the pillars in his church. He was a friendly, open man and both he and his "maid"—who was quite pretty—lived simply. I do not know what became of this clergyman, but since that time, I have been informed that St. Christopher never truly existed and was only a pious legend who performed miracles in the company of St. George, who, as it turns out, likewise did not exist. What I can say with certainty is that on that July day of 1948, the twenty-fifth to be exact, we sang our hearts out during High Mass and we all attended the traditional benediction.

There was something dignified and touching in this ceremony that the Church now considers a vestige of an unworthy superstition. But it is true that the Church has not yet reached the point of renouncing it entirely. And if I joke about a St. Christopher who never existed yet performed miracles, it is because I know it is necessary to see beyond the official versions spread *urbi et orbi* by figures who have abrogated infallible rights never claimed by the first apostles. We are all Christophers, or at least should all be carriers of Christ—not the Crucified One but the Anointed One—and thus inspire miracles that, rather than being supernatural acts, will become a part of everyday life.

That said, on this July 25, 1948, under the noonday sun as we returned to Puchay, the Vexin tablelands glowed with all their fires. A wind came up and swept the wheat as it swept waves of the sea. I loved this land. I loved this wind that brought me the first intimations of the ocean. I loved these paths that crossed through the middle of the fields; I could envision travelers from olden times making their way on foot toward the setting sun, carrying with them all their joys and sorrows. At every crossroads they would gather around a cross or a statue of St. Christopher, at that same spot where their Gallic ancestors worshiped the god of the double or triple face who protected those traveling toward distant lands. The Order of the Templars, I knew, had been created, at least officially, to protect the roads of pilgrimage to the Holy Land, and had subsequently overseen the great paths of communication linking all parts of Western Europe. But what did the Templars matter to me then? During the evening, we buried ourselves anew in our fantasies about who might find the buried treasure of Gisors, Bézu-Saint-Éloi, Neaufles, or even Mortemer. I have vivid memories of these too short hours; they are among the most cherished moments of my life.

I have often returned to Gisors, the Epte Valley, and the Vexin tablelands. Each time I have felt the same wonder, the same profound nostalgia, the same ferocious will to plunge deeper into the shadows that can be half glimpsed through the openings in the leaves.

This land appears more Celtic to me now than ever. It bears an inexplicable imprint from the dawn of time, a commingling of all civilizations that has been crystallized into a large mysterious halo. The Vexin was the territory of the Gallic people known as the Veliocassians, who merely established themselves in a region that had already been settled by earlier peoples. At the time of the Roman conquest, Vexin formed part of Belgian Gaul, as did everything north of the Seine. It was a region of transit, certainly, a part of the great plain of Northern Europe, a junction between the North Sea and the roads leading to the Atlantic coast, between the east and west running valleys and the English Channel, once known as the British Sea. It is a crossroads region where winds have blown from every direction and where, like a strange spinal column, the Roman Way (a paved Gallic path) from Lutece (Paris) to Rotomagnus (Rouen, the "plain of the wheel," or the "round plain") can sometimes be found beneath the foundations of Highway 14. It is a historical region where the Franks and Viking pirates met, followed by the kings of France with their vassals, and the Anglo-Norman kings. In the midst of all this, in a land divvied up by the Saint-Clair-sur-Epte Treaty of 911 c.e., the fortress of Gisors shines like a beacon coveted by all those who are caught in its luminous beam.

There were three different ways I could enter this privileged domain: from Chaumont-en-Vexin and Trie-Château (I have mentioned their French fortresses that overlook Gisors); from the direction of Magny-en-Vexin after a stopover at the Guiry-en-Vexin museum, which testifies to the ancient nature of this rural region; and by small lazy roads that wind through the charming valleys of Vexin in seeming isolation from the world. It was on this route that I discovered astounding village names like Haute-Souris, and one that led me to the banks of the Epte: Bray-Lû.

In Trie-Château I always made a kind of pilgrimage to the famous covered alley, somewhat out of the way but retaining intact that magnetic power that can be felt in every exceptional sacred construction. The alley is extremely well preserved and presents a relatively unique feature: The support that blocks the entrance—in opposition to its use—is pierced with a circular hole. Certainly there are other covered alleys in the Parisian region presenting this same feature—one can be found, for instance, at the Pontoise museum as well as in the old moat around the Museum of National Antiquities in Saint-Germain-en-Laye—but here in Trie-Château, the monument remains on its original site, which makes it all the more moving.

I must mention that on certain dates, even now, somewhat secret ceremonies and obscure initiation rituals take place there. If my informants are to be believed, the participants in these ceremonies have ties—

or at least claim to have ties—to the Templars. I cannot, however, suppress a smile at this. Initiation into what? Rituals that emerged from whose imagination? Syncretism ravaged the declining, if not rotting, final years of the twentieth century, during which the confusion of beliefs and values reached such heights that nothing could be recognized for what it once was. We know nothing of any secret Templar ritual—if there ever was one, which is far from being proved—for the good reason that it has remained secret. We know nothing, or almost nothing, of the religion of the megalith builders because no *legible* document has come down to us from their time stretching back to the second and third millennia B.C.

Some archaeologists have dubbed this hole in the support of the Trie-Château covered alley the Hole of the Soul, indicating the belief, perhaps, that the soul of the deceased interred within the covered alley could, after a certain period of time, leave the body and continue on to another world. It has been noted that there exist holes in a good number of the skulls found in megalithic monuments, obviously resulting from trepanning. Whether this was a surgical operation intended to heal a patient or a ritual trepanning performed on the deceased with a religious objective in mind, such as permitting the soul to escape from the cranium, no one can answer. It so happens that among the accusations lodged against the Templars and based more on myth than reality is one concerning the worship of an idol in the form of a head, the famous *baphomet*. The covered alley of Trie-Château will always hold a mystery for me, and long may it continue to do so.

When I arrived in the region around Gisors by way of Magny-en-Vexin, I never tired of admiring this market town's old houses and coaching inns from the time of the stagecoaches. Today these structures slumber, closed to the noisy world of motor vehicles that roar past them in scorn. For me they provided an entry into a past that gradually revealed itself as if I were turning the pages of a book no one else had ever read before. I continued on my path through Saint-Clair-sur-Epte, where the Roman choir of the cathedral took me further back in time to that fabulous image from my childhood of Rollon and Charles the Simple. It was a strange area where, still lurking, were the shadows of those who signed a treaty with such weighty consequences for Western European history.

Immediately upon leaving this village I found myself surrounded by factories that had been erected on the banks of the Epte in a spot bearing the name of Bordeaux-Saint-Clair, appropriately enough. [Bordeaux means "water's edge" in French. —*Trans.*] There is a level crossing nearby where the rails of a totally obsolete railroad lie rusting. This is the point of entrance into Normandy. On the hill overlooking the town the fortress of Château-sur-Epte stands—at least, what remains of it, including some fortifications and the keep crumbling in the midst of vegetation grown wild and certain parts of the buildings that have been used by local residents for agricultural purposes. It is truly a shame that this château has been left abandoned in this way, for it was one of the most beautiful in Normandy and one of the key pieces in the Norman defense system on the Epte frontier.

My favorite itinerary, however, took me through Bray-Lû. The miasma caused by the Parisian agglomeration was a distant memory by the time I reached the roads out of Meulan that wound alongside the hills through flower-filled valleys. Because no one at the time used plant-specific herbicides, there were poppies peeking through the wheat and daisies grew on the roadsides of routes that the truckers hadn't yet discovered. Entering Normandy, I was greeted by the fresh aroma of orchards and tucked-away vegetable gardens.

But I didn't linger long in the valley. I quickly followed the course of the Epte up to Aveny, climbing up the slope of the plateau in the direction of Dampsmesnil. Somewhat out of the way, in the midst of the copse on a sloping rise, there was a covered alley, which, although definitely less imposing and not as well preserved as the one in Trie-Château, was just as evocative of the mysticism and dark ages of prehistory. What is most striking about it is the carving depicting two woman's breasts and a necklace of several rows. This image is not unique to this spot and can be found on other megaliths in the area as well as inside some of the Neolithic caves in the Petit-Morin Valley, namely in Coizard. This kind of illustration, halfway between figurative and symbolic, is characteristic of dolmen art and can be compared to the carvings found on the supports of many of the monuments in Morbihan. The female form in Aveny has an obvious kinship with the famous idol "in the form of a cooking pot" of Pierre-Plates in Locmariaquer and with the goddess of the hair and necklace depicted several times in the mound on the isle of Gavrinis. She is most likely a funeral goddess, for the dolmens and covered alleys are tombs, but she also seems to be a deity of life, given the context and the flowering, decorative elements evoking the sea and plant life. An elaborate metaphysical thought may be inferred from this: Life and death are but two complementary aspects of a single reality.

Whatever speculations they engender, symbols are always intended to express a specific meaning. The necklace is a sign of potency and the breasts denote abundance. The message can be summed up as follows: Life is triumphant. Why, then, is there need for more questions? The covered alley in Aveny is sufficient by itself, and when you have remained there for a while with your back pressed up against the stone, you eventually gain the feeling that everything is possible because the energy emanating from the earth in this spot is so strong that it leaps out, like a flash of lightning, toward the sky through the trees. I am convinced that the megaliths of Trie-Château and Aveny are necessary keys to opening the real doors of Gisors—those that are within us. More direct routes to ourselves lead only to the void of obtrusive vanities.

I often remained by the covered alley in Aveny for hours. At that time, the number of visitors who had noted the monument in the tourist guides and decided to see what it was all about were relatively few. Generally these visitors left quickly, adding a heap of stones to their collection of images from the trip. I have seen those, however, who examined the stone, photographed it, and became imbued with its inspiration. Likewise, when I felt I had been "recharged" with my fill of indispensable vital forces, I resumed my journey on the path that threaded its way through the trees.

On returning to the valley, I could then better perceive its romantic and timeless aspect. The Epte Valley, I was convinced, had ceased belonging to the world for at least a century; it seemed forgotten, a place where it would be nice to fall asleep some spring evening when the lilacs are flowering and not reawaken until the end of time when the apple trees of the isle of Avalon are producing their fruits that are ripe year-round. I could smell the water of the Epte when standing on the old bridge that crossed the river. The village of Aveny lay basking in the sun before me like a painting by Claude Monet—who, by the way, lived for a long time in the Epte Valley, in Giverny. You may still visit his house and gardens, not far from the confluence of the Epte and the Seine, which carries its lazy waters toward the wide open sea and the drunken boats. Impressionism, Symbolism, the "fin-de-siècle" style, the howls of Rimbaud, who attempted to reawaken the fairies slumbering beneath the wisteria of houses ravaged by times past: It is all there, everything is ready for a dive toward the dawn of time when the divine light still permeated the golden particles raining down upon the earth.

From Aveny I ascended the road following the course of the Epte, a path hardly suitable for heavy traffic. It followed the river and was also parallel to the railroad connecting Vernon to Gisors, which featured some occasionally bizarre-looking level crossings. The timeworn nature of these railroad tracks always reminded me of a science-fiction scenario involving a train straying onto some rails that are no longer used and plunging into the mists of another world. Indeed, it possesses a decided atmosphere of unreality. Can we be sure that the houses in the hamlet of Berthenonville are inhabited by human beings? It is so quiet on the edge of both this road and this railroad that the question becomes inevitable. The same can be asked in the village of Château-sur-Epte—in fact, the unreal atmosphere is emphasized by the phantomlike ruins of the fortress, which seem to mock the traveler. It hardly seemed to matter that this fortress was built by William the Red at the end of the eleventh century and that for a long time it bore the name of Château-Neuf while the group of houses tucked away on its slopes was called Fuscelmont. In my mind, the château was much closer to being one of those castles that can be vaguely glimpsed in the Arthurian romances, one of those in which extraordinary trials await the knight who dares to accept the risk they offer. In the morning, though, after he has spent the night defending himself against malefic beings, he sees that the fortress is devoid of inhabitants, that the courtyards have been invaded by brambles and the buildings are in ruins, as if they had not been occupied for centuries. Was it in such a castle that Perceval witnessed the mysterious Grail Procession?

The atmosphere changes completely when one arrives at Bordeaux-Saint-Clair. Because of the frequent use it receives, the Paris–Rouen road breaks the dream that permeates the bottom of the valley. Yet the factories themselves have a certain familiar, old-fashioned charm. They can almost be overlooked given the riot of vegetation that grows over them, but it is thanks to them that the railroad still exists, like a valuable remnant of the past. I cannot help but feel a bit nostalgic when thinking about Bordeaux-Saint-Clair and recalling a specific spring evening in 1971. When crossing the Epte, it seems that we cross the border of what the Celts called the Other World, a world inhabited by strange beings who are identical to human beings and who hide in the mist at the very moment we seem to have them in our grasp. What message was she trying to deliver to me, that woman using a name that was not hers? More important, just who was she—a flesh-and-blood individual or one of those ghosts who pursued me relentlessly when I was a child? I do not know, but I am haunted by bridges, fords, and all passages that can lead *elsewhere*. Perhaps she was simply a symbol of the enchantment cast by the Vexin, a land that is not mine but, like a flame, lures me to pitifully burn my wings.

When climbing along the course of the Epte, I also stopped at Guerny, whose Breton name is clearly Celtic and evokes the alder or the marsh. In fact, the valley that extends to the east on the French side is occupied by large pastures that most likely were created by the draining of an ancient wetlands. The village of Guerny is as tranquil and withdrawn as Aveny or Berthenonville. I find here the same mystery and the same impression of having escaped from the weight of time. From here what is only a footpath leads me up the slope of the plateau toward the town of Vesly. In its ancient church there are some old statues from the fourteenth and fifteenth centuries as well as a beautiful seventeenth-century retable that excite my curiosity. The Vexin region holds many surprises when it comes to religious art. Just a little north of Gisors, Mainneville is home to the famous statue of St. Louis, whose now classic image has spread throughout the world.

Returning to the valley, I climbed back toward the larger town of Dangu, whose partially Roman church was renovated in the sixteenth century. Next to it there is a magnificent Norman house with the half-timbered walls characteristic of the ancient construction of this region. Dangu, which stretches between the banks of the Epte and the summit of the plateau, holds a privileged place that testifies to its strategic importance. There is a Gallic fort on its heights and a Roman camp in the valley.

Following the treaty of 911, the site became a bastion of Norman defense, with its fortress controlling the Epte Valley as far south as Gisors. A town then grew around the castle but was intentionally burned to the ground by Robert de Chandos to prevent it from falling into the hands of the French king Louis VI (the Fat). At the end of the tenth century Dangu was the theater of ferocious battles between the Anglo-Normans and the French. It changed hands between the two several times and was obviously pillaged each of these times. Finally, in 1400, the ancient fortress was abandoned by Jacques de Bourbon, who had another castle built. Under the Second Empire, this castle, renovated and restored several times, belonged to the count of Lagrange, who arranged for Napoleon III's horses to be trained there. All that remain of this building are the cellars. On the other hand, another castle has dominated the town since 1908—the castle that Madame de Pompadour had constructed in Montretout and then transported, stone by stone, to its present location.

Though a site of war and history, Dangu has retained something from the era when the druids performed their worship in surroundings unblemished by any construction of the *nemeton:* a sacred clearing in the middle of the forest. The sanctuary was obviously Christianized. Now, as Notre-Dame-du-Chêne [Our Lady of the Oak —*Trans.*] it sits in the middle of a woods, accessible only by a simple path, and is the object of an annual pilgrimage. The place is frequented by many, as testify the impressive number of *ex-votos* that can be found there. From druidic sanctuary to Christian pilgrimage site, the shadow of the divine mother in the middle of the oaks perpetuates the permanence of beliefs and rituals through the centuries despite the changes and upheavals in the world.

When heading toward Gisors, a detour can be made to Neaufles-Saint-Martin. On this road there is a strange cross, which, from a distance, looks like a Celtic cross like those found in Ireland. In fact, it is an inscribed cross from the fourteenth century whose presence is no doubt linked to the existence of an ancient sanctuary. It sits out in the open on the top of the plateau, where it dominates the monotonous countryside and seems to scratch the sky. A keep can be seen farther away, beyond Neaufles, the final remnant of the important fortress that preceded Gisors, but which, because of its less advantageous situation, did not allow for effective surveillance of the Epte Valley. Legend maintains that it is connected by an underground tunnel to the Gisors keep. What we know for sure is that the castle of Neaufles was the residence of a White Lady, the famous queen Blanche of Evreux.

In truth, anything is possible in this land of half tones, the place of predilection for so many painters. I have mentioned Claude Monet in connection with the lower Epte Valley, but the memory of Pablo Picasso also lives in a hamlet of Gisors, where he lived for a time, and we can still see the house of Camille Pissarro, whose paintings were often inspired by the landscapes and scenes of the region in the upper Epte Valley. The Epte, rising toward Gournay, has always formed a natural border between Normandy and France proper. Little flower-filled villages with small, melancholy churches stretch along the valley. Picardy is on the French side, and to the north is the Brays region, with its pasture-covered, undulating hills.

Remnants of forests are scattered about this land and remind the traveler that Lyon-la-Forêt is the center of the most beautiful beech groves in France. Elsewhere, though, it is hard to picture the Vexin at a time when the loggers had not yet finished their work of systematic destruction. How many sacred clearings of the druids were thus surrendered to the light? Because of the absolute rule of the permanence of worship, the majority of churches and chapels that can be seen today were built on the very sites of these sanctuaries. The sacred, then, never dies; it merely changes shape. And it is always the same wind that blows over the harvest-rich plateaus. The ancient goddess of the dolmens has simply adopted new names over the course of the ages. As in Brittany and Britain, saints from other lands have struck the ground with their pilgrim's staff, causing the gushing of springs that assuaged the thirst of those who have suffered under the yoke of successive invaders: the Gauls, of course, then the Romans and their legions, the Franks, the Vikings, and so many others. The lands that are the most historically charged are those that have suffered the most. It is by virtue of this history and these sufferings that they are worthy of interest. They inspire seekers, provoking the impassioned quest for what is not always obvious and for everything concealed beneath the ruins, for there is always something beneath a collapsed monument, even if it is only the dream of those who can never satisfy themselves with appearances.

This is how Gisors seemed to me at the time I was desperately struggling to climb up the Epte Valley.

2

The Glory Days of Gisors

IT IS LIKELY that on the hill where the castle of Gisors currently sits, one of those fortress-refuges characteristic of Celtic civilization was located during the Gallic era. We know that Gallic society was essentially rural, with habitations dispersed along rivers, on the plains, or on the edges of the forest. Villages in the sense that we conceive of them were practically nonexistent among the Celts. Rather, there were fortresses where the inhabitants of the surrounding area could live in the event of war. It was only in the first century B.C.E., just prior to the Roman conquest, that some of these fortresses became market towns because they allowed large segments of the population to gather together. Some artisans, blacksmiths mainly, took on the habit of settling there. This was the case in Rouen and Laon, and even in Mont-Beuvray, the ancient Bibractus, and in Gergovie, the capital of Arvernes. It is easy to imagine, then, the makeup of Gisors during the Gallic era: one fortress on the hill and another on the banks of the Epte, with dwellings in between and around them occupied by farmers and shepherds. The very name of Gisors, Gisortium in its most ancient form, tends to prove this conjecture: What we find in the second syllable is the well-known Celtic toponym *rit-* (the Latin form is *ritum*), meaning "ford," and the entire name can be translated as "the Pasture of the Ford." It is certain, in any event, that below the castle on the hill there was a ford allowing a path coming from Beauvais and Laon—which subsequently became a Roman road—to cross the Epte in the direction of Rouen.

Also certain is the importance of the Roman occupation in Gisors. From various digs and numerous restorations of the church, many traces of the Roman presence have been discovered. Gisors was already a strategic site beyond the Seine Valley—it permitted the Romans to effectively survey the heavily forested hinterlands that were still inhabited by unknown peoples. The town probably began to develop at this time of the Roman occupation, within the curve of the Epte that forms a natural defense to the confluence of the Troesne.

It seems the village grew considerably during the Merovingian era. We know that the largest part of Gisors territory was dependent on the chapter house of Rouen Cathedral because of the donation of King Clotaire II.[1] Important traces from this time have been rediscovered, namely a cemetery located under the rue des Épousées north of the church. The fortuitous discovery of this cemetery in 1947 during the restoration and expansion work necessitated by bombing damage from the war, as well as the discovery of an ancient underground tunnel connecting the church to the castle, was sufficient to revive all the old rumors of underground tunnels, all the more so because the existence of numerous sarcophaguses was a proven fact. This is why I heard so many stories about underground passageways in the Vexin during my stay there in 1948. From there it was only a short step to the talk of treasures buried beneath Gisors—a step quickly taken.

During the Carolingian era, Gisors took an active part in the political life centered in Laon and the religious life for which Rouen was the hub. As an important point on the road from Laon to Rouen, and no doubt the junction, as well, of a road out of Paris that reached Rouen by way of Chaumont, Gisors could not fail to increase in both renown and military importance, especially during the Norman invasions. We know

---

1. Clotaire II, king of the Frankish realms of Neustria and Austrasia, was compelled in 614 to grant a charter giving extensive privileges to the nobility and clergy in his realm. The clergy of Rouen would thus have received the power to administer the territories such as Gisors that were dependent on their chapter house. —*Trans.*

that the Normans, primarily sailors, used streams and rivers as their invasion routes, a method they also used to traverse Russia, incidentally. Though it has never been mentioned anywhere, it's quite probable that the Normans who had settled in the Lower Seine region came up into the Epte Valley in the same way that they reached the Eure Valley.

But Gisors' true importance in European political struggles is a direct consequence of the Saint-Clair-sur-Epte treaty signed in 911 and, in 1066, the conquest of England by a Norman duke, following the victory at Hastings, which completely altered the balance of power on the Continent and was one of the remote causes of the Hundred Years War.

If we truly seek to understand the importance of Gisors and to shed some light on the mystery surrounding its fortress, we must pick up its history right at the beginning with the arrival of the Norsemen. We know that the Viking raids were felt in three main sectors of the Continent: in Brittany at the mouth of the Loire, in Frisia (the future Netherlands), and in Neustria (western France) at the mouth of the Seine. It is this last sector that concerns us.

In the year 820 C.E., thirteen longboats from Scandinavia landed for the first time in the Bay of the Seine. Nine Norsemen met their deaths there in a pitched battle with those Bretons and others who guarded the shore. We must not overlook the fact that the left bank of the mouth of the Seine was an ecclesiastical enclave affiliated with the bishopric-abbey of Dol-de-Bretagne.

On May 12, 841, a veritable war expedition led by the Norse chief Asgeir arrived in this same location and shortly after, on May 14, Asgeir captured Rouen. Ten days later he burned down the Irish-founded monastery of Jumièges and then was paid a ransom for sparing the Saint-Wandrille Monastery, which at that time still bore the name of Fontenelle. Four years after the arrival of Asgeir, in 845, another chief, Ragnar, arrived with one hundred twenty ships and six thousand men. He sailed up the Seine and reached Paris on March 28, Easter Eve. The Carolingian king, Charles the Bald, paid him a ransom of seven thousand pounds so that he would spare the city, but during his journey back he raped and pillaged the Seine Valley.

Asgeir's return in 851 led to the destruction of the monastery of Saint-Wandrille on January 9, 852. After this, he settled in Rouen, from which he launched raids into the Vexin and the Beauvais. To avoid a counterattack by the Franks, he wintered on the heavily fortified island of Jeufosse, between Vernon and Bonnières.

Another raiding expedition picked up where Asgeir left off, directed this time by Siegfried and Godfried. Charles the Bald tried to attack the Norsemen but could not manage to dislodge them from their stronghold on Jeufosse. As a result, in 853 he decided to negotiate a treaty with Godfried, who, in return for a large sum of money, left the area. But Siegfried, who did not sign the accord, remained and pillaged regularly. In 857 Chartres fell into the hands of the Vikings and was sacked. Finally, on Easter, April 3, 858, it was the turn of Paris to succumb to the pressure of the Norsemen and pay them a ransom. Once again Charles the Bald attempted to attack them on Jeufosse, but then decided to change tactics, negotiating with Veland, another Viking chief, and giving him the mission of driving out the bands who had established themselves in the Lower Seine region.

Veland formed a blockade around Jeufosse with two hundred ships. The besieged on the island, short of foodstuffs, paid him a ransom, after which Veland and his defeated compatriots evacuated the area. When the contract binding him to Charles the Bald expired, however, Veland ended his allegiance and started operating for his own benefit, accompanied by his former adversaries. He spent the winter of 861–862 on the other side of Paris, in Meulan, while the French built a fortified dam at Pont-de-l'Arche, which was not able to prevent a fleet of seven hundred ships from sailing up the Seine in 885 and laying siege to Paris.

The new king, Charles the Fat, found himself forced to pay a stiff ransom, and the invaders' fleet sailed back out to sea in 887. This did not mean, however, that all the Vikings left. A good number had settled along the Seine, namely in Rouen. Leading them was a tenacious and daring chief by the name of Hrolfur, now customarily known as Rollon. It was under this name that he imposed himself as chief over all the Vikings in the Lower Seine region. He mocked the Franks even as they began to regroup and reorganize, birthing a new hierarchical system—which will lead to feudalism—in which the king increasingly *ruled* while the nobles *governed* the territories entrusted to them.

This new system had been set up at the time when Hrolfur, leaving his Norman bases, laid siege to Chartres. A Frankish army led by Robert de Neustrie, Richard de Bourgogne, and Ebles de Poitiers fell upon Hrolfur's men. It is claimed that six thousand Vikings died on the battlefield, which seems quite an exaggeration. Nevertheless, Hrolfur was forced to lift his siege and fell back to the Seine, but displayed no intention of leaving Gaul. Quite the contrary, he entrenched himself in his bases at the bends of the river.

It was at this point that young King Charles III, known as the Simple, stepped in. He had not taken part in the battle of Chartres but used the potentially short-lived victories of the nobles to find a political solution that would allow him to definitively remove the Viking threat in both the short and the long term. His reasoning followed an implacable logic: Hrolfur had been beaten but not totally defeated. He thus constituted an ever-present menace that would be sufficiently tamed if transformed into a safeguard. Because the Viking leader had a solid hold on Rouen and the surrounding region, it could be considered necessary to officially recognize him as the count of Rouen—provided he convert to Christianity and protect the land given him against any new incursion by the Norsemen—and allow him to enter with full rights into the Frankish kingdom. The Romans dealt in the same way with certain British peoples in northern Britain so as to reduce the threat presented by the Scottish Picts.

Thus was concluded, and in very short order, the treaty of Saint-Clair-sur-Epte. The king accepted the fealty and homage of the Christian convert Hrolfur/Rollon (who, incidentally, adopted the name of Robert) by naming him Count of Rouen and bestowing several *pagi*[2] around the earldom of Rouen. These extended to a border marked by the Epte, north of the Seine, and the Eure and the Avre Rivers in the south, an area basically corresponding to the current region of Upper

---

2. The *pagus* (countryside) is a Gallo-Roman territory corresponding to the area occupied by a Gallic people before the conquest.

Normandy. The part remaining in Frankish control formed the small earldom of Ivry (Ivry-la-Bataille), and the eastern portion of pagus Velcassini became the French Vexin (as distinct from the Norman Vexin.) Subsequently, Rollon added to this territory what today consists of the departments of the Orne and Calvados. His successors added the Cotentin (taken from the Bretons) and the Passais (the region of Domfront). Thus Normandy was born.

Everyone was satisfied with the accord reached in Saint-Clair-sur-Epte. The title of count of Rouen meant that Rollon was the sole legitimate power holder among the Vikings. He was also their sole representative in negotiations with the king. But he was also the legal "Frankish" count facing the Gallo-Frankish populace of his territory. The king did not have to negotiate with the Vikings or the Gallo-Franks of the new territory. His sole partner was the count of Rouen, who could organize "his" land as he saw fit.

Everyone knows what followed. Normandy, which was sparsely populated at that time, was partially devastated. The entire southern and eastern portions of the land were covered again by dense forests. The banks of the Seine, which had been quite prosperous during the Gallo-Roman era, became semi-deserted. This was where the Vikings essentially settled, as well as in the Pays de Caux and the Caen plain. Later, Norwegian immigrants from Ireland settled in the north of Cotentin, making it possible for a linguistic line of Scandinavian influence to be traced following the toponomy from Granville to Gisors by way of Argentan and Conches. South of this line there was only sporadic Viking occupation. Gradually the Norsemen, converted to Christianity, melted into the Gallo-Frankish populace, abandoning the Scandinavian for the Roman tongue, but leaving it marked by a great many words and idiomatic expressions.

Of course, this does not mean that relations were now completely smooth between the Franks and the Vikings. In 925 new conflicts set Rollon at odds with the Frankish aristocracy, and for a long time the very Christian count of Rouen never hesitated to call upon the aid of Danish pagans in his struggles with the king of France. Furthermore, the Vikings of the Loire committed crime upon crime and ravaged Brittany. In this way, the danger they represented was thus a permanent one. This is why the Carolingian king and the Frankish nobility finally resolved to more or less abandon everything north of the Neustria—the land between the Seine and the Loire—to the Normans of Rouen, on condition that they conquer the lands of the Loire Normans as well as those of the Bretons. The famous contentions regarding Brittany stem from this date. Brittany was never a fief of the Frankish crown, but the Carolingian sovereigns handed it to the Normans as a backward region, provided they conquer it—which they could not do.

This policy, however, singularly reinforced the power and influence of the counts of Rouen, who would become the dukes of Normandy. These counts were, of course, prepared to recognize the authority of the Church as well as that of the king, and accepted the incorporation of themselves and their vassals into the kingdom's aristocracy. This was the result of an incontestably successful policy that would, in the long term, lead to uniting the kingdom of France. But the Rouen counts were also strong because of their acknowledged importance, which led to their protracted tendency to play their own game and do whatever they wanted. This reality would become even more tangible when they became the kings of England, to the great displeasure of the Capetian kings, who thus found themselves confronted by a vassal whose power was practically double their own.

It is in this fairly unique and specific context that we find Gisors and the role it played for more than three centuries until the annexation of Normandy by Philip Augustus. Situated halfway between Paris and Rouen, two capitals of the kingdom, Gisors happened to be on the road leading to the bishoprics of Picardy, the Valois, and Champagne, the sole bishoprics that mattered during that era,[3] the ones that could make or

---

3. During the thirteenth century, six of the twelve peers of France were ecclesiastics. These were the Archbishop of Reims and the bishops of Beauvais, Noyon, Laon, Châlons, and Langres. This reveals the importance of a state of affairs going back to the Carolingian Era: the predominance of high Gallo-Frankish church authorities over the other bishops in the kingdom. It was these bishops, for instance, who removed the Merovingian dynasty in favor of the Capetians, and it was under the impetus of the Archbishop of Rouen that Hugh Capet was acclaimed in Senlis and crowned in Noyon.

break a king. Therefore Gisors, alternately in the hands of the French and the Normans, was always the object of determined bargaining, if not merciless struggles, though these in no way prevented meetings there between the king of France and the king of England in attempts to find solutions to their quarrels.

Existing in Gisors at that time was an old elm, an *ormeteau ferré* (meaning it was propped up by iron rods), the chronicles of that time explain. It sat in the middle of a field, close to the current location of the railway station, on the left bank of the Epte, which is the French side. This elm was the pride of the village inhabitants, who compared it to another famous elm, one that could be found in Paris in front of the church of Saint-Gervais-Saint-Protais. Much speculation and legend has circulated about this elm and its connections with the Knights Templar, but what we discover is that the elm tree in Paris is right on the border of the Temple property and the parish church of Gisors carries the same name of Saint-Gervais-Saint-Protais. Coincidence? We know for certain that the Gisors elm was a symbol and that the parleys between the kings of France and England took place beneath its branches. Charles Nodier, who, though he often got carried away by his romantic enthusiasm, was not such an innocent when it came to hermetic traditions, spoke of the tree with strong emotion:

> Its foliage served as a pavilion for kings and as canopy for pontiffs and confessors. Beneath its shade Calixtus and Innocent had put aside the worries of their crowns and the pomp of Rome. St. Bernard mused in solitude there. St. Thomas of Canterbury there prepared himself to face his martyrdom. William, the Archbishop of Tyre, preached the Crusade there, where his eloquence dragged Philip Augustus and Philip of Flanders into the holy war.[4]

It should be added that William of Tyre was the first up to that time to have left a record of the founding of the Order of the Temple, al-

---

4. Nodier and Taylor, *Voyages pittoresques et romantiques dans l'ancienne France: Normandie*, 1820, 1825, and 1878.

though, and this is the least that can be said, he held many reservations about the military order and never held the Templars dear in his heart.

The fact remains that in 1031, on the occasion of the death of the second Capetian king, Robert II (the Pious), the young dynasty was shaken by internal struggles. The crown had come down to the eldest of Robert's three sons, Henry I. But Robert's widow, Constance d'Arles, showed a marked preference for one of her younger sons, Robert, who would become the duke of Burgundy, and she did not hesitate to turn the princes of the kingdom against their sovereign. Henry, alone and at bay, sought refuge in Fécamp, where he asked assistance from the duke of Normandy, Robert the Magnificent, who had not taken part in the revolt, and the duke promised to help his suzerain. Victory then swung back to the other side and Henry I was enthroned in his royal duties. As thanks to his faithful ally, Henry ceded the French Vexin to the duke. Normandy now extended to the banks of the Oise, and for a time Gisors would lose its strategic importance.

Later, King Philippe I, aware of the dangers represented by the Norman duchy so close to Paris, occupied the French Vexin, determined never to surrender it. William the Conqueror went to the king to demand the return of what he considered one of his territories, but his request was in vain. William then marched on Paris and it seemed the Capetian king was at the point of defeat when the duke of Normandy was wounded before the town of Mantes and died in Rouen several days later, on December 7, 1087. Because his successor did not press his claim to the French Vexin, it became definitively attached to the royal domain, and thus was Gisors restored to its former importance.

On the French side, Chaumont and Trie-Château were formidable fortresses that not only protected the road to Paris but also served as bases for raids into Normandy. On the Norman side, with the main road now passing through Gisors, Château-sur-Epte had lost its usefulness. As for the castle of Neaufles-Saint-Martin, although extremely well fortified, it was now too far away from the Epte. This was why in 1097, the duke-king William the Red decided to build a fortress at Gisors itself. The plans were drawn up by the architect Leufroy and its construction entrusted to Robert de Bellesme, a Norman knight who combined his knowledge of engineering with a justified reputation as a formidable warrior.

It is difficult, if not impossible, to know what the original plans of the castle looked like because the building we see today dates largely from the end of the twelfth century and has undergone many subsequent renovations. Because military architecture has constantly evolved, any citadel provides evidence of successive renovations. For example, we know that the current castle of Montségur was completely renovated by French troops well after the famous siege of 1244. Thus it is practically impossible for us to know the castle that was erected at the beginning of the thirteenth century at the request of the Cathars. This same problem holds true for Gisors.

It is likely that at the beginning of construction the fortress was confined to a mound topped by a wooden keep surrounded by a wall. Later, under the reign of Henry II Plantagenet, the keep was rebuilt in stone and the defense system was strengthened. The large encircling walls we see today were erected in 1123, following a riot of the populace of Gisors against the garrison.

It has been reported that the overall plan of the fortress at Gisors obeys strange astronomical and astrological laws. The same has been said of Montségur and of other, similar examples of twelfth-century military construction. The builders of castles were the same as those who built cathedrals. They had their own rules, distinctive techniques, and construction secrets, which they transferred to one another within the framework of guilds and apprenticeships, but they especially possessed their own state of mind, which is considered essentially *esoteric*. This is a cold, hard fact—and the secret and mysterious components of medieval architecture cannot be denied under the pretext that we cannot understand them. Therefore, we can dispense with making extravagant claims in interpreting this construction; there is no shame in admitting ignorance, and despite all that can be said about medieval architecture, all interpretation of it, whether religious, civil, or military, remains in the realm of conjecture.

It is obvious that the fortress of Gisors is built according to a predetermined blueprint. The encircling walls make up a twelve-sided poly-gon. This has been sufficient evidence for some to insist it is a represen-tation of the twelve signs of the zodiac. By this reckoning, and given the fact that all numbers have a symbolic value in what can be called the Tradition, it is quite obvious to some that there is an esoteric explana-tion for virtually any building. But such people do not stop there; they must discover those who inspired such blueprints—and they believe that in the Templars they have discovered them.

This conclusion, however, overlooks the fact that in 1097, the date construction of the Gisors castle began, the Templars did not yet exist. It is true that the Templars occupied the castle, but not until 1158, and they remained there for only three years. They are not the ones, then, who had the castle built and there is no indication that they undertook any work on a building that did not belong to them and of which they had only temporary charge. It is undeniably true that the Templars brought back builders from the East and that they provided sure, effec-tive protection for the guilds of masons and stone cutters. They can even be considered enthusiastic propagators of Gothic architecture, and while they did not invent the ogival cathedral, they were certainly its ardent partisans, though for reasons that were more political than religious or esoteric. But that is another story. The essential task is confirming what can be proved by archaeology and art history: The Templars never had a specific style. Delirious hypotheses have been widespread on this topic, but the reality is much simpler. When the Templars needed to build a military, religious, or civil structure, they were content to use the styles and modes of construction that were the custom of their time and per-haps to introduce them into countries where they were not yet known.

In 1108, when Louis the Fat became king of France he concluded a treaty with Henry I, the king of England. Under the terms of the treaty, a certain knight de Payens or de Payns was put in charge of Gisors, but in 1109 Henry I took the citadel back from him. Louis VI immediately de-clared war against the English king to force him to respect the treaty. Henry I totally repudiated this demand and hostilities dragged on for years until the king of France was finally beaten in Brennenville in 1119.

It was then that Pope Calixtus II, who had come to France for the Council of Reims, offered to mediate between the two kings. At Gisors he imposed a peace treaty according to which the heir of Henry I, William the Aetheling (who would become a victim of the shipwreck of the *White Ship*),[5] owed homage to the king of France for Normandy. In return, Gisors became a Norman town.

While all of this is part of the historical record, it is permissible to add a few facts for consideration. The date of the founding of the original Order of the Temple by nine knights who simply called themselves "Poor Knights of Christ" is, in fact, 1119. The chief instigator of this founding and the incontestable head of this new militia was named Hugues de Payen or de Payns. We do not know the first name of the knight who was entrusted with charge of Gisors, but we might wonder if he and Hugues de Payen are the same person.

It was in 1123 that the revolt of the town's inhabitants against governor Robert de Chandos occurred, supported by several Norman lords. Robert set fires to repel the conspirators and prevent them from reaching the castle, but unfortunately the blaze spread, destroying part of the town as well as the church. Following this event, the now famous wall was erected, which we can still see today, and the town was rebuilt and continued developing from that point forward. The tanneries, which had constituted the principal source of wealth for Gisors, declined, but other activities appeared on the scene. Most prominent was the burst of religious fervor that was responsible for the creation of several monasteries. Originally within the walls there was only a Benedictine priory under the control of the abbey of Marmoutier. Now there were the monasteries of Récollets, the Ursulines, the Annonciades, and the Carmelites, and, outside the walls, a house of Trinitarians and a lepers colony.

---

5. The sinking of the *White Ship* occurred on November 25, 1120, and was largely responsible for the civil war that followed in England: The heirs to most of the major estates in England drowned in this disaster, leaving their posts open to successors. The ship sank off the coast of Brittany while en route to England, carrying with it the English treasury and 140 knights. Poor visibility and the crew's and passengers' heavy drinking and subsequent inebriation caused the mishap. Among the victims was the sole son and heir of Henry I (Beauclerc), Guillaume, better known as William the Aetheling. —*Trans.*

The death of Henry Beauclerc provided the king of France an opportunity to reclaim Gisors and the Vexin. After William the Aetheling died in 1120, a victim of the sinking of the *White Ship*, Étienne de Blois, grandson of William the Conqueror, took possession of the English throne. However, the daughter of Henry Beauclerc, Empress Mathilda, widow of the emperor of Germany, held control of the duchy of Normandy. She had remarried and her new husband, the count of Anjou, Geoffrey Plantagenet, known as the Handsome One, therefore considered himself to be the duke of Normandy, though the Normans detested him because of all he exacted from them by extortion. As an act of diplomacy, on his return from the Crusades, which he had joined in the company of the king of France, Louis VII, he gave the duchy to the son he had with Mathilda, Henry Plantagenet. In 1151, under the watchful eye of Eleanor of Aquitaine, still queen of France,[6] Geoffrey Plantagenet concluded a treaty with Louis VII, and Henry II paid homage to the king of France in exchange for the duchy of Normandy. This submission cost Henry little, for he had already set his sights on two things: Eleanor and her duchy of Aquitaine, and the rights he held, through his mother, to the English throne.

In the following year, 1152, the Council of Beaugency annulled the marriage of Louis VII and Eleanor of Aquitaine, who, several weeks later, wed Henry Plantagenet, to whom she brought as dowry almost half of the territory that is France today. In addition to this, in 1154, through completely legal means, Henry Plantagenet became king of England. In this way Gisors found itself not only at the center of the quarrels between Louis VII and Henry II, but also at the very heart of the intrigues that were hatched around the French throne.

In fact, the Capetian monarch Henry had no male heirs. With Eleanor he had two daughters, Marie and Alix, who allied with the house of Champagne, and with his second wife, Constance de Castille, he had another two daughters, Marguerite and Adélaïde. It was only in 1165 that a son would be born to him from his third wife, Adèle de Champagne,

---

6. I have extensively analyzed the part played by Eleanor in the relationship between the Capetians and the Plantagenets, as well as her ambiguous attitude regarding her strange "divorce," in my book *Aliénor d'Aquitaine,* 4th ed. (Paris: Payot, 1983).

the future Philip Augustus. During this period, Eleanor's intrigues—her dream was to see her Plantagenet children ruling France—led to these arrangements: Marguerite was engaged to the elder Plantagenet son, Henry the Younger, and Adélaïde to the second son, the future Richard the Lion-Hearted. It seemed clear that one day or another the throne of France would be assumed by a Plantagenet. Thomas à Becket, who was then the English chancellor, had negotiated these engagements and, following a great deal of back and forth and the intervention of both English and French Templars, a treaty was concluded in 1158. Because of the maneuvers of Eleanor and Henry II, however, the agreement amounted to a conning of the king of France.

The crown of France truly was the prize, but so was the possession of Gisors, a key position in the balance of power between the kingdoms of France and England. The main actors in this drama were Henry the Younger, son of Eleanor and her Plantagenet husband, and Marguerite, daughter of Louis VII. Marguerite's dowry was to include Gisors and the Vexin, but in 1158, because both members of the engaged couple were just over three years old, it was far too soon to celebrate a marriage. It was decided then that Gisors should be neutralized until it was possible for the marriage to take place. Thus the fortress was sequestered and entrusted to an apparently neutral third party, the Order of the Templars, which delegated three of its knights to accept this trust: Robert de Pirou, Tostes de Saint-Omer, and Richard of Hastings. These were the only three Templars—at least with the title of knight—to occupy the castle of Gisors, and they stayed there for less than three years. From this fact, we can see that considering Gisors as a Templar fortress and viewing the castle as a sanctuary of the Temple and a secret place of either Templar treasure or archives is not merely a step, but a precipice. The historical reality is implacable, however unfortunate this is for the fantasies of some authors in need of something to write about.

It remains nonetheless true that the Templars played a role in this affair, and this in no way prejudices the conclusions that can be drawn concerning the profound and *secret* motives of the Templar Order. There would be no mystery surrounding the Templars if the order had not meddled in several matters that were obscure, to say the least, and for which the true reasons for their involvement cannot always be discerned.

In any case, the treaty of 1158 stipulated that the young couple could not wed before the age of seven years and that a dispensation would be required from the pope. The Church thus served as guarantor of the accord. Meanwhile, the Vexin—minus the neutralized Gisors and several fiefs granted to the king of England—belonged to the king of France. If Marguerite died before the marriage took place, the Vexin would remain in French hands, with the exception of those fiefs given to the English king. Everything appeared to be clear and simple.

In 1160 the accord was made official in a treaty specifying that the little Marguerite would bring as dowry the fortresses of Gisors, Neaufles, and Neufchâtel, and that the marriage would take place in three years. It so happened, however, that several months later, in November of that same year, Eleanor and Henry Plantagenet celebrated the completely legal marriage of the two royal children in Rouen, with all the necessary dispensations from the ecclesiastical authorities. Immediately the three Templars who had been entrusted with the charge of Gisors returned their keys to Henry II, who did not fail to install a strong garrison in their place. This was a wise move on his part, for Louis VII, who felt he had been gulled, prepared to start hostilities against his vassal, who happened to be king of England.

Legend claims that the king of France saw to it that the three Templars in charge of Gisors were arrested at their home in Éragny, a short distance from Gisors, and were hanged from a tree. The reality, however, is quite different. Robert de Pirou, Tostes de Saint-Omer, and Robert of Hastings were simply driven out of France—in other words, forbidden to stay there—and took refuge in the territory of Henry II, who, according to the news of the time, heaped them with favors. It is true enough that having shown a particular enthusiasm for the king of England, they deserved a good reward. The formerly Poor Knights of Christ, who had become the Knights of the Temple of Jerusalem and secondarily, bankers of kings, may perhaps have taken a vow of poverty, but the order itself could receive gifts—and it did not turn them down. This was not so exceptional in that era, for the Cistercians, after a period of decline, had become quite wealthy and the Mendicant orders followed their example in the following century.

When a monastic order is wealthy (all the more so when it concerns soldier-monks), while the members of that order theoretically own nothing, they are nonetheless free from want. From the chronicles and accounts of the first half of the twelfth century, we are perfectly aware that the Templars gained enormous sums from the two pretenders to the English throne, Étienne de Blois and the empress Mathilda, Henry II's mother. Entrusted with mediating between the two rivals, they profited by "cashing in on all sides"—allowing the situation to deteriorate until the death of Étienne de Blois and taking care not to adopt an official position. Why didn't Mathilda's son also bestow his largess on the Templar Order, which was as solidly established in London as it was in Paris?

As we can see, the role played by the Templars in the Gisors affair and the marriage of the two royal children is far from clear. It transpired much like secret negotiations were being carried out behind the back of the unfortunate French king, who was doubly duped by his first wife—first by her marriage into the Plantagenets, then by the hastily arranged marriage between the two children. It is permissible to assume that the Templar commandery in London, installed inside the city and devoted to the Anglo-Norman sovereigns who were the chief sponsors of the Crusades, was allowed to negotiate directly with the Temple of Paris, "headquarters" of the order, regarding this marriage. Some historians accuse the Templars of having received subsidies for accelerating the time of the marriage and surrendering Gisors. This is obvious, but is undoubtedly not the only reason for their actions here.

It is forgotten by almost everyone that while the Knights Templar—and even the other members of the order—owed blind obedience to the grand master, he in turn took his orders *directly* and *absolutely* from the pope. While the Templars showed a visible preference for the king of England, it is not conceivable they would have done so without the order of the sovereign pontiff—or at least his consent. So the explanation for their involvement in accelerating the marriage must be sought in

Rome. Furthermore, only the pope could grant dispensation for the age of the royal children at the time of marriage. Arnoul, the bishop of Lisieux, who took part in the negotiations, left behind a testimonial, which also serves as a confession. According to this seemingly sincere ecclesiastic, "never would the papal legates have granted this dispensation [for the marriage] if they had not been compelled by necessity and the inestimable good that would result from it."

This much is clear: In 1160, though France would always be "the eldest daughter of the Church" (these beautiful turns of phrase are always amusing), the papacy chose the Plantagenet dynasty over the Capet dynasty, which was believed to be on the path to extinction. Furthermore, and this is an element that carries weight, the pursuit of the Crusades essentially depended on the Anglo-Norman nobility, for they provided the largest contingents of troops and the surest source of subsidies. In the Machiavellian policy it adopted before it came to dominate Europe and the Mediterranean world, the papacy played both sides against the middle when it was not playing both sides against each other—in complete Christian fraternity, of course. An earlier example of this was when Rome literally delivered the British into the hands of the Anglo-Saxons in the seventh century in order to counter the growing influence of Celtic Christianity in the British Isles and delivered the Irish into the power of Henry II Plantagenet in the twelfth century. The least that can be said is that the Irish, probably the most "papist" of all Catholics, did not show the fault of being resentful. It is true that the designs of God are unexplainable, especially when individuals assume the right to speak in his name.

This is where the Templars assumed their essential role. Officially created to protect the pilgrimage roads in the Holy Land, the Order of the Temple became in 1160 an enormous machine with operations everywhere—in the Holy Land, of course, but also in Spain, where it ensured the "reconquista," and throughout the whole of Europe to Ireland, maintaining a complex system of relay stations, bank branches, and strategic positions along the great channels of communication, and, secondarily, within sanctuaries. In 1160, benefiting from countless gifts, sponsored by the highest dignitaries of the Church, and *justified* by Bernard de Clairvaux, who was the true master of Christianity during the first half of the century, the formerly Poor Knights of Christ were at the height of their power. They constituted a formidable force endowed with an efficient hierarchy, one that could act on the ground without paying attention to borders or lordly domains. It was an international force that was, I should repeat, at the exclusive service of the pope.

The Order of the Temple was solicited by everyone, whether to rule on lawsuits, negotiate treaties, or serve as mediator in disputes. The Templars were necessary to ensuring the optimum functioning of the Crusades, necessary for realizing the transport of funds between Europe and Palestine, necessary for administering certain royal and noble treasuries, necessary for lending money during an era when usury was banned—but tolerated on the part of the Jews, those evildoers!—and necessary to establishing contact between various people. It is no secret that Normandy, which held several important Templar establishments, was a wealthy land as well as being what would be called today a buffer state. It was in the interests of the Temple, and thus the papacy, to establish a solid presence in Normandy in order to play a predominant political role. To do this, it was necessary to contrive a balance between the two rivals for Normandy, France and England, in such a way as to draw the maximum benefits from both the French and the English. The restoration of the Vexin to English control weakened the king of France and discouraged any potential lust he might have for expanding his territory. It was enough to advise the king of England to benefit from his possession without taking any undue advantage of it, for if he did, the balance of power might swing back in favor of the French. This system reinforced Normandy's autonomy and is illustrative of the same kind of high politics transacted when the kingdom of Belgium was created during the nineteenth century.

Gisors was now in the hands of Henry II Plantagenet. The work he called for involving the conversion of the fortress lasted until 1184. In 1169, Thomas à Becket, who was by this time former chancellor of the kingdom of England and had retired to Pontigny Abbey following his rift with Henry Plantagenet, made a stop at Gisors. It seems Louis VII had reconciled with the English king and asked Becket to reassume his position of primate archbishop over England and Normandy in Canterbury. We know that Becket dies on the altar steps of the cathedral there, assassinated under the no doubt misinterpreted orders of Henry II. Thomas à Becket was eventually canonized and the ruins of a chapel erected in his honor within the Gisors keep are still visible. During his stay in Gisors, Thomas à Becket met an influential Templar by the name of Jean de Gisors, with whom he had numerous conversations. As there is no record of what they discussed, a certain number of people have not missed an opportunity to embroider upon a possible understanding between the primate of Canterbury and the Order of the Knights Templar. No conclusion, however, can be drawn from this relationship, already problematic enough on its own, with all due respect to those who view this Jean de Gisors as the architect of a rift within the heart of the Templar Order, said to have occurred in 1188 beneath the famous Gisors elm tree.

This brings us precisely to 1188, when, beneath this same tree, Henry II Plantagenet found himself in the field with the leaders of his army. Also present were the new king of France, Philip II, who would be known as Auguste, along with his top military personnel. The guest of honor was William, archbishop of Tyre, the same person who left us the first communication concerning the founding of the Templars. William was there to exhort support for a new Crusade, which would be the third. His enthusiasm won over all those in attendance. The barons took up the Cross with shouts of "It's the will of God!" This event would cast a long shadow and it is from that date that the coat of arms for the town of Gisors was adopted: "the engrailed cross, gold on a field of azure," beneath a crown upon which the year 1188 is inscribed. Later, in 1555, King Henry II of France would grant Gisors the right to add three gold "lilies in chief" (*fleur de lys en chef*) to its coat of arms as thanks for the city's loyalty and the solemn reception afforded him by its inhabitants.

But magnanimous enthusiasm was soon replaced by discord. A discussion between the old Plantagenet, Henry II, and the young Capetian, Philip II, still beneath the famous elm, turned sour. The stories relating this affair vary to some extent. According to one of the versions, the elm offered the only possible source of shade in the field, but the shadow it cast was quite large as it took nine men with their arms fully extended to barely span the circumference of the trunk. Henry Plantagenet arrived first and, because it was a torrid day, settled in comfortably with his companions beneath the tree's branches. When Philip Augustus arrived late, he had to make do with a place in the sun. With the help of the weather, tempers grew heated. Insults were exchanged between the Anglo-Normans and the French, which soon led to blows. Because the French were more numerous, the Anglo-Normans were forced to seek refuge in the fortress. Philip Augustus, in a fit of anger, had the secular elm cut down and, it is said, returned to Paris grumbling: "I did not come here to be a woodchopper!"

A colorful story, obviously. Another version claims that the French king, annoyed by the symbolic importance the elm held for the Anglo-Normans, had threatened to have it chopped down. The king of England then had the trunk of the tree reinforced with iron bars (*ormeteau ferré*). The next day a detachment of Frenchmen armed with slings, axes, and clubs gathered in the field to fell the tree. The Anglo-Normans, led by Richard the Lion-Hearted, attempted to oppose them. The battle lasted until nightfall but the French, who remained in control of the ground, succeeded in chopping down the elm.

Whatever the truth of the circumstances surrounding this matter, it is incontestable that the Gisors elm, a symbol of dialogue between the Anglo-Normans and the French, was felled on the occasion of a quarrel over prestige between the two sovereigns—no doubt a simple incident of travel on the difficult parallel paths taken by the Capetians and the Plantagenets. But after the event, something strange occurred. It was seized upon later as the departure point of a serialized historical fiction novel. Under the pretext of a kinship between the name of the tree [*elm* is *orme* in French —*Trans.*] and that of a certain Ormus, a so-called Egyptian mystic who was converted by St. Mark and became founder of a Gnostic sect (in reality it must be Ormuzd, or Ahura-Mazda, of the Persian Mazdean tradition), it was imagined that the chopping down of the elm tree symbolized a separation between the official Templar Order and a phantom "Priory de Sion" that was an integral part of the Templar Order since its origin until this fateful time in 1188.

However, after the death of Henry II, his son Richard the Lion-Hearted went to war in the Holy Land, accompanied by Philip Augustus, who arranged his own return from the Crusades ahead of Richard by secretly concluding an agreement with the emperor to hold the English king prisoner. This allowed him to reach an understanding with Richard's brother, John Lackland, who was ever ready to assume the responsibility of continuing the Plantagenet dynasty. Gisors' Norman governor subsequently turned over Gisors to Philip Augustus with the complicity of John Lackland in 1193. Philip then took advantage of his possession of the fortress to renovate the castle, but Richard, once freed from captivity, wished to gain back what he considered his rightful property. He began by considerably fortifying Château-Gaillard in order to be ready for any eventuality and started harassing the French king throughout the Vexin region. Philip was defeated in 1198 during a battle that took place between Vernon and Garnaches. He was beaten again a little later between Courcelles and Gisors. Forced to flee, he managed to reach Gisors with his forces in disarray. At the moment the French king was crossing the bridge over the Epte, it collapsed under the weight of his soldiers. Philip almost drowned and legend says that he was saved thanks to a pledge he made to erect a golden statue of the Virgin on the site where this tragedy took place. We know he kept his word and a recent statue on a bridge over the Epte, though on another part of the river, recalls this event.

While he was still absolute master of Gisors—as of the whole of Normandy because of John Lackland's fall from power—Philip Augustus turned the fortress into a stronghold intended not only for keeping watch over the back regions but also for protecting the Parisian area from any aggression out of the northwest. He had the second enceinte wall enlarged and a tower constructed known as the Prisoner's Tower, which overlooks the moat on the southeastern side of the castle. It is eighty-seven feet high by forty-two feet in diameter and consists of three rooms, one on top of the other. The first room is a guard room with a large fireplace and the second beneath it was intended for archival storage. The third room, most likely a prison and reached by a narrow staircase, is quite dark, with its only source of light being the four murder holes in its walls, which are covered with graffiti that some have claimed to be of Templar inspiration, and with small sculptures depicting religious themes, comparable to those carvings found in churches. It has been presumed that the prisoners lodged there were either clergy or those who had worked on church decoration.

There is a legend associated with this prison, one perhaps based on actual fact. A certain Nicolas Poulain, who was the queen's lover—we are not told which queen—was locked up in this room, but managed to escape by digging a tunnel connecting to some underground passageways among which a mysterious chapel was located: "He entered a room close to the cage and from there shimmied up a stone wall, broke through a floorboard and entered a room near the Saint-Catherine Chapel, and then entered said chapel in which was stored the artillery of our said castle."[7] Many searched for this chapel intently during the 1950s and 1960s because it allegedly held either the Templar treasure or its secret archives.

The legend also claims that Nicolas Poulain, after emerging from his prison, stupidly let himself be killed by a castle guard who fired his harquebus the moment Nicolas was preparing to cross the moat to rejoin the queen. This obvious fable is quite intriguing. Who was this mysterious prisoner, Nicolas Poulain? The name Poulain—in fact, a nickname, for during that era patronymics were not yet fixed—lends itself to analysis in that it means a Christian who had established roots in the Holy Land during the Crusades. The Templars had a certain number of *poulains* in their ranks who were quite valuable for their knowledge of the West. Might not this Nicolas Poulain hide, if not a person, at least a message left by the Templars? Though not impossible, there is no proof. What's more, the graffiti in the Prisoner's Tower are not very convincing

---

7. From a 1375 manuscript preserved in the Archives Nationales (JJ 106, folio 406), quoted by J.-L. Chaumeil, *Le Trésor du Triangle d'Or* (Paris: A. Lefeuvre, 1979). I hold great reservations about the interpretations provided in this book.

in regard to their alleged Templar origin. Religious themes were common property during the Middle Ages, and everyone made use of them according to his individual convictions.

Whatever the case may be, Gisors remained a French possession until the Hundred Years War. It was only in 1419 that King Henry V of England gained control of the castle after a three-week siege. A number of military operations took place around Gisors and throughout the Vexin region up to 1449, when the English captain Richard Merbury surrendered it to the seneschal Pierre de Brézé. In 1465, during the troubles caused by the War of the Public Weal,[8] the town and castle of Gisors were taken by the duc de Calabre, but after this time, peace reigned and the town prospered. The inhabitants took advantage of this respite to rebuild their church, which had suffered many cruel battles.

The choir and its two aisles were the same as those in place in 1249. At the end of the choir was a flat wall pierced by a large broken arch with no capital that had been extended by the chapel's ambulatories. Construction of the Chapel of the Assumption was begun north of the nave and it wasn't until 1515 that the transept and south portal were reconstructed and in 1567 that the large western portal and the large south tower were rebuilt. The tower was never finished, however, because of the troubles caused by the Wars of Religion.[9] What distinguishes this church, Saint-Gervais-Saint-Protais, is that it includes five naves like a cathedral, two rows of lateral chapels, a transept with two portals, and, replacing the apse, a choir with a passageway behind the altar. The monument we see today has been almost entirely restored after the 1940 bombings, which destroyed almost three quarters of the building, leaving only the essential structure.

It was during this same period of time, the mid-sixteenth century,

---

8. The War of the Public Weal refers to the conflict of 1465 between Charles the Bold, duke of Burgundy, and Louis XI of France, in which Burgundy recaptured some of its territory from the French. —*Trans.*

9. The Wars of Religion refer to the open hostilities between French Catholics and Protestants (Huguenots) that lasted from 1562 until the Edict of Nantes was declared in 1598, giving legal standing and toleration to the Huguenots. This edict was modified in 1629, then revoked entirely by Louis XIV, who declared France an entirely Catholic nation. —*Trans.*

that the mysterious Saint-Catherine Chapel was built. The location of this chapel is the subject of much speculation; it has been placed almost everywhere—under the mound of the keep, under the church, or in an underground passageway connecting the church and the castle. It has not been rediscovered, but in 1898, when work on the church was being done, a retable was found that in all likelihood had formed part of this forgotten or concealed chapel. Of course, the mystery surrounding its location has contributed a great deal to the nourishment of the stories about treasure and secret documents. All that can be known for certain, based on unimpeachable sources, is that the Saint-Catherine Chapel was built around 1530; that its donor and founders were members of the Fouilleuses family, lords of Flavacourt; and that, before it could be located, it was probably destroyed by unknown causes south of the nave of the church, near the chapel contiguous to the southern portal. What is also certain is that King Henry II of France made his entry into Gisors on St. Catherine's feast day in 1555 and bestowed the compliment of three lilies to the town's coat of arms. Is this simply a coincidence?

During the Religious Wars, Gisors remained loyal to the Catholic faith and even revealed a ferociously anti-Huguenot spirit. When Henry IV wished to enter the town following his solemn renunciation of St. Denis, the inhabitants demanded certain guarantees, among which was the insistance of the curé of Gisors, Pierre Neveu, that the king publicly disavow the "evil doctrines" he had previously followed before he would be allowed to enter the church. It appears that Henry of Navarre (Henry IV) recanted with good grace, after which he is supposed to have said: "Here I am now, king of Gisors!"

In fact, in 1528 the earldom of Gisors had been given in dowry by François I to his sister-in-law Renée, daughter of Louis XII and Anne of Brittany, and, let me say in passing, the true heiress to the duchy of Brittany.[10] Renée married Hector d'Este, who became duke of Ferrare, which subsequently made the earldom the property of the houses of Ferrare and Savoy before it was returned to the royal crown in 1707. But in 1718

10. I have presented the arguments in support of this hypothesis in my book *Anne de Bretagne* (Paris: Hachette, 1980).

the marquis-maréchal of Belle-Île ceded to the king his Brittany island, a piece of land with important strategic value against a number of different territories, among which was the earldom of Gisors. It so happens that the person who became count of Gisors was the grandson of the disgraced Nicolas Fouquet, who is always enveloped by an air of mystery. Fouquet was also the individual more or less directly connected to the very obscure Razès affair, over which the shadow of the Templars looms large.[11] Is this another coincidence? Whatever the case may be, the earldom of Gisors was soon promoted to a dukedom-peerage and its last title holders were the comte d'Eu and the duc de Penthièvre.

Gisors declined in importance during the Revolution. Les Andelys was chosen instead to be the district capital. However, because Gisors was a small provincial town some forty-five miles from Paris, it still incurred great suffering during wartime. In 1870 [during the Franco-Prussian War —*Trans.*] numerous battles took place there. In 1940 three quarters of the town was destroyed by German bombing, which did not prevent the Resistance from creating a solid organization there, thereby greatly aiding in its own liberation by the British army in August 1944. Did any of the English soldiers recall that Gisors had once been the advance bastion of the United Kingdom in its drive toward the heart of France?

The past of Gisors is rich with all kinds of events, testifying to the importance of its site—lands of no value, after all, are not subjects of dispute. It also testifies to the permanence of an ideal of knighthood that can be labeled as chivalrous and, in that regard, it is not so surprising that we find there, if only episodically, the Knights Templar. They were obligatorily tied to the political life of their time, and as Gisors has constituted a political pivot of the first magnitude, it is only natural to find them there, although imagination concerning the extent of their involvement may soar far beyond historical reality. While the past is the property of everyone, it is necessary to know exactly what to make of it.

But what remains visible of this past in Gisors? Definitely not much,

---

11. For further information, see J. Markale, *Montségur et l'énigme cathare* (Paris: Pygmalion, 1986). English translation forthcoming in 2003 from Inner Traditions.

and yet these precious traces are lacking in neither grandeur nor interest. First we have the castle. It is one of the best-preserved and most handsome examples of twelfth- and thirteenth-century military architecture. Its walls are imposing. While the famous Prisoner's Tower holds an unassailable air of mystery, another tower, square in this instance, known as the Governor's Tower, forms the main entrance to the town. From there we can reach a staircase that ends at a small street called the ruelle du Grand Monarque. This name can be a source of some surprise as it has a connotation that cannot repudiate the contentions of the esotericists from every school. Millennarianism, prophecy, hermeticism—all seem to rendezvous here in the hope that He who will unify the brotherhood of all men will finally appear. Alas, the explanation is much more prosaic. This passageway of the great monarch is named thus because it follows the path taken by good King Henry IV when he became "the king of Gisors."

What attracts most attention at the castle is the keep. To tell the truth, it is quite impressive. Built atop a man-made mound in the center of the fortress, it once could be reached only by a stairway ascending straight up. But this stairway is now vanished and has been replaced by a path that climbs its winding way around the mound, ushering the visitor into a polygonal courtyard surrounded by a wall that is around six feet thick. On the right side of the courtyard remnants of the twelfth-century chapel dedicated to St. Thomas à Becket can still be seen. A spiral staircase of one hundred steps that is anchored on the eastern face will take one to the top of the keep. From there it can easily be seen what a magnificent observation post this keep made. Not only does it overlook the entire town and Epte Valley, but one can also see what is transpiring on the facing sides of Trie-Château and France can easily be determined. It is understandable that the kings of England and France fought so long for possession of this castle.

The painstaking restoration of the Church of Saint-Gervais-Saint-Protais is quite moving. Its fairly grandiose overall plan bears witness to the different stages of its construction. In answer to the radiating Gothic pillars of the choir, the pillars of the nave, without capitals, simply jut straight up eighty-seven feet, like the huge beech trees of the nearby Lyon Forest, to vanish into the arches. The pillars of the south aisle are remarkably original: Here we can see the spiral-shaped pillar of the dolphins, St. Jacques' pillar with its scallop shells, and, most important, the pillar donated in 1525 by the tanners guild—for a long time made up of the richest craftsmen in Gisors—which carries scenes of their craft on its four sides. A sixteenth-century fresco of the Transfiguration can be seen there as well as a stained-glass window of St. Claude, the patron saint of the tanners guild. There are other old windows dedicated to St. Crépin and St. Crépinien, the patron saints of cobblers. Within this church that has suffered so much at the hands of fratricidal violence, the essential was preserved, and that is not such a bad thing.

For the rest, the town itself offers few traces of its rich past aside from the portal of the leprosarium, some medieval facades in the Passage du Grand Monarque, and the famous Norman wash house on the banks of an arm of the Epte that flows peacefully under rows of flower-filled windows. Gisors seems to be asleep. But beneath its apparent torpor, inside this battered land, there is the sense of another world pulsing, a world full of shadows that are hard to define. It is a fact that there are passageways beneath Gisors, so all that is told in story is not always merely legend. Who knows what there is to be revealed in these mysterious galleries where the sun never shines?

3

The Treasure of Gisors

IT WAS IN 1962 that widespread public attention was brought to Gisors because of objects and secret documents discovered in the numerous underground passageways beneath the town, mainly between the keep and the parish church. The possible existence of a "treasure" was connected to the town for the first time with the release of a document that we were assured came from the Vatican archives.[1] Fanning the flames of this exceptional enthusiasm was the publication of a book by Gérard de Sède, *Les Templiers sont parmi nous* (The Templars Are among Us).[2] The success of this hypothesis is cause for surprise, considering that it rests on the lone statement of a single Templar, a certain Jean de Chalon, concerning three carts that allegedly left the Paris Temple on the eve of October 13, 1307, with contents intended for shipment abroad on vessels belonging to the order. It is suggested that these carts, in passing through Gisors, may have gone no farther on their journey, and this was

---

1. This document was allegedly given to Gérard de Sède by the Vatican librarian as a result of the request of the French ambassador and the cultural attaché at the embassy in Rome. While the author provides a photographic reproduction of it in his book, it is very hard to form an opinion on the actual value of the document and its authenticity.

2. *Les Templiers sont parmi nous* (Paris: Julliard, 1962). This book has been continuously in print since its first publication.

grounds enough to suggest that the Templars' treasure would be found buried somewhere beneath the town.[3]

From this point on, the question of a hidden treasure was not merely raised, but raised publicly. Because a question does exist and answers have been proposed and reservations concerning these answers have been raised, it would be stupid and even dishonest to skirt the issue and stubbornly deny the reality of a treasure.

The story concerning the treasure of Gisors has a long history, and it is likely that ever since the Middle Ages a certain number of seekers have ceaselessly explored the lower reaches of the town in search of gold, precious gems, and even documents. But if any of these seekers ever found anything, they certainly refrained from announcing their discovery and were simply content to profit from it themselves. This scenario takes place to some extent almost everywhere there are ancient structures. It is very well known, for example, that numerous dolmens and covered alleys have been "explored" and emptied of their contents. However, several historians and archaeologists have taken a specific interest in Gisors and its surrounding area.

In 1857, a local archaeologist named Gédéon Dubreuil declared that underground passageways extended westward from the Gisors keep toward the keep at Neaufles-Saint-Martin. Yet no one officially deemed it necessary to verify his contention. On the other hand, the location of an underground passageway connecting the keep to the Gisors church is very well known, having been revealed following the bombing of areas that have since been filled in. According to archaeologist Eugène Pépin, there is a veritable "network of underground caves, consisting of a central corridor forty-six yards long with an east–west orientation and two perpendicular corridors." Deep niches set within groined vaults on the

---

3. Speaking of the three Templars, who for several months, as a result of the agreement between Henry Plantagenet and Louis VII, occupied Gisors castle, historian Alain Demurger adds, in *Vie et mort de l'Ordre du Temple* (Paris: Le Seuil, 1985), 195: "The duration of their sojourn is inversely proportional to the tons of stupidities written or spoken by all the media who have weighed in on the subject." This harsh judgment is aimed much more at what followed the publication of Gérard de Sède's book than at the book itself. I will abstain from making any comment myself on the subject, satisfiying myself with simply adding the work to the files of the Gisors affair.

left and right of these corridors must have served as provision storage for the castle.

After the castle ceased to be inhabited, these underground tunnels were forgotten and only rediscovered when the gardens were laid out. A Gisors historian of the time relates how "people strolled through them with torches during festival days." One part of the central corridor could well date from the twelfth century. The corridor perpendicular to it is of a more recent date and appears to have been built to connect the inhabited area with the old corridor. Another part of an underground tunnel has been spotted within the cellars of the houses on the rue de Vienne. It heads in a southern direction, toward the ruelle des Épousées—in other words, toward the church. This was where German bombs exposed an area within which a Merovingian cemetery was discovered, though it has since been filled in and walled.

There are definitely underground tunnels, then, beneath the town of Gisors beween the church and the castle, that are known not only through vague legends but through chance discoveries as well. On March 23, 1950, according to an article by the archaeologist Eugène Anne in the paper *Paris-Normandie* (March 25, 1950), construction workers engaged in the task of enlarging the ruelle des Épousées north of the church brought to light "within the very axis of the portal, four stone sarcophaguses." The archaeologist ended his article hypothesizing that at the end of the fourteenth century:

> [T]he Gisors cemetery became the north side of the church. In order to continue the construction and build the north portal, it was decided to get rid of this cemetery. Another location was chosen southwest of the church. All the remains from the closed cemetery were placed in an ossuary while the sarcophaguses were left on site. No doubt they were the sepulchres of important figures.

Meanwhile, construction continued. Several days later the workers' pickaxes broke through a vault revealing a large excavation. According to Eugène Anne:

The opening was enlarged and people went down through it. Six yards below, an astonishing underground tunnel was discovered that looked like a crossroads. Between thick walls of solid and well-constructed masonry, four large niches topped by groined vaults opened, each the height of a man. A remarkable keystone at the top of the crossroads connected skillfully constructed Roman arcades, built with well cut stones that were solidly assembled. The whole thing was in perfect condition and the limestone was still almost white. It certainly appears that this place was only a stopping point in the middle of an underground road leading from the nearby fortress to the church. In fact, to the right of the third niche a dark passageway half choked with rubble opened up, which, as recent research has shown, crosses beneath the ground of the main street and ends up in the extremely ancient cellars of two houses built on this site that were spared during the war. Here again niches can be found and even columns with sculpted capitals. Bombing destroyed any exit that once existed toward the church.

It so happens that following this construction and discoveries, the entire thing was sealed back up and no efforts were made to protect these remnants of a remote era.

This was all it took to set fire to the imagination. What was concealed in these ancient underground corridors? A treasure? Documents? Both? And why was there so much haste to fill in the hole and continue with this urban construction project? There is a great temptation to view this as a maneuver of systematic obstruction: It was important that no one know just what was once concealed therein. It was only one small step from this view to talk of occult intervention and the deliberate intention *to hide something*. And after all, why not imagine a universal conspiracy intended to maintain silence over the entire matter, with, as in any good spy novel, the intervention of mysterious figures claiming to be the heirs or continuers of great initiatic lineages? All this was imagined, with the principal result being an increase in the mysterious atmosphere surrounding Gisors.

However, it is good to remember a few essential points. Following the Second World War and throughout the 1950s, the majority of municipalities spared little thought toward the protection of archaeological sites whose worth was not always obvious. First and foremost was the reconstruction of towns in adaptation to the needs of modern life. The rest was archaeologist business and the municipal aediles of any town generally viewed with a jaundiced eye the intervention of archaeologists in their affairs, especially because such interference was accompanied by bureaucrats and regulations.

Things played out everywhere this way and not only in Gisors. To avoid administrative problems and delays in urban construction, numerous municipalities filled in "holes" containing historical or archaeological remains. While this is regrettable, it does not provide grounds for shouting about universal conspiracies or stubbornly insisting on discreet interventions by occult powers. Furthermore, scientific excavations operating with all safeguards are expensive and the budgets available for this kind of activity have been quite reduced. If there are riches in the underground tunnels of Gisors, they are in a safe place and perhaps may be brought to light at a time when conditions are more favorable.

However, the imagination cannot be satisfied by such base material considerations. At all costs an explanation must be found that can feed the fantasies of the treasure seekers and other "initiates" of some more or less secret doctrine. Not one but several such answers have been discovered, the majority being obviously unverifiable and contradictory to boot. With these arguments, great pains were taken to exploit the most minor documents, even if known only through second or third hand. There was much talk about a priest who obtained from one of his colleagues—a Father Hoffet, whose name, not by chance, is connected to the Rennes-le-Château affair—the copy of a seventeenth-century manuscript, the author of which was a certain Alexandre Bourdet. This author, in his *Remarques sur l'histoire de Gisors,* revealed the existence of an underground chapel beneath the mound of the keep and provided its plans and a cross section of it. Support was also taken from a letter attributed to the canon Vaillant, senior priest of Gisors, in which he asked a correspondent for the return of "a Latin document of the year 1500" concerning thirty iron chests that had been found in the Gisors church. Most important in this regard, though, is a perfectly authentic archaeological discovery from 1898 revised for contemporary tastes with carefully selected esoteric embellishments.

According to Louis Régnier in the newspaper *Le Vexin* dated November 20, 1898, on November 7 of that same year, while engaged in repaving the Notre-Dame-de-l'Assomption chapel inside the Gisors church, "several paving stones of fairly large size bearing raised sculpture on the other side" were spotted. Unfortunately, in pulling them up, the workers broke the stones into multiple pieces. However, after they were successfully reassembled it became clear that they were the retable of an altar measuring fifty-two inches high by seventy-one inches wide. It was decorated with objects sculpted en haut or in bas-relief, according to their location, and framed "within an architecture of François I style, composed of three arcades or fully groined arches that separated the pilasters." Obviously there was enough here to justify the enthusiasm raised by this discovery.

Here are descriptions of the sculptures from the article in *Le Vexin*:

In the center are two standing figures, though missing their heads, that probably depict Jesus bidding his mother farewell, a subject borrowed from the apocryphal gospels that sixteenth-century image makers and painters happily reproduced. A good example can be seen in the beautiful glass work in the church in Conches. On the left are some apostles (St. Peter, St. John, and a third, for whom only the lower half of the body remains) standing behind a balustrade. Before them and much smaller in size, in accordance with medieval and Renaissance custom, the kneeling donor can be seen. On the right side and in much better shape, the donor's wife is in prayer, while ascending behind another balustrade are St. Madeleine and another figure who is unidentifiable, as is the open book she carries as her attribute. The entrance of Jesus into Jerusalem is depicted in the center. It is only recognizable today because of the figure of Yave, still visible in the tree he has climbed in order to get a better view of the person for whom Jerusalem was providing such an enthusiastic reception. All these sculptures were originally covered with paint and gilding, some traces of which still remain.

What has yet to be determined is the origin of these retable fragments, which, by all evidence, were reused following the destruction of an older edifice, though from a time no earlier than the era of François I. As it happens, the historian Louis Régnier, to whom we owe the description of this discovery, has provided an answer. This retable was part of a Saint-Catherine Chapel that had been built around 1530 south of the nave in the Gisors church and destroyed sometime after 1629. In fact, in 1629 a pewterer named Antoine Dorival composed a poem in which he describes this chapel, "with its altar table all covered with beaten gold," which he then goes on to describe:

> Among these, we find, as in our sculptures, Jesus and the Virgin, the scene in the Olive Garden, and St. Madeleine, but also there can be seen the meeting with the Good Samaritan and St. Thomas' display of disbelief, whereas the author of the poem doesn't mention the two individuals in prayer, nor St. Peter, nor the entry into Jerusalem.

Louis Régnier also quoted Antoine Dorival's poem:

> Gold, the luminous gleam yet shining
> of the altar table, all covered in beaten gold
> Shines so clearly that the entire chapel
> Resembles daybreak or a beautiful dawn.
> Near the well of Jacob, a lover of humanity
> Rested in his weariness, when from the Samaritans
> A woman arrived, whom God in his glory
> As if in need humbly asked for a drink
> Which she refused him, and he received from his bounty
> Water drawn from the shoot of his divinity . . .

From the tomb emerged the resurrected Jesus.
But dear Uranus, delay a while your course
And, as you have taken the Virgin for your guiding star
At the time you set sail,
Take her Son as your pilot.

There is nothing original about Antoine Dorival's poem. It is written in the precious style of the salons of that era, and even includes the allusion to Uranus so dear to Vincent Voiture, Malleville, and the other regular visitors to the salons of Madame de Rambouillet and Mademoiselle de Scudéry. Rather than view this as some sort of cryptogram, it is better to see it as an example of the elegant banter on a vaguely religious theme that was a popular style of the time. But the metaphors of the Son as pilot and the Virgin as the "guiding star," as in the Big Dipper, along with the different biblical citations Dorival includes, all provide excellent food for those seeking esoteric keys even where there are none. Dorival's poem has thus become for such people a sacred text for rediscovering the road to the Gisors treasure, which obviously can only be found in the Saint-Catherine Chapel.

Conveniently, this chapel no longer exists, thus anyone is free to say anything about it. It is theorized by some, however, that it no longer exists because it was made to utterly vanish—someone did not wish for the secrets deposited there to be spread over the surface of the world. So the universal conspiracy theory is still present, as is the notion of the intervention of occult powers. Dorival's manuscript, known only through the fragment published by Louis Régnier, was allegedly stolen from the Eure archives, where it had been stored. As for the retable rediscovered in 1898, it has vanished without a trace. The only remaining proof of its existence is Régnier's description and a photograph, which, while being quite strange, in no way gives anyone the right to claim that within this altar table "sleeps a secret that, to this time, only the initiates could decipher."

What is most annoying about this talk of *initiates* is that we are never told *what* exactly they were initiates of. But this allows the speaker to appear "in the know," as they say, and to present as realities what are simply work-ing hypotheses. The Gisors Saint-Catherine Chapel, however, actually existed. It was demolished for reasons unknown, and it is likely that the fragments of the retable discovered in 1898 have not been lost completely. There is a very discreet breed of art collector for finds such as these.

At the center of the affair of the Gisors treasure is a certain Roger Lhomoy, who was Gérard de Sède's informant for de Sède's book *Les Templiers sont parmi nous*. According to the rather conflicting testimo-nies about Lhomoy, it appears that this figure, who died in abject pov-erty in 1974, was a fanatical treasure hunter. During his youth he carried out clandestine digs throughout the Vexin region and apparently sold the curiosities he discovered to collectors. But these near-illegal activi-ties did not enrich him and he managed to get hired on as a gardener-cum-guide for the castle of Gisors, a position with no responsibilities, especially at that time, which allowed him all the time he needed to explore his favorite passion. He was not ignorant of the fact that under-ground tunnels existed beneath the fortress and the town of Gisors. In fact, he made a number of excavations, but always clandestinely and without revealing whatever he unearthed. Furthermore, he claimed that his activities were encouraged by the local clergy, but this declaration has never been confirmed. According to the picture that emerges from all the testimonies, Roger Lhomoy was a slightly uncultivated but sin-cere and stubborn peasant, a man who was somewhat of a crank and a naïf who often mistook his desires for realities. Those who knew him preserve touching, tender memories. By all evidence he was the sort of person everyone calls "a nice guy," but the activities he allegedly engaged in were so suspect that it is difficult to separate fact from fiction and anything said of him is probably best expressed in the conditional tense.

During the Liberation, from D-Day to August 24, 1944, when the Germans surrendered Paris, Roger Lhomoy carried out systematic, al-though nocturnal and solitary, excavations beneath the castle keep. He knew that during the German Occupation the Wehrmacht had installed a tank holding fifteen thousand liters of gasoline and a garage for repair-ing assault tanks. The construction projects that accomplished this may have provided the opportunity for some chance discoveries. While it has never been officially verified, in 1944 a German military mission arrived in Gisors with the objective of exploring the basement of the keep. Excavations, however, were never started, perhaps because of the complete collapse of Germany during the summer of 1944. Nevertheless, during the Occupation, in the Salle du Tournoi [the Tourney Room] located beneath the keep, collaborators who were no doubt militiamen tortured and shot twenty-seven Resistance members belonging to a network led by a jockey of Neaufles-Saint-Martin who was of English origin. This murky affair has never been truly cleared up, but it seems surprising that Resistance members would have been shot by firing squad—especially a French firing squad—inside the castle when the Germans were occupying the structure. It seems the Germans would have preferred handling this task themselves, and on the outside. All of this reveals under what conditions and in what a singular climate Roger Lhomoy performed his searches.

Lhomoy claims to have turned over yard upon square yard of dirt and hollowed out a vertical gallery along the former well, up to the day when a cave-in almost cost him his life. He escaped with a broken leg and then resumed his work, now digging horizontal galleries from the foot of the mound on which the keep was built. In his words, it was a veritable rabbit warren, a labyrinth of passageways that were not shored up and that were extremely narrow and impractical for a person of normal size. It is a source of amazement that Lhomoy could have carried out such excavation without being dispatched by another cave-in, especially because it appears that he took no particular precautions. It can also arouse a certain skepticism when we realize that an individual would risk sudden asphyxiation in such underground passageways if he or she were to remain in them for any length of time.

However, one day in March 1946, Roger Lhomoy appeared before the Gisors municipal council to declare that he had discovered an underground chapel. This is the narrative he apparently gave:

> I have recently discovered beneath the keep a Roman chapel made with stone from Louvecienne. The structure is thirty yards long,

again as wide, and in the area of four and one half yards high to the key stone in the arch. The altar is made of stone, as is the tabernacle. Halfway up the walls, supported by stone corbels, are statues of Christ and the twelve apostles. Along the walls, resting on the ground, are nineteen stone sarcophaguses two yards long by twenty-four inches wide and in the nave there are thirty metal chests lined up in rows of ten.

Here is food for wild speculation! The municipal aediles met at the foot of the keep, the place to which Lhomoy had directed them. But because it was impossible to enter the hole, the majority retraced their steps, saying the gardener was a madman. One of them—the fire chief, who later became mayor of Gisors—did try to enter the vertical gallery, but he was unable to get very far. The result of the entire expedition was that Roger Lhomoy was considered to be a liar. Orders were given to a team of German prisoners of war to seal up the open galleries, for they presented a very real danger to anyone who might venture around the encircling wall of the castle.

But Lhomoy did not see himself as beaten. He applied for and received an excavation permit from the State Ministry of Cultural Affairs. But then the entire municipality set itself against him, preventing him from carrying out his excavations and even threatening to bury him inside them. His permit was revoked and he was forbidden to frequent Gisors. In 1952 Lhomoy, who had not renounced his intentions, joined with two inhabitants of Versailles and obtained a new excavation permit. This time, while the municipality did not turn him down, it demanded a security fee so high that the three treasure seekers abandoned their plan. But Roger Lhomoy would sometimes return to dig at night, at least this is what he said, and he eventually met Gérard de Sède, who listened to him attentively and became enthusiastic about the whole business. The result was *Les Templiers sont parmi nous.*

Here we enter a zone of total obscurity. Gérard de Sède claims he was threatened by a strange figure calling himself the guardian of the Temple, who firmly advised him to abandon his research. He even recounts how one fine morning his car door was sprayed with buckshot. Where is the truth concealed? Does this guardian of the Temple really exist? If he does, where did he come from and what was he doing on the scene, given that Lhomoy had never uttered the name of the Templars? It is natural that we should ask who established the connection between the alleged discovery of the underground chapel and the events of 1307, during which the Templars caused the disappearance of at least some compromising documents, if not treasure. Roger Lhomoy, dragged onto television by Gérard de Sède, confirmed his story of the discovery of the chapel and his conviction that many other mysteries existed in the regions beneath Gisors.

Of course there was a storm of protest and denials from veteran academics, particularly from those who had been in charge of the monuments in Gisors. There is no need to quote these reactions; they were a unanimous, pure, and simple rejection of Lhomoy's allegations. However, on orders from Minister of Culture André Malraux, the keep of the castle was sealed and three months later excavations were started, which were officially described as simply "routine and unconnected to the Sède affair." But these digs turned up nothing and the openings were soon closed off again by order of the municipality.

On October 12, 1962, Roger Lhomoy was summoned to appear before the press. Several other figures gathered near the keep. They requested that he go down the hole to the place where he'd left his tools and the journalists who were present noted that the tunnel ended in a cul-de-sac. Lhomoy stuck by his story and claimed there was still a yard and a half to be dug to find the crypt. But his effort up to that time was for nothing. Convinced that enough time and money had been wasted listening to the ravings of a mythomaniac, the officials determined that the case had been decided and gave the order to depart. The excavated gallery would be filled in. It was not until 1964, though, after a new series of excavations conducted under orders from the ministry, that this work would be abandoned once and for all due to the fact that fissures had appeared in the keep, endangering the building's stability. Cement was then poured into every cavity that had been dug.

All those who believed in the existence of the underground chapel cried that the truth was being squelched because it frightened some people. The others, skeptics and naysayers alike, retorted in vain that this was the only means of protecting the building and ensuring the safety of the site's many visitors. Care was taken to avoid mentioning the cistern that might contain fifteen thousand liters of gasoline! In any case, there was food enough here to both nourish polemics and feed the boldest and most contradictory hypotheses. And despite the sealing of the excavation, countless clandestine seekers conducted their own discreet and illegal explorations over the following years—with no result, of course, unless you believe certain "initiates" who repeat the secret information that the treasure has been discovered and is now stored in a safe location.

The problem is knowing whether or not Roger Lhomoy discovered an underground chapel beneath the keep. Because he is the only one to have seen it and, as the saying goes, a single witness is no witness, we can only have doubts, even if we remain convinced overall that the underground passageways of Gisors have not surrendered all their secrets.

It seems that Roger Lhomoy subsequently allowed a few confidential confessions to slip, the most significant being his declaration that the excavations he had undertaken had led to nothing and that he invented the chests.[4]

The relentless nature of his excavating activities and his stubborn attempts to see to it that his findings were recognized are hardly actions compatible with his confessed behavior of lying. What, then, is the truth? Perhaps this renunciation of his findings can be seen as a sign of his deep bitterness. We cannot know. There are people who are more convinced than ever that Lhomoy had spoken the truth when claiming to have found a crypt containing the chests because his description of them corresponded to a description found in an ancient document, but there is

4. "What I told Gérard de Sède and others is not true. The excavations I undertook led to nothing . . . The chests, I invented them." These are Lhomoy's words as reported by Robert Charroux during an interview with Jean-Luc Chaumeil in 1974. From J.-L. Chaumeil, *Du premier au dernier Templier* (Paris: Henri Veyrier, 1985), 235. It should be noted that this is secondhand testimony.

nothing upon which to base this connection. There are also those who believe that Lhomoy embellished a few insignificant discoveries he may have made in the course of his digging, but neither can this be proved.

All of this confusion rests on the fact that no one has been able to pinpoint the actual location of the famous crypt in question. Furthermore, no one is very sure whether it is a crypt, a chapel, or a simple underground chamber in which the chests were stored. It seems that everyone has his own version of the facts in this affair that does not take into account the fact that there are so many versions. Added to this is the fierce attitude of obstinate rejection on the part of some of those individuals who think it is all a hoax.

One thing is certain: There was never a chapel beneath the Gisors keep, but there was one elsewhere, probably beneath the parish church. Its existence has been proved and a description of it has even been left for us. It has absolutely no connection with the Templars, however, for that order disappeared—at least officially—in 1312 and the Saint-Catherine Chapel dates from 1530.

The sole tenable hypothesis is this: Sometime during the sixteenth century, someone transported and concealed within the chapel objects and documents of Templar origin that had been stored elsewhere before that time. This would not be the first time archives were moved for reasons of security. After all, the sixteenth century was the era of the Religious Wars. Having accepted the existence of Templar documents that possibly compromised the Roman Catholic Church, certain Catholics might have deemed it wise to see to it that these documents disappeared or were stored in a secure location. But is a highly visible, recently constructed chapel a secure location?

So many questions! According to the private confidences he shared, Roger Lhomoy gave the impression of having been encouraged in his research by an ecclesiastic. This is not impossible. We know a certain number of clergy members in the region took an interest in the history of Gisors and knew of the existence of a crypt in which chests were stored, though having no precise information concerning the nature of these chests. One of these individuals, without stepping forward publicly, could therefore have encouraged Lhomoy to undertake some discreet excavations.

But if this was the case, why steer Lhomoy toward the castle keep when the ecclesiastics knew full well that the chapel could only be located near the church? This piece of the puzzle does not make sense unless we look at this guidance as an operation of diversion. Lhomoy would have served as a red herring by attracting attention to his digs at the castle while secret explorations were taking place next to the church. All of this would make an excellent plot for a spy film were it not for all the loose ends. In any event, everyone in Gisors and the surrounding area had long known there were underground tunnels that would likely reveal if not treasure, then at least some archaeological curiosities. The probable existence of a chapel beneath the church or its immediate neighborhood was, in sum, an open secret.

We could pose the question another way: If Lhomoy was truly manipulated to conduct excavations beneath the castle, who was manipulating him and for what purpose? And this begs another question: Why, even if Lhomoy lied, did those with official authority visibly prevent the continuation of his explorations that may have provided proof, if only proof that he was a liar? There are no answers to these questions.

How and where do the Templars fit into all of this? They are indeed present behind this obstinately drawn curtain. The great fascination explorers of the past hold for the Templars is that following the official annihilation of the order in 1314, they disappeared without a trace. The same fascination is held for the druids, who melted into their natural surroundings following the Roman conquest. Under these conditions it is hardly surprising that from time to time souvenirs—real or imaginary—of both of these groups are found in the more obscure though abundant corridors of history. Ghosts have a hard life, whatever the more rational minds may think, and manifest under very altered appearances. In Brittany, folk tradition says that the Templars, known there as the red monks or cursed monks, still haunt the places where they committed their crimes. This speaks volumes about the reputation of the Templars, which excellent authors wish at any cost to portray as saints and the unfortunate victims of an arbitrary authority. But that's another issue.

The interesting hypothesis presented by Gérard de Sède in *Les Templiers sont parmi nous,* which has the merit of prompting a reaction, is that Gisors is the place where the Templars buried their treasure and secret documents the night before their arrest.

It is true that when the agents of Philip the Fair, on the morning of October 13, 1307, went to arrest the Templars and confiscate the property of the Temple, they found nothing—neither gold, nor precious vessels, nor objects of worship, nor documents of any kind. It is a valid assumption, then, that the Templars, who had been warned in advance about the date of the arrest, had been able to find a safe haven for what they most valued. This was a setback for Philip the Fair, who thought to take possession not only of the Templars' wealth—however much there may have been—but also of compromising documents that would have permitted a speedy trial of the Templars and a condemnation of the order not subject to appeal. At the Paris Temple, the mother house of the order, for example, the king's archers could find neither treasure nor documents, but only men.

A tenacious tradition, apparently based on the document published by Gérard de Sède, claims that during the night before the arrest, heavy carts left the Paris Temple in a westerly direction, toward Gisors, naturally, where their contents would have been concealed within a crypt of the castle whose location was known only to the Templars. In other words, the famous chapel beneath the keep, which Roger Lhomoy and many others since have sought, is said to have contained the treasure and/or the Templar archives. Unfortunately, this ingenious theory does not stand up to analysis.

First, it is doubtful that a number of carts could have left the Paris Temple the eve of the arrest without attracting the attention of Parisians, or at least of Philip the Fair's spies. Next, if we suppose that the carts could have slipped through the net spread by the king's police, why would they have deposited their cargo at Gisors, in a *royal* castle guarded by *royal* troops? Unless we accept the explanation that the best hiding place is in the very jaws of the wolf, such a plan appears quite astonishing.

And even if the carts did leave Paris—which is not an impossibility, after all—it would be much more likely they would have gone in the direction of foreign territory not dependent upon the king of France. Because the Holy Empire, Aragon, and Brittany were too far away, only England could have served as a Templar storage site. In this regard, incidentally, it should be noted that while much hunting for the Templar treasure goes on in France, the question of whether or not the treasure exists is totally ignored in England.

There remains the theory of a first-stage site—not in a Templar commandery, because all the Templar establishments were under surveillance, but in an abbey or castle near Gisors, or at Gisors itself—followed by a gradual transfer to a further destination. This is not impossible, but how are we to know for certain?

It is also plausible that Pope Clement V managed to forewarn Grand Master Jacques de Molay of the plot being hatched against the Templars. According to testimony collected during the trial, Jacques de Molay was thrilled that he managed to cause the secret Rule of the Temple to disappear before the fateful day. Furthermore, it would be cause for surprise if the pope himself, sole superior of the Templar Order, had not taken certain precautions before accepting the incarceration and torture of the Templars. The legitimate relationship between the pope and the Templar Order should have left some trace of its presence, but none has been found.

So there is an impassable divide between what is known for certain and the claims that the Temple's treasure and the archives of the order were buried in a crypt beneath the castle of Gisors or in the Saint-Catherine Chapel (which, if you recall, was built two centuries after the disappearance of the Temple). The scenario is not without charm, but it has no relationship to either historical reality or archaeological evidence. And the alleged documents of 1307—the origin of which is a subject of controversy and the discovery of which is entirely shrouded in fog—cannot be used to support any certainty.

However, in the field of historical enigmas, nothing is ever really lost and another theory can be found to make up for the weaknesses of a preceding one. The theory of the Templar treasure buried at Gisors is a fragile one and rests solely on assumptions, but some offer another hypothesis that in this case, it is said, is supported by numerous documents: The chests that should be located in the Saint-Catherine Chapel (the crypt whose existence is incontestable) did not contain the archives and/or treasure of the Templars, but held instead the secret archives of a mysterious order founded by Godefroy de Bouillon—the Priory de Sion. This order would have been older than the Temple, contributing secretly to the Temple's creation and separating from it in 1188, at the time of the famous incident of the Gisors elm. The existence of this Priory de Sion would have paralleled that of the Knights Templar Order that has survived into the present. The order allegedly stored its documents in the famous crypt of Gisors, later adding several documents concerning the Templars specifically. This theory is no more absurd than any other. The problem is that the documents allegedly presented by the Priory de Sion and published as part of a secret dossier appear to be of dubious or at least totally unverifiable authenticity.[5]

It is always a delicate matter to pass judgment on documents that emerge from the remote past and appear by chance just when there is a need for them. We may consider strange the attitude of a small group who, at a certain moment, decide to make public what had been kept hidden for centuries.[6] Obviously, discoveries of this kind occur from time to time and historians are happy to avail themselves of the contribution they present. But before all else, the origin of such documents must be clear. A valid theory cannot be constructed without support from verifiable foundations, especially if we are led to accept a number of conclusions from lack of certainty.

---

5. *Le Charivari,* no. 18, devoted to the Priory de Sion, contains certain allegedly secret documents and numerous commentaries. For more on some of these documents, read Richard Bordes, *Les Mérovingiens et Rennes-le-Château* (P. Schrauben, 1984). There is enough here to feed skepticism.

6. Some of the secret documents have been published by the Priory de Sion itself in a work entitled *Le Livre des Constitutions* (Geneva: Éditions des Commanderies de Genève, 1956). Those calling themselves members of the Priory claimed that the time was right to divulge what had once been kept secret.

History is full of examples of documents fabricated after the fact to meet the needs of a particular cause: postdated maps, imaginary testimonies, and skillfully aged "parchments." During the Middle Ages the monks of certain abbeys were specialists in this kind of work, which raised the prestige of their abbey, attracted pilgrims, exempted themselves from taxes, and returned favors to noble patrons. In Glastonbury, England, under the aegis of Henry II Plantagenet, monks fabricated out of whole cloth a report detailing the supposed exhumation of the corpses of King Arthur and Queen Guinivere. Even today a visitor can stop to gather his thoughts before the tombs of these legendary figures—a good example of why it pays to be extremely prudent in judging the verity of certain documents claiming to shed new light on a historical enigma.

Outside of these secret documents, not a single document or any work on the knightly orders talks about the Priory de Sion, astonishing for an order supposedly founded so long ago and for one that played such an important role in history. According to the documents, it is Godefroy de Bouillon himself who is said to have established this order in Jerusalem in 1099 and its first seat is said to have been the abbey Notre-Dame-du-Mont-de-Sion. An order such as this would not have been founded by chance, but would have been tied to an even older sect about which the documents give us no information. Furthermore, it is likely that Godefroy de Bouillon would have had contact with the mysterious Brothers of the Red Cross. The Red Cross was an emblem, we are told, of the Sages of the Light, an initiatory fraternity with Gnostic tendencies that was allegedly established by a certain Ormus or Ormessus, an Alexandrian converted to Christianity by St. Mark.

But this connection alone was not enough to ensure an authentic initiatory lineage for this new order. Thus we are assured that the Priory de Sion was born of the fusion of the Brotherhood of the Red Cross, Essene groups, and Godefroy de Bouillon's group. In this way the Priory de Sion is given a connection to the Johannites. What indeed would become of esoteric sects, prudently called "philosophical circles," if they could not be placed under the protection of St. John? Whether the protector is John the Baptist, John the Apostle, or the John who wrote the

Apocalypse (John of Patmos), we are assured, is of no importance. In any case, the rule of thumb seems to be to set in opposition John, keeper of the true message of love, and the perverted church of Peter, the church that has succumbed to a diabolical exotericism by vulgarizing itself in its present embodiment. Of course, the institution of this opposition overlooks the fact that the true and authentic founder of the Christian church is not Peter, the famous phrase from the Gospels notwithstanding, but St. Paul, whose Epistles, older than the Gospels, are the absolute departure point for Roman Catholic doctrine. But that is neither here nor there. Once we presume the existence of Johannine tendencies in medieval Christianity, it is very easy to accept that the Priory de Sion—if indeed it truly existed—had a solid connection to it.

This Priory de Sion would thereby have spread out from Jerusalem, but in a secret fashion until its leaders recognized the fact that in order to act with any validity, they needed an official organization that could be integrated into ordinary life. This was how, at the behest of mysterious "superiors," the first Order of the Poor Knights of Christ—the original Order of the Temple—was founded. Added to this is the allegation by the partisans of this theory that three of the Temple's founders, Hugues de Payns, Bisol de Saint-Omer, and Hugues de Champagne, were themselves members of the Priory de Sion. The Temple, an *exoteric* creation of an *esoteric* order, became a kind of militia that was launched during the twelfth century, but was subject in all respects to the venerable Priory de Sion, which reserved the right to make all necessary decisions and define the actual objectives pursued by the Temple.

To be sure, all this brings to mind the plot of a good spy novel. But do not be deceived; within this scenario there is a well-founded religious and metaphysical aspect, even though it may seem a little suspect at times.

Because John's patronage was not enough to establish the authenticity of the order's direct descent from Gnostic tradition, steps were taken to include in the Priory de Sion's lineage everything possible concerning the mysterious Ormus. Of course this Gnostic tradition was based on the earlier Mazdaism: The Sages of the Light are necessarily the Sons of Light—in other words, the descendants of the partisans of the great

Persian god Ahura Mazda, symbol of the Light that wages unending war against the forces of darkness represented by Ahriman, whom the Christians incorporated into their doctrine under the name of Satan. Ahura Mazda is generally better known in the West under his contracted name Ormuzd. How surprising it is to find the great god of the Persians in the somewhat mythical figure of Ormus! Syncretism always pays off when it comes to religious matters—especially religious "mysteries." There is no great distance between this "luminous" Ormus-Ormuzd and the elm [*orme* in French —*Trans.*] of Gisors—and let's not overlook the elm in Paris in front of the church of St. Gervais, a place, it appears, that was frequented quite regularly by the Freemasons. But haven't trees always held a symbolic value?

Whatever the case may be, we are assured that the Priory de Sion, after creating the Temple, discreetly merged into the new order. It is also declared that when the kingdom of Jerusalem had been lost once and for all, the brothers of Ormus settled at the great priory of Saint-Samson of Orléans, while others freely integrated into the Templars, as well as into the small priory of Mont-de-Sion in Saint-Jean-le-Blanc near Orléans. This is why what had been known as the Order of Sion was, after that date, called the Priory de Sion—at least this is what is said in the famous secret dossiers.

But there is more. In 1188 the elm [*orme*] was destroyed at Gisors, though not, apparently, because of a quarrel between Philip Augustus and Henry II Plantagenet, as historians commonly and mistakenly believe. According to the documents, it was actually during a veritable ceremony of rupture between the Knights Templar and the knights of the Priory de Sion that this event took place. The reasons for this break are quite logical. We know for a fact that following the loss of Jerusalem, the attitude of the Templars in general and specifically of its grand master, Gérard de Ridefort, had been more than suspicious. Ridefort was accused of having betrayed and even of having renounced Christianity in order to save his own life. However, nothing can be proved in this regard and Gérard de Ridefort remains a mysterious figure—this is a fact. According to the secret documents, the anonymous superiors of the

Priory de Sion held the Templars responsible for the Christian defeat. The Templars had fallen into disfavor, betrayed their mission, and somehow renounced the plan of Godefroy de Bouillon. The members of the Priory de Sion thus decided to separate from the Temple and allow that order to follow its own destiny with no further intervention on their part. Their decision, apparently, was to form an independent and secret order once again. This is a strange breach of truth but one that would explain why no voice was lifted in defense of the Templars when they were abolished. Accordingly, the Priory's documents seem to suggest that the Templars' fate was a just punishment. We are finally told that the Priory de Sion elected its own grand master, a certain Jean de Gisors, who took the name John II because the title of John I was traditionally reserved for Christ. Again we find ourselves in the shadow of John. It seems that all the grand masters of the Priory de Sion who succeeded him also bore this name, or rather this sacred title. A list of these grand masters follows, among whom we are not surprised to find such cultural giants as Nicolas Flamel, Leonardo da Vinci, Victor Hugo, and even Claude Debussy and Jean Cocteau.

At the time of the disappearance of the Temple, the Priory of Sion would have survived thanks to the extreme discretion surrounding it. As shown by the admission in the secret documents that one of the goals of this clandestine organization was to put an authentic heir of the Merovingians back on the French throne (in this instance, a descendant of a lineage going back to Dagobert II), the Priory worked in the shadows toward the destruction of all usurpers. We may then ask in good faith if the Priory de Sion may not have incited the dukes of Lorraine, descendants of Godefroy de Bouillon, to claim the crown of France; if it may have inspired the assassinations of Henry III and Henry IV; if it compelled Nicolas Poussin to paint his mysterious work *The Shepherds of Arcadia,* then to whisper into the ear of Nicolas Fouquet a dangerous secret that would be the cause of Fouquet's downfall; and—why not?— if it had a hand in the condemning to death of Louis XVI. Anything is possible. There are shadowy zones in history inside which we long to shine a light. After all, why not see the discreet presence of the Priory de

Sion in the seventeenth-century Brotherhood of the Holy Sacrament, the famous Cabal of Devotees, who, among other things, worked so hard to save Fouquet? Is everyone aware that the three heads of this brotherhood were Vincent de Paul; Jean-Jacques Olier, founder of Saint-Sulpice; and Nicolas Pavillon, bishop of Alet? Vincent de Paul was far from being very forthcoming about his relationships, and his career is full of unexplained intervals. As for Saint-Sulpice and Alet—not far from Rennes-les-Bains—the Priory seems to have been involved in both, or at least its possible influence has been noted. How true it is that history is a great whole in which the same figures reappear consistently.

But in this instance history has been subjected to a little manhandling:

> If Godefroy de Bouillon actually founded an "abbey of Mount Zion"[Priory de Sion], nowhere is it said that it served as the seat for any order. In reality it existed in Jerusalem until 1187, at which point it was transferred to Saint Leonard's in Acre. The last of the monks who lived in Acre died in Sicily in 1291. Louis VII returned from the Crusades with several clergymen of Mount Zion and established them at Saint-Samson of Orléans, the former Saint-Symphorien that the king had recently offered to the House of Jerusalem. Louis VII's donation was confirmed in 1152 by Pope Adrian, who bestowed on the Orleans clergy the Rule of St. Augustine. The monks remained at Saint-Samson until 1519, the year of their reformation, and in 1617 the church and its properties passed into the hands of the Jesuits, who founded the royal college of Orléans. In fact, Saint-Samson had been in full decline since the end of the thirteenth century. It had no more than two capitular canons in 1289 and only one in 1291.[7]

This is a long way from the Templars, and even farther from the Priory de Sion. In reality—because there always is a reality—the source of

---

7. Jean Robin, *Rennes-le-Château, la colline envoûtée* (Paris: Guy Trédaniel, 1982), 87.

certain documents concerning the Priory de Sion is now known full well:

> The history of the Priory de Sion was drawn from the texts of Jacques-Étienne Marconis of Nègre, nineteenth-century Freemason and brilliant French writer of works on a number of subjects, who was twice expelled from the Rite of Misraïm (first in Paris under the name of Marconis and second in Lyon under the name of Nègre!) which led him to found his own rite, that of Memphis.[8]

Just what does this actually mean? According to Marconis, the apostle St. Mark converted to Christianity a "Sephardic priest" named Ormus, who was living in Alexandria. Then it is told that with six colleagues, Ormus created an initiatory society of the Sages of the Light in Egypt. The Essenes were allegedly connected with Ormus and his disciples until 1181, the year in which they would have communicated their secrets to the Knights of Palestine, when Garimont was patriarch of Jerusalem. An order of Oriental Masons settled in Edinburgh in 1150, and it was not until 1814 that the order was introduced into France by a mysterious figure named Samuel Honis.

In the period from 1839 to 1854, Marconis revisited this legend, personally altering the name Ormus to Ormesius. On these foundations, he established in 1839 the Oriental Rite of Memphis, consisting of ninety-five degrees, with the Hierophant being the ninety-sixth.[9] The Templars are singularly absent from this legend hastily strung together by Jacques-Étienne Marconis de Nègre. So is the Priory de Sion. But it is easy to see through this transparent manipulation. It was simple enough to replace the Oriental Masons who settled in Edinburgh with the monks who established themselves at Saint-Jean-le-Blanc. Once this trick had been pulled off, the Priory de Sion could fly on its own power, survive through the centuries, and even provide—why not make use of it?—logical

---

8. Jean Robin, *Rennes-le-Château, la colline envoutée* (Paris: Guy Trédaniel, 1982), 84.

9. Jean-Pierre Bayard, *Le Symbolism maçonnique des hauts grades* (Paris: Éd. du Prisme, 1975), 259.

explanations for the creation of the Temple.[10] It is often useful to make discoveries in the depths of library books or manuscripts no one knows about, volumes whose contents will never be verified by anyone. In this way they can be exploited, generally in ways never anticipated by their authors.

What should we think of the revised and corrected history as presented in these documents? One immediate reaction leaps forward: Lump it in the fiction category, along with the iron mask or the unfortunate Louis XVII. But that is too easy. Throwing away a debatable theory is not enough to eliminate the mystery it is attempting to explain. After all, as the saying goes, there is no smoke without fire.

What is annoying about the possibly fabricated history of the Priory de Sion is that we never manage to discover the motive behind this fabrication. That there may have been the discreet presence of an earlier order at the time of the founding of the Templars is entirely possible. That the personal action of Godefroy de Bouillon played a part in the formation of this mysterious order is perfectly acceptable. The figure of Godefroy de Bouillon remains an enigma, to say the least. It should not be overlooked that he or those around him spread the assertion that he was the descendant of Lohengrin, the famous Swan Knight, son of Parzival. Godefroy de Bouillon sought—or others sought for him—a clear connection to the Grail lineage. This desire for association is not an exception: The Lusignan spared no effort to show proof of their descent from the mysterious Melusine and Henry II Plantagenet clearly wished to be considered King Arthur's rightful heir.

The theory of the Priory de Sion, whatever its truth, necessarily rests on something, even if some documents appear to be hardly trustworthy.

---

10. I should also mention the "inspired hill" of Sion-Vaudémont in Lorraine. During the nineteenth century, a priest who was somewhat of a crackpot endeavored to make the hill of Sion a spiritual Mecca. This priest, Léopold Baillard, aided by his two brothers, managed, after many difficulties, to create there an Institute of the Brothers of Our Lady of Sion-Vaudémont—which was not well looked upon by the ecclesiastical authorities. It is true that this affair cast shadows that were somewhat suspect, yet Maurice Barrès took advantage of Baillard's endeavors to popularize this inspired hill of Sion, whose name would become quite symbolic. It is no cause for surprise that the name Sion would have been employed for such an operation.

So, under these conditions, why not imagine the following hypothesis: The Gisors affair would have been fabricated from whole cloth to incite searches and perhaps permit the discovery of documents, genuine in this case, that were to be found buried in the underground tunnels of Gisors. This would explain Roger Lhomoy's tenacity in continuing his excavations, the relationship of the Gisors treasure to the Templars, and the opportune publication of the secret documents of the Priory de Sion. Most important in this affair is to know who is manipulating whom.

Gisors is the focal point of an inextricable tangle of probabilities, uncertainties, and suppositions. But it is also the crossroads and intersection of all the paths that might lead to a coherent explanation for the Templar mystery. There is not or, rather, there is no longer a Saint-Catherine Chapel. But the underground tunnels of Gisors certainly exist and they have never been entirely excavated. Furthermore, each time an entrance to them has been opened, it has been vigilantly sealed again—even to the extent of being filled with cement. For what reason? We know a Merovingian cemetery is located just north of the church, but we are zealously prevented from knowing what exactly it contains. We know that the Templars occupied the castle of Gisors for only several months, so they could not have undertaken any serious construction projects there. But we also know that the Templars have always played a role in Gisors, even if only to serve as mediators between the Anglo-Normans and the French. We know that this same Gisors castle was begun before the founding of the Temple, thus making it impossible for the Templars to have had any influence on its general design—but certain characteristics of the surrounding wall and the keep present similarities to other Templar monuments. We know that the graffiti in the Prisoner's Tower are largely of later provenance than the Templars, and that in any case the fictitious Nicolas Poulain could not have been a member of the order—but the graffiti are nonetheless of Templar inspiration. We know that areas beneath the castle and beneath the church of Gisors have been excavated but have never officially led to any precise discoveries, and that no efforts have been made to enable these searches to reach a positive outcome.

Is the reason for this to allow for any hypothesis on the treasure hidden in the basement of Gisors? Does knowing that the plan of the castle corresponds to the position of the sun and the stars in the sky on December 25, 1090, help us to solve the mystery? Will learned exegeses of the numbers read from the castle and the church of Gisors hold the key we need to open "the open door to the sealed palace of the king"? Everything depends on what will actually be discovered in the time to come, when the decision has been made to clear away the ruins of the Temple.

In an affair where the "almosts" sometimes have the value of certainties, why couldn't we indulge in a few word games? This practice was common during the Middle Ages, the time of the Templars, and was employed by authors of serious reputation. It was believed that in the underground passages of the castle lay gold [gisent ors], but this was incorrect. The Templars' treasure and archives, if they ever existed or if they still exist, lie outside [gisent hors]. It is perhaps up to us to discover in what part of memory they have been buried.

4

The Temple Is Elsewhere
and Everywhere

GIVEN THE FACT that the Templar Order was founded in Palestine for the express purpose of protecting pilgrims on their way to Jerusalem, logically it is in the Holy Land that Templar establishments should be sought. They are there to be found, of course, and they held great importance at the time of the Crusades. They can also be found in Cyprus, which served as an indispensable departure base and surveillance station for the Middle East. But we cannot help but be surprised by the impressive number of Templar sites found throughout the whole of Western Europe—in Spain, England, Ireland, and especially France. In the case of Spain, a Templar presence is justified by the reconquest of the peninsula from the Muslims. The combat undertaken there by the Templars was the same as that which they waged in Palestine. But what of the other countries? Ireland, as far as we know, was never in any danger of being assailed by the "infidels"—unless these "infidels" were other than Muslim. Yet it is a fact that from the middle of the twelfth century on, a large portion of Western Europe was seeded—even riddled—with Templar establishments: sanctuaries, commanderies, simple houses or "barns" (meaning farms), and fortresses, with all buildings being inseparable from lands whose extent expanded ceaselessly.

But what were the Templars doing in territories so far from the Middle East?

Historians generally have a short and simple answer to this question: Ensuring the material means necessary for propaganda and the struggle against the "infidels," as well as recruitment for the Crusades and Christian settlement of Palestine, required the Templars' solid presence in the countries of Western Europe. Their presence enabled the inhabitants of these lands to show solidarity with the Christians of the East. That the strongest Templar presence corresponded to the great crossroads and communication paths of Western Europe was no coincidence, but was in response to an absolute necessity: to ensure the rapid transport of men, foodstuffs, and material toward the Mediterranean ports from which they could embark to the Middle East. This is all quite logical, but is it the only explanation?

The existence of Templar establishments across the map of Europe is not due to chance. Following its official recognition by the Council of Troyes in 1128, the Order of the Temple certainly received numerous gifts from great lords who desired participating in the Crusades, and the gifts of buildings and lands were quite scattered. It should be noted that the majority of these gifts were fallow lands, portions of territories that had not yet been exploited. But the Templars, who, by the unanimous opinion of their observers, were excellent administrators, practiced what is today called the reconstitution of scattered properties. They worked out exchanges, sold certain domains in order to acquire others, and used the monies they received as payments to acquire property. All of this appears to have been orchestrated in accordance with a master plan intended to situate the Templar establishments near the main roads of commerce, making them the necessary links between the most far-flung regions of Europe and Mediterranean ports. It is a fact that the majority of Templar commanderies are located at strategic points governing the economic, social, and political life of Europe.

Further, while it is true that the Templars' presence can be justified by a need for efficacy in the achievement of their goal, we might still ask just what exactly that goal was. Much has been written about double meanings in what the Templars said. But before looking for esoteric reasons for it, perhaps we should focus on the simple political reasons behind it. After all, the Templar Order was created *to watch the roads*—in Palestine, of course, but why not in Europe as well? Why couldn't a uniquely fine-tuned structure operating under the best circumstances serve two parallel goals that did not conflict? The Templars' obligation, then, to provide a specific supply of resources from the European continent, could easily have been coupled with a more veiled obligation: It was in the complete interest of the papacy to monitor Europe's highways if it wished to make often rebellious sovereigns bow to its ideals. He who holds the roads holds the country—a perspective that should be kept in mind if we wish to have a good idea of both the greatness of the Order of the Temple and its brutal fall. In any event, it is not a negligible hypothesis.

That said, the Templar network sheds light on certain strongholds occupied by the famous commanderies whose traces can be found today not only in ruins and in preserved or restored buildings, but in toponyms as well. It is said that place-names persist even after the disappearance of the social group that created the name. The name of Paris, for instance, comes from the name of a Gallic people, the Parisii, who occupied this area during the time of Caesar and Vercingetorix.

However, we must exercise the greatest prudence when creating a map of the exact locations where the Templars built their edifices, where they occupied preexisting buildings, and where they merely possessed lands. Of course, a place called the temple has a strong chance of having belonged to the order, this appellation being the most widespread and the most characteristic. But it is not the only term that designated a Templar establishment and, being a common term before the existence of the order, often referring to Roman ruins or even an ancient sanctuary from pagan times, its presence in a toponym is not necessarily proof of a connection to the Knights of the Red Cross. For instance, on the outskirts of the town of Alésia in the Doubs region, possible site of the genuine Alésia of Vercingetorix, there is a place called Temple Belin, which is recognized as the former site of a sanctuary dedicated to the Gallic sun god Belenos. There are many other examples of this sort. In addition, the influence of Protestantism should not be overlooked. In certain regions the term *temple* simply designates a place where members of the Reform Church gathered, particularly during the time that Protestants, persecuted by the official church and royal police, were forced to worship clandestinely.

Because the term *temple* by itself is insufficient to confirm a Templar presence, it can be confirmed in certain places only through local history. We should also be aware that the word *temple* as appropriated to a building does not necessarily imply that the structure was a religious one. It may simply have been a house or farm or piece of land owned by the Templar Order, sometimes far removed from any important establishment. This especially does not mean, counter to general belief, that there was a commandery in the location. Commanderies were not located everywhere, but instead were a specific region's sort of headquarters to which a number of secondary, more or less remote establishments were connected. In the Lot-et-Garonne region, the modern township of Temple-sur-Lot corresponds precisely to a former commandery whose buildings still exist. A neighboring township bears the name Granges-sur-Lot, which shows us that there were farms dependent on this commandery. On the other hand, in the Loire Atlantique region, there was never a commandery nor even any Templars in the township called Temple-de-Bretagne. As for legends, they are countless. For example, in the Lower Alps, the charming thermal spa of Gréoux-les-Bains prides itself on its historical connection to the Templars: It is said that the admirable castle there, naturally defended by the Verdon ravine, was built by the Knights Templar. It is a quadrilaterally shaped fortress reinforced on the west by two towers, a beautiful example of medieval military architecture, but—unfortunately for some—dating from the middle of the fourteenth century and attributed to the Knights Hospitallers of St. John of Jerusalem, the other order of soldier-monks who took possession of the property of the Templars in 1312. Local tradition has it, though, that this castle is haunted by the ghost of a Templar who was immured within its walls. This is not the only example of a Templar tradition in places where the Knights Templar never resided.

Of course, only the rich are touched on for loans, as demonstrated by the privileged place occupied by the Templars in the collective memory. Long after their official disappearance, they continued to be seen everywhere. In Paris, for example, the grand master of the Hospitallers, the heirs and successors of the Templars, was continuously referred to as the grand master of the Temple of Paris, and the famous red monks of Breton oral tradition refer not only to the Templars but also to the Hospitallers. This confusion is normal; how could the average people of that time distinguish between the Knights of the Temple and the Knights of St. John of Jerusalem? Both were orders of soldier-monks and their missions were apparently identical, which does make more difficult research of sites that were actually built or at least occupied by the Templars and gives credence to the fact that the presence of the word *temple* in a toponym is not enough to prove a Templar presence, especially if archives and local history do not also confirm it.

On the other hand, toponyms of the red cross are very strong clues to a Templar presence and, in the majority of cases, indicate direct Templar connection to a place (even in the case of a single field). We know for a fact that the red cross was officially the emblem of the Templars beginning in 1148, while the white cross was the emblem of the Hospitallers of St. John. So wherever we see *red cross* in a name, we may assume connection to the Templars; wherever we see *white cross,* we may assume connection to the Hospitallers, provided we are certain that the place-names are quite old.

We cannot so easily discern the history of the places called the commandery. Of course, there is a large chance that the foundations in question are due to the Templars, but they could just as easily be Hospitaller works, or the work of other orders consisting of hierarchies with commanders, such as the Knights Hospitallers of the Holy Spirit and St. Anthony of the Viennese. It is also difficult to know whether place-names such as La Chevalerie and La Cavalerie designate a site where horses were raised, a fiefdom of knights, or a commandery. The same holds true for the numerous Le Chevalier or Les Chevaliers. The term *grange* appears to have been used more than *farm* by the Templars, but it is not safe enough ground on which to base assumptions. La Ferme [Farm] du Temple can be found next to La Grange du Temple. Place-names like Villeneuve-du-Temple and Bourg-des-Templiers should also be considered. While there may not have been a commandery in each of these places, the Templars did lead some sort of activity there. As for appellations such as La Villedieu, Masdieu, L'Hôpital, L'Hospitalet, and La Maladerie, if they can be attributed to the Templars, as is the case with the Mas Deu in the Roussillon region, they are common to the Temple and other orders that take responsibility for providing shelter to pilgrims or the sick.

Special mention should be made of a toponym that others have ig-nored: La Bachellerie. This term, which derives from the Latin *baccalaria,* originally meaning "a land concession in return for rent," designates an extremely important medieval position responsible for maintaining the roads, ports, and earthen levees, especially in the western regions of France. The role of *bachelier* was entrusted to lords, monks, and even commoners, who were then exempt from taxes. It so happens that the most important bacheliers of the twelfth and thirteenth centuries were the Templars. Therefore, we have every chance of finding a trace of the Templar presence when visiting any place called Bachellerie. This only reinforces the theory that the Templars located themselves along routes of communication in a network intended to maintain surveillance over European roads—an extension of the Templars' original mission in Pal-estine. Because the Templars were devoted heart and soul to the papacy, this surveillance of the roads was not always well received by heads of state, which explains, at least partially, why Philip the Fair displayed such an unrelenting effort to destroy the Temple after seemingly attempt-ing to take control of it.

The Templars' geographic connections and holdings reveal a per-fectly tuned and smoothly functioning European infrastructure. It is to this weblike system that the Templar Order owed its smooth operations—especially in sending knights to the Holy Land—as well as its economic power and consequently its political role. All studies to date on the op-eration of the Templar Order show that the knights' timely and efficient action was very advanced for its age. But this is the diurnal face of the order, the exposed portion of the iceberg. The nocturnal face, the submerged part, is what we are gradually discovering. Apart from a few privileged individuals, the contemporaries of the Templars were incapable of recognizing or even presuming their existence. A tremendous ambiguity must be acknowledged concerning the system put in place by the Templars, which led to their downfall, whatever the reality of their secret activities. This is why the Templars remain such an intriguing subject for seekers. They all know there is something to be discovered beneath appearances.

The quintessential symbol of this powerful ambiguity of the Temple is the commandery. The word has left a strange resonance in our minds. Of course, during the Templar era, *house* was used much more frequently than *commandery*. But it was not simply a house; it was a coherent whole of great complexity: primarily a sanctuary, of course, a church or simple chapel, sometime a place of inspiration known only to a few, but also

> [s]imultaneously a convent, a concern of the noble type, the center of a network of relationships and clientele. The men found there were a diverse lot: their positions, their station, their roles all differed, but all were brothers or men of the Temple. The commandery provided protection and shelter for the large Templar family.[1]

For this reason, a place like Gisors cannot be eliminated from the list of places where the Templars had a presence, even if, officially, only three Templars lived there for only a few months. The commitments of the three Templars in Gisors were the commitments of the commandery to which they belonged and, through that, of the entire order. The very structure of the order did not permit the slightest deviation from its operational procedures (the private lives of the members of the Templar Order were another matter). Everything was connected, and while Gisors was never a commandery or Templar fortress, or even a secret sanctuary, the castle and its underground passages formed part of the Templars'

---

1. Alain Demurger, *Vie et mort de l'Ordre du Temple* (Paris: Seuil, 1985), 129.

giant web. Further, there are several strongholds and places that are explained by the Templar presence at Gisors.

Let's examine several of the more interesting or notable examples of these places, for it is impossible to provide an exhaustive examination of every one. It is said that the Temple had nine thousand commanderies in Europe at its disposal, meaning the countries of France, England, Ireland, Germany, Italy, Spain, and Portugal. Of course this figure is exaggerated or, rather, it represents the total of commanderies and their annexes. France, where the Temple enjoyed its greatest success and inspired extraordinary donations, and which appears to be the cradle of the order in the West, counted only around seven hundred commanderies, each including, on an average, a dozen domains, independent of houses, scattered fields, and even entire villages.[2] Of these seven hundred commanderies spread over the territory of what is now France, which, in the Templars' time, meant the territories dependent on the French crown, the Holy Roman Empire, the earldom of Toulouse, the duchy of Brittany, and the kingdom of England, some played only a minor role, but others were of true importance.

In order to understand the role of Gisors, it is important to understand the Templar presence around the famous fortress. As it so happens, the region of Normandy has the greatest wealth of Templar commanderies and houses. This is no cause for surprise when we consider that it was the hinge connecting the Anglo-Norman kingdom with that of France, which is yet another indication of the political aspect of the Order of the Temple and, with all due respect to some, that it was an order rooted in everyday life even if we can glimpse in the background motives of a more esoteric nature. It is not by chance that Templar establishments of primary importance were placed on the Lower Seine in the strategic zone that was the subject of such bitter contention between the two kingdoms. The closest commanderies to Gisors and the Epte frontier were Saint-Étienne-de-Renneville, Chanu, Brettemare, and Bourgoult in what is now the department of the Eure. A little farther away we find

---

2. Georges Bordonove, *La Vie quotidienne des Templiers au XIIIe siècle* (Paris: Hachette, 1975), 117–18.

Sainte-Vaubourg, near Rouen, and La Genetay in the forest of Roumare, in what is today the department of the Seine-Maritime. In the rest of Normandy we can point out the commanderies of Bretteville-le-Rabel (Calvados), Baugy and Bayeux in Calvados, Volcanville and Coutances in La Manche, Fresneaux near Séez, and Villadieu-sous-Grandvilliers near Trun in the Orne region.

The commandery of Bourgoult, near Gisors, is the former dependency of the Rouen diocese, parish of the archdeacons of the Norman Vexin, viscounty and poll of Vernon, parliament and treasury jurisdiction of Rouen. One of its founders was a certain Robert Crespin, son of Gosselin, baron of Étrépagny, and lord of Dangu. During the Middle Ages the family of Crespin-Dangu was the rival of the Harcourt family, which multiplied its donations in favor of the Templars. Wishing not to be left behind, in 1219 Robert Crespin offered the Templars a sixty-acre property in the parish of Harquency, in the woods of Bourgoult. Other members of the family made additional donations that the commandery used to expand and enrich itself, establishing annexes, notably in Andelys, Cahaignes, Saint-Vincent-des-bois, and Dangu. In Bourgoult itself, headquarters of the commanderies, the Templars erected a manor and chapel dedicated to Saint-Jean-Baptistes on the side of a hill in the township of Harquency. These buildings were destroyed during the eighteenth century by the Knights of Malta, which was the new name of the Knights Hospitallers of St. John. These knights rebuilt the sanctuary in 1768 and on the site of the former chapel they constructed the farmer's house. Currently the thirteenth-century commandery is located on private property, but nothing remains of the original buildings. If we accept the fact that the treasure of the Temple of Paris was transported west through Gisors on the night of October 13, 1307, we can also theorize that it could have passed through the Bourgoult commandery before being securely stashed elsewhere, probably in England. On the other hand, as the commandery of Bourgoult was not founded until the beginning of the thirteenth century, it is impossible to attribute to it any kind of role in the affair of the three Templars of Gisors or in the episode of the felled elm in 1188.

The commandery of Saint-Étienne-de-Renneville in the township of

Sainte-Colombe-la-Campagne was by far the oldest and most important of the region. In 1147, Richard d'Harcourt, member of one of the noblest and most powerful Norman families, had built a Saint-Étienne chapel at Sainte-Colombe in the Evreux diocese, which he then gave, with its fief, to the Templars, along with the vast number of furnishings and the patronage of Saint-Pierre-d'Épreville near Neubourg. Richard d'Harcourt did not confine himself to donating lands, but also donned the habit of the Templars. He should not be confused with his nephew, also named Richard d'Harcourt, who fought in the Holy Land and took part in the siege of Saint John of Acre and whose name figures as a witness on letters of marque used by the English king Richard the Lion-Hearted to confirm to the grand masters of the Temple all the alms, immunities, franchises, and customs that had been granted them in his states. As for the first Richard d'Harcourt, he ended his days as a Templar and was laid to rest in the choir of the commandery of Renneville, where he still lies.

In 1200, another member of the family, Robert d'Harcourt, bought confirmation of the donation of Saint-Étienne-de-Renneville. In this one act he also confirmed the donations made by his predecessors as well as all the properties that his knights, vassals, and their vassals had conceded to the Knights Templar, and renounced in their favor all the rights of justice and lordship that had been reserved for him. In addition he gifted the Templars with the church of Tilleul-Lambert, including its revenues and the two-acre dependent domain of Hémard, from which the order had long profited.

All of these donations illustrate that the commandery of Saint-Étienne-de-Renneville was the wealthiest and most powerful in Normandy, by both the extent of its holdings and the amount of revenue it earned from them. Other donations were added in the thirteenth century to those made by the Harcourt family. We know that in 1312, when Templar property was turned over to the Hospitallers, the Renneville commandery owned lands amounting to one hundred ninety plowed acres earning twenty *sols tournois* an acre, a fairly considerable sum. The commandery meted out justice for moderate and petty crimes and held certain rights over the neighboring parishes.

The commandery's seat consisted of a large manor flanked by two towers, a beautiful chapel dedicated to Saint Étienne, a farmyard with lodging for the farmer, including a courtyard, garden, and groves, as well as eighteen acres of land surrounded by tall hedges and moats located along the road from Neubourg to Saint-Melin. The manor was subsequently rebuilt by the commander of the Hospitallers, Philippe de Mailly, at the end of the fourteenth century. Spared from the turmoil of the Revolution, the edifice was inexplicably demolished in 1847. All that remain are scattered stones and several shafts of fluted columns. Search for the chapel's location has been fruitless, and though there may be caverns and underground passageways, no excavations have been undertaken to find remnants of what was once the wealthiest and oldest commandery in Upper Normandy. Could this be the result of a deliberate intention to hide something?

The location of Saint-Étienne-de-Renneville, its importance at the time of the quarrels between the Plantagenets and the Capetians, its influence over the region, even its very age, all prompt us to ask certain questions: Couldn't this location conceal some long-sleeping secret, still buried and stubbornly guarded? Isn't it possible to imagine that this commandery might have held all or some of the problematic treasure moved from the Paris Temple? The remoteness of this commandery, the fact that under the new management of the Hospitallers it was kept in good order, then carefully enlarged, and especially the fact that it was demolished for no valid reason and notable interest are all food for thought. Perhaps attention was diverted to Gisors while Renneville has been, all along, a more likely source of Templar remnants. This is simply a hypothesis, but a reasonable one.

Another important commandery in this region was Sainte-Vaubourg, also known as Val-de-la-Haye, near Rouen on the right bank of the Seine. Since the time of the founding of the order, the Templars were established in Rouen, an important center of maritime and land-based commerce. Their original establishment, which may well not have been a commandery, was located in what is now the rue des Cordeliers. The Templars also owned a town house on the rue de Basnage, near the Saint-Laurent

Church. It was not until 1173 that King Henry II Plantagenet gifted the Temple with his manor and park of Sainte-Vaubourg. The abbey of Bec-Hallouin and the monks of its monastery, which had jurisdiction over this site, gave their approval. In 1194 and 1199 Richard the Lion-Hearted and John Lackland confirmed the donation and granted letters of amortization that joined their father's donation to all others they were eligible to receive in Normandy. The commandery expanded its territory considerably with various fiefs and urban properties, notably in Rouen and Caudebec-en-Caux. The house of Caudebec—at least its magnificent facade—still exists, but the Sainte-Vaubourg establishment has vanished. Not a single stone remains of the chapel today, though by happy chance its stained-glass windows have been preserved. They were, in fact, removed and transported to the Abbey of Saint-Denis, and they have since been restored and transferred to a more advantageous site: the Templar chapel of the Villedieu-les-Maurepas commandery, located today in the new town of Saint-Quentin-en-Yvesline. These are the only known Templar stained-glass windows at present. Notable in particular is one depicting a majestic Virgin and a kneeling Templar clad in a blue robe with a white hood and wearing a small cross in a red circle. Other windows depict Knights Templar, with a true representation of the color of their uniforms: white for knights and black for sergeants, squires, and formerly married knights. Each of them wears a large red cross.

What is known as the commandery of Genetay, in the Roumare Forest near Saint-Martin-de-Boscherville, was in fact only a subsidiary Templar house of Sainte-Vaubourg. But in this case, while not intact, the structure and outline of the building is perfectly known.[3]

There is a very handsome thirteenth-century main building with enormous chimneys, the largest of which takes up the entire south gable. The walls are quarried stone. The building is a single story with a vaulted cellar. In front of the house there sits a well with a round coping, and a round tower attached to the house conceals a spiral stone staircase. It is

---

3. This building currently belongs to a member of the International Group of Templar Studies, who is carefully restoring it—which is a hopeful sign that this stirring Templar remnant will be preserved and its true value recognized.

thought that this tower was once higher, serving as a lookout post. The house, which is built on a height, overlooks a bend in the Seine.[4] Remnants of quarried stone construction can be seen in the nearby vicinity.

While this structure is not a commandery, its importance is such that it is impossible to regard it as merely a farm. Unfortunately, for lack of any documentation, any questions we have about this Templar establishment must remain unanswered. In Genetay, as in Gisors, the Templar mystery is stronger than ever. Genetay could also have served in 1307 as a very discreet relay station in the transport of the Templar treasure in the direction of England, for it was little known during that time and not officially a Templar site. The trajectory from Paris to a port of embarkation could easily have passed through Gisors, Bourgoult, and Le Genetay. All hypotheses are valid.

As a general rule, Templar establishments received much support and protection from the Anglo-Norman sovereigns and equal favor from the papacy. Let us not forget that it was the Anglo-Norman knighthood who provided the largest contingents for the Crusades (in the twelfth century, at least). The commanderies and various houses of the Templars in Normandy formed excellent stopovers, as well as strategic points on the road to London, home of a powerful commandery whose members exercised a ceaseless influence on the Plantagenet kings.

However, it was in Paris that the most significant Templar establishment in the whole of Europe was located. Well known to all through the tragedy of the French Revolution because its tower served as a prison to the royal family, the Paris Temple was a city within a city during the thirteenth century, a state within a state. It was the visible, physical symbol of the actual power of the Templar Order.

It was in about 1143 that King Louis VII conceded the grounds near the Place de Grève to the Templars. Here they erected buildings and their own private port on the Seine. Shortly thereafter they acquired uncleared marshlands in what is called the Marais, a neighborhood that

---

4. An outline and cross section of this Templar house can be seen in the magazine *Heimdal*, no. 26 (1978), as well as in an article by Michel Bertrand titled "The Templars in Normandy."

forms the major portion of the third and fourth arrondissements of Paris. They cleared, drained, and decontaminated the overly wet areas, practiced intense cultivation—employing for this purpose numerous Parisians who thereby became secular members of the Temple—and had their famous enclosure constructed. This consisted of a large quadrilateral area bordered by twenty-four-foot-high crenellated walls defended by round towers. There was only one door into the enclosed area, framed by two large towers and located at the end of a drawbridge facing what is now the rue des Fontaines-du-Temple. The keep was no less than three stories high and flanked by four small towers, one of which contained the stairway. It was located on the southern end of the enclosure, on the site of the rue Eugène-Spuller, between the north wing of the mairie [the French equivalent of a town or borough hall —*Trans.*] of the third arrondissement and the railing of the Temple square.

Why did the Templars build such an impressive fortified enclosure in the center of Paris? Why did they seek to be an entity apart from the rest of the city, while considerably expanding the ground they occupied outside the enclosure even to the detriment of the occupants of certain neighborhoods, which they did not fail to expropriate? From the moment the Holy Land was lost and the Templars were forced to retreat to Europe, they sought to make the Paris commandery the head house of the order and organized it as such. What is odd is that they built their fortress to be equal in strength to their most powerful castles in Palestine. Under the reign of St. Louis, however, they ensured the protection of the French king and at first glance seem not to have had much to fear from inside Paris.

We can see in this construction the imprint of grandeur and even a kind of challenge thrown at the king. As we now know, following the emancipation of the towns, the bourgeois, freed of the supervision of lords and bishops, immediately constructed belfries in front of the keeps of the castles and in the bell towers of cathedrals as symbols of their own importance. Why shouldn't the Templars, too, as a show of their independence with respect to the monarchy and the church, have sought to make a clear statement of their strength for all to see?

There was, however, a practical reason for this proud and formidable display: Their head house was located in a section of Paris that was not very secure. The people of the immediate surroundings hardly enjoyed good reputations. Those who lived there then were what might today be called *heteroclite fauna* [literally "strange animals" or unsavory characters —*Trans.*] capable of anything. The area of what is today the rue des Francs-Bourgeois was then a veritable Court of Miracles swarming with pickpockets and cutthroats. People there thieved, assaulted, and murdered to their heart's content and the king's archers weren't able to do much about it. Furthermore, especially at the beginning of the thirteenth century, the Temple of Paris had become the central bank of the order—and even the royal treasury was housed there. This all helps explain why the Templars built such substantial defenses around the Paris Temple. The Temple Commandery in London, which also served as a bank, was invaded and pillaged by bandits on several occasions; it is quite obvious that the Templars would seek to avoid similar incidents occurring in Paris. Finally, the Templars' reputation was at stake: Would any confidence be placed in bankers who did not protect their vaults?

In fact, the Templars, ex–Poor Knights of Christ, had become, purely and simply, the bankers of Europe, which somewhat overshadowed their original purpose. As Georges Bordonove noted, "It is impossible to completely deny the intention of asserting Templar power and its elevated place in the feudal hierarchy." And we may take this interpretation even further to say that having become an influential first-rate economic and political power, and including an incontestable military reserve, the Temple provoked resentment and envy and could expect reversals if new circumstances came into play. It could almost be said that the Templar Order had long anticipated what would happen in 1307—a confrontation with royal power. But when the expected confrontation occurred, they were unable to, or did not wish to, profit from their acquired advantage.

There was, of course, a church within the Paris Temple enclosure. Originally it was a simple Roman chapel, a rotunda with a dome supported by six columns. Then, during the thirteenth century, different elements were added to the sanctuary, expanding it considerably. The chapel became an actual church in which the original edifice could hardly be detected.

Many questions have been raised about this Roman chapel with its circular rotunda because it was the only example of its kind in France, excepting the mysterious Temple of Lanleff (Côtes-du-Nord), which has absolutely nothing to do with the Templars. This model has several examples in the English Templar churches, though, the Temple of London in particular. Some have tried to insist that this be viewed as a specifically Templar kind of construction, which is absurd, for in addition to the Temple of Lanleff, there are sanctuaries known to have been started long before the founding of the Templar Order yet composed of similar characteristics, such as the church of Neuvy-Saint-Sépulchre, which dates from 1042, and even that of Sélestat, dating from 1094. The model is Eastern, quite simply the Anastasis of the Holy Sepulcher of Jerusalem, which had already inspired the Palatine Chapel of Aix-la-Chapelle. Others besides the Templars made subsequent use of this model, as can be seen in the churches of Cambridge and Northhampton. "The desire to imitate the Anastasis combines here with an Anglo-Norman tradition, which as Élie Lambert says, is more generally an old Celtic tradition that is occulted elsewhere."[5]

The circular sanctuary could only have been an immense satisfaction to converted Celts, recalling to them the ancestral memory of the *nemeton,* the circular sacred clearing in the center of the forest, the only authentic sanctuary tolerated by the druids and considered a symbol of a portion of the sky *(nem)* projected upon the earth. The famous and mysterious Temple of Lanleff belongs in this category of Romanesque architecture characterized by a circular rotunda. It was believed to have been a Roman temple, but is simply a Roman church built at the beginning of the twelfth century with a rotunda and curved aisles, a plan that is also found in the basilica of Sainte-Croix-de-Quimperelé (Finistère). There is nothing strictly Templar in any of this; the original chapel of the Paris Temple was simply following a certain style of the times.

---

5. Alain Demurger, *Vie et mort de l'Ordre du Temple* (Paris: Seuil, 1985), 155.

Practically nothing remains of the Paris Temple. The Knights Hospitallers of St. John, when they took over the enclosure following the dissolution of the Templar Order, continued to occupy it and of course modified it as necessary. The customs connected to this site remained until the Revolution, particularly the right of asylum. As Sébastien Mercier said in *Les Nuits de Paris:*

> [T]here the bailiff's work was nullified, the warrant commanding the arrest of a person expired on the threshold. The debtor could talk with his creditors on this same threshold, hail them, and shake their hands. If he took one step further outside, he would be taken. Everything possible was done to entice him out, but he was careful not to fall into the trap.

This is sufficient indication of the considerable privileges connected to the Temple domains. But stones grow old, and the respect they are due is not always granted. The modernization of Paris during the nineteenth century and the large urban renovations undertaken by Baron Haussmann prevailed once and for all over what had been the most important Templar establishment in Europe. Currently, beyond the names of the streets that faithfully retain the name of the Knights of the Red Cross, only several scattered remnants of their presence can be recognized, such as the lower portion of a corner tower of the former enclosing wall located between 32, rue de Picardie and 73, rue Charlot, or vestiges of the Hôtel des Barres, built by the Templars during the thirteenth century, at 56, rue de l'Hôtel de Ville. At this site we can see an ogival cellar with two bays. One of the arch keystones of the first bay bears a coat of arms with the Templar cross. One keystone of the second bay is decorated with a leafy rosette. It is claimed that this was a secret place where initiations and ceremonies reserved for certain dignitaries of the order took place—but how are we to know? It could just as well have been storage for dry goods. What is certain, though, is that it is an authentic Templar remnant.

Near Paris, in Maurepas (now in the new town of Saint-Quentin-en-Yvesline), there remain buildings of what was once an old and important commandery. The chapel, which was sold as national property during the Revolution, was used as a farm until, one fine day, it was decided to restore it and make it and the others buildings a cultural center. The structures are characteristic of military architecture, with the bell tower of the chapel having also served as a watchtower. Three farm buildings lie in the immediate vicinity, an indication that this Villedieu commandery was likely the center of important agricultural activity in the Beauce wheat fields, and must have been a veritable granary for the Templar organization.

The same is true for Coulommiers in Brie, where the commandery still appears today as a magnificent set of twelfth- and thirteenth-century buildings. Turned into a farm, this commandery was scheduled for demolition to make way for worker housing. But thanks to the concerted efforts of historians, archaeologists, and the inhabitants of Coulommiers themselves, this magnificent evidence of the Templar presence was spared and its restoration undertaken through the effective collaboration of young people from all over Europe. The chapel and the commander's lodge were thus restored to a state that allows the imagination to view what they once were. Here again the commandery has become a cultural center, often the sole means of protecting the past.

In Brie, in Provins, there was another, similar commandery. It is well known that during the Middle Ages, Provins was one of the three most important cities in France, along with Paris and Rouen, and it held fairs frequented by people from all of Europe. The Provins commandery, specializing primarily in the wine trade, was quite wealthy and also owned, in the Val near the hamlet of Fontaine-Rialule, a large house in the upper town of Madeleine and another across from the Sainte-Croix Church, not to mention the lands surrounding the town. Further, as a result of numerous donations made by the counts of Champagne, the order was the proprietor of seventy houses and shops in Provins, the majority accompanied by gardens and located on the most commercial streets of the town. The Templars realized substantial revenue from the rental of these dwellings and also owned most of the region's mills, another significant source of income. As they customarily practiced attractive pricing, the Templars' clientele was constantly growing, to the point of prompting numerous complaints from their competitors of unfair trade practices. These examples of their economic proficiency demonstrate how the Templars wisely managed their domains, and show how they could expand them thanks to the resources they drew from them, all while giving the local economy an added lift that primarily benefited consumers. In short, the Templars contributed to a better distribution of products through all classes of society, thus paving the way for what is called today the consumer society.

But this economic activity, indispensable not only for the Crusades, but for the very survival of the order as well, did not exempt its members from their religious activities. This becomes apparent when we draw up a list of the sanctuaries that belonged to the Templars, were built by them, or were built for them.

The most beautiful example is the Temple of Laon. Currently the best-preserved Templar sanctuary, it is the chapel of a commandery founded in the twelfth century in the southern half of the upper city. The sanctuary is a Roman-style octagonal construction with a gabled bell tower, an altar niche located directly facing the entrance, and a choir ending in a demi-cupola apse.[6] This polygon church, allegedly a characteristic example of so-called Templar art, has nothing at all in common with the Holy Sepulcher of Jerusalem, though, and while the Templars often employed this kind of construction in their sanctuaries, it was not specific to them, having existed long before them. Some have sought to connect this style to the Lord's Temple of Jerusalem, the Dome of the Rock, which, as we know, is octagonal. In fact an octagon chapel tradition exists throughout Western Europe, primarily expressed in cemetery chapels such as the Montmorillon octagon long falsely attributed to the Templars and actually predating them. The Templar chapel in Laon is clearly one of this type, with eight sides, a lantern-shaped roof, and no circular ambulatory. "But its model is not to be looked for in the Orient. It is in Laon itself, in the cemetery of the Saint-Vincent Abbey, where an octagonal chapel was built before the arrival of the Templars in the city."[7]

---

6. A plan of the Templar chapel in Laon can be seen in *Heimdal*, no. 26 (1978): 9.

7. Alain Demurger, *Vie et mort de l'Ordre du Temple* (Paris: Seuil, 1985), 155.

The octagon seems to have a meaning linked to its original presence in cemeteries: In the old symbolism of the zodiac, the number eight, corresponding to the sign Leo, evokes the idea of resurrection.

It is thought that the twelfth-century Metz chapel located near the Arsenal could be of Templar origin. This has not been proved, though we find in its structure the characteristic feature of an octagon, with each of its eight sides pierced by fully arched windows and one side opening on to a square choir that is an extension of the apse. It is quite certain that here the idea of resurrection is being emphasized. Given this example, it is tempting to see in the octagonal shape of the Gisors keep at least the influence of the Templars, if not their very hand. It should be kept in mind, however, that the builders of fortresses were also the builders of chapels and cathedrals at that time. Furthermore, the fundamental distinction we make between the sacred and the profane, the religious domain and the secular domain, did not exist then. Consequently, we can maintain the theory that all construction with a material objective, including military construction, also had a spiritual objective. But here again, such action involved a general phenomenon, a state of mind common to all in the Middle Ages. There is nothing specific to indicate a deliberate and unique intention on the part of the Templars.

Yet this is what some have deduced from the Sours commandery in the center of the Beauce region near Chartres, the founding of which goes back to 1192, when Adèle de Champagne, widow of Thibaud, count of Blois and former seneschal of France, granted her lands and its habitations in Sours to the Order of the Temple. This donation was approved by her children and confirmed by Philip Augustus.

Sours, therefore, became an important establishment on which the Templar house of Chartres soon depended after it was created in about 1225, the same time the cathedral was under construction. It is said in certain so-called hermetic milieus that Sours was the principal site of the Templar mysteries and that secret initiatory ceremonies were celebrated there for several privileged members of the order who held the true reins of power. It has even been specified that Sours formed the Center of Centers, the absolute Mecca for all Templar esotericism. Unfortunately, however, there is not a single shred of proof for any of this, although it is easy to establish a connection between this unverifiable Templar tradition and the verifiable historical tradition going back to Julius Caesar. According to the Roman leader, the land of the Carnutes—in other words, the Chartres region—once covered by thick forest, was the religious center for all the druids of Gaul. It was here, still according to Caesar, that the druids gathered each year in a secret sanctuary at the center of the forest (in a *nemeton*) to settle all problems that were of concern to them. Because some in hermetic and esoteric circles wished wholeheartedly that the Templar doctrine was in some part a legacy of druidism, it was quite tempting to claim that Sours, located in the middle of the Beauce region and thus in the very sanctuary of the ancient druids, was the center of Templar initiation. The problem is that we have a very poor understanding of druidism and know almost nothing at all of the Templar doctrine.

Somewhat similar claims have been made of Payns, the native home of the founder and first grand master of the Templar Order, Hugues de Payen, or de Payns, and of the Orient Forest neighboring Payns. This forest is divided into four sections: The northwest is known as the Little Orient, the center is the Large Orient, the northeast is the Spur, and the southeast is known as the Forest of the Temple. It is true enough that the Templars occupied this forest and built their centers, houses, fortresses, and farms there and that the wood constituted a safe and remote retreat, well protected by entangled trees and marshes. It is an ideal place for *hiding something* and no doubt there have been many who think that the Templar treasure could be found buried somewhere within it. The Holy Grail sought by some at Montségur or Glastonbury (and perhaps in Brocéliande) has been placed by some in this Orient Forest, which, in their opinion, is the true Brocéliande Forest.

It is also true that the Orient Forest is not so far from Troyes, the land of Chrétien de Troyes, the first French author to speak of the Grail and its mysterious procession. A theory doesn't require much more to be accredited. Further, given the fact that part of the forest is called Large Orient (or Grand Orient), some have sought to prove a connection between Freemasonry and the Templars, and then between these two and the quest for the Grail. The Templar treasure, therefore, being not a physical treasure but one of an intellectual and initiatory order, would simply be the Grail. Why not, after all? When Chrétien de Troyes described the Grail procession, he clearly refrained from revealing *what was in the vessel*. It has been up to us to fill this grail. With Hugues de Payns, founder of the Templars, being lord of the region and Troyes being the place where the official statutes of the Temple were promulgated by the council in 1128, we are at liberty to assume many things. The main thing is not to jump too hastily to conclusions.

Some claim that the Templar treasure is neither in the Orient Forest nor in Gisors, maintaining instead that it is in a feudal castle located in the commune of Chantenay, in the Rhône region near Villeneuve-sur-Saône. A local tradition going far back in time does, in fact, declare that the treasure—or a treasure—of the Templars could be found in the keep known as the Tour des Béatitudes [Tower of Bliss —*Trans.*], because it is pierced by eight openings that are symmetrically placed in relation to the center. Here we find again the famous number eight, which, we should recall, is the sign of Leo in the zodiac, the symbol of resurrection. But there is no indication that this tower was built by the Templars.

Because there is no documentation to support this tradition, experiments that, frankly speaking, clearly fall into the realm of the irrational have been conducted in support of it. It appears that a famous esotericist held ritual ceremonies at the château of Arginy to summon the eleven Templars who, according to the same tradition, guarded the treasure buried in the keep. Alas, despite all precautions and the pains taken in observance of the rituals, the "spirits" refused to divulge the place where the guarded treasure lay; they simply left the impression that it was not of coin and was nothing less than the Philosopher's Stone. (It is true that the Templars were suspected of practicing alchemy.) The same esotericist, obviously a stubborn individual, apparently continued his spells and summoned the shade of the Templar grand master Guillaume de Beaujeu because a document dated 1745 puts forth the possibility that the coffin holding the grand master's remains may have been transferred to the Arginy region. Whatever the case may be, the evanescent shade of the

Templar, entreated to reveal the Great Secret, apparently responded that the time of the Apocalypse was too near to commit such an indiscretion—which is why the Templar treasure of Arginy has not been recovered. For the record, it seems appropriate to point out that the etymological meaning of the word *apocalypse* is "revelation."

Ultimately, none of these experiments provides any solution to the mystery posed by the Templars. Instead, each threatens to divert attention from the strikingly real questions that remain unresolved—such as those related to La Rochelle. Normally, all the Templars' efforts to branch out were guided by a single objective: facilitating communication with Mediterranean ports in order to permit embarkation of men, matériel, and provisions to the Holy Land. It is known that La Rochelle was home to an important commandery and that the Templars maintained a commercial fleet there. However, it is obvious that La Rochelle is not on the route to the Middle East. Certainly the claim can be made that the fleet there—maintained at great expense and consisting of numerous vessels, each with a retinue of sailors who belonged *de jure* to the Order of the Temple—ensured liaisons among France, England, and Portugal, and even the part of Brittany that was not part of the kingdom of France. But neither was La Rochelle part of France. During the twelfth century the city and its port were under the jurisdiction of the Plantagenet empire. So what was the purpose of the Templar fleet stationed there and what became of it after the order was dissolved?

No one knows. Interestingly enough, however, the Templars' Red Cross was to be seen again on the first vessels to reach America, namely those of Christopher Columbus. From this small strand an entire epic has been woven. The Templars, so this tale goes, apparently sailed for America—long after the Vikings, of course, whose voyage is now proven fact, but well before Christopher Columbus and Vasco da Gama. A curious connection has even been made between this Templar fleet and the Irish Celts. The departure point for this "epic" is the Mexican tradition brought back by the first conquistadors and their priests. According to this tradition, the remote ancestors of the Maya of the Yucatán and Guatemala had witnessed the arrival of white men on their shores. Their ships were shining and the men themselves were large, handsome, and blue-eyed. They wore strange clothing adorned on the front with an emblem that resembled two interlaced serpents. Once ashore, these men settled with the Maya and educated them. Much later, a stranger landed in the Yucatán bearing in that country's language the name of Quetzelcoatl, or "serpent-bird," and in the Mayan tongue the name Kulkulcan, or "the feathered serpent." As a prisoner of war in Chichén Itzá, he was thrown into a well but managed to survive. Once freed from the well, this strange man, who wore a beard, was apparently considered a sacred being.

That is the Amerindian legend. It has its intrinsic worth and is widely believed throughout Central America. The fault lies with those ingenious commentators who have grafted onto it other legends of Welsh and Irish origin, such as the story of Myrddin (Merlin), who, according to one of the *Triads of the British Isles,* departed over the sea accompanied by other bards in the direction of the City of Glass and never returned.[8] This detail is purely mythological, however; the "City of Glass" in the Celtic context clearly means finding fulfillment in the Other World. There is a second legend, though, with a greater connection to history, that has also been incorporated into the Amerindian legend. This involves Madawg (Madoc), son of the Welsh chieftain Owein Gwynedd, who died in 1169. This Madawg and three hundred men set out to sea on ten ships. No one knows where they went.[9] Interestingly, a fairly ancient and odd monument constructed along the lines of the famous Temple of Lanleff has been discovered in North America, and there is good reason to consider the possibility that Celtic navigators landed on the American continent durng the twelfth century. This theory is not an absurdity.

It so happens that by taking support from another legend—an Irish one in this instance, concerning the famous hero Cuchulainn, who would

---

8. This is, in fact, another version of Merlin's imprisonment by the fairy Vivian inside an invisible castle. See my book *Merlin: Priest of Nature* (Rochester, Vt.: Inner Traditions, 1995), 54 and 101–12.

9. Jean Markale, *The Celts* (Rochester, Vt.: Inner Traditions, 1993), 189–90.

be none other than the Kulkulcan of Mayan tradition[10]—some commentators have constructed a curious hypothesis:

> If it turns out . . . that around the eleventh or twelfth century some other bearded "White" man stepped ashore on the Yucatán from a vessel that must certainly have had a strong resemblance to a *drak,* or feathered serpent, and if the bearded White man overcame a difficult test such as surviving in a well, would it be so surprising that he would be considered as an emissary of the legendary god Kulkulcan?

We know that Templars were obliged to wear beards. We also know that they possessed a great deal of silver, specifically a lot of silver coinage. Because this metal was quite rare during the Middle Ages, it raises the question: Where did the Templars find so much silver? This led one commentator to the following: "Is it impossible that the Templars may have landed in America, specifically in the Yucatán, where there are silver mines?"[11] The question is not as outlandish as it appears. It is necessary, after all, to explain the origin of the Templars' silver and the exact role of their fleet in La Rochelle. And we should remember that at the arrival of Christopher Columbus's caravels bearing the Templar cross, the indigenous peoples showed not the least sign of surprise at this symbol, which they appeared to recognize. While it is true that the cross is a universal figure that does not pertain strictly to Christianity,[12] this hypothesis should not be rejected outright, if for no other reason than it has the merit of raising questions that are generally evaded.

It is apparent that there is no need to call upon the intervention of

---

10. This is not impossible. Irish legends from the high Middle Ages are filled with marvelous voyages and arrivals in strange lands. The problem is extricating the elements that may be historical remembrances from the mythic structure itself. See my *Epics of Celtic Ireland* (Rochester, Vt.: Inner Traditions, 2000), 115–19.

11. Louis Charpentier, *Les Mystères templiers* (Paris: R. Laffont, 1967).

12. With the exception of the Latin cross, representation of the crucifixion, which both the Cathars and the Templars rejected.

"invisible powers" in order for us to lose our way among the numerous enigmas posed by the Templars. Their presence in French territory is itself surrounded by so many obscurities that it is difficult to know with any certainty what their activities were and which places they actually established. Also, as can never be repeated enough, the Templars, at least the Knights of the Temple, were not numerous, especially in Europe, where there were primarily a few dignitaries, some specialists, convalescing wounded or sick knights, and those too old to fight in Palestine. The others who formed part of the order to varying degrees—the squires, the workers, the peasants, even the serfs—are only male, and sometimes female, subordinates or allies of the Knights Templar. This only adds to the confusion.

In a land like Brittany, then, the Templar presence still remains a mystery despite the documentation at our disposal and in spite of the somewhat negative notoriety that has clung to the Templar name in popular memory. It appears they had six preceptories of the Temple there. They also owned property in about one hundred locations around Brittany—chaplaincies, chapels, barns, mills, and isolated houses. The most important commanderies were La Guerche, which included the Temples of Rennes and Vitré, and La Nouée-en-Yvignac (Côtes-du-Nord). There were also important establishments in Carentoir (Morbihan) and La Feuillée (Finistère), as well as in Nantes and Clisson (Loire-Atlantique). Tradition maintains that La Guerche stud farm provided the armies for the Holy Land while La Nouée was an initiation site for the monk-knights, and that the roads entering Pont-Melvez from Quentin (Côtes-du-Nord) were lined with red crosses. It should be noted that military orders often sought to establish themselves near the old Roman roads and along the shore, perhaps for holding the land and sea routes toward Saint-Jacques of Compostella. Still, much uncertainty remains.

Toponymy preserves countless traces of the Templar presence in Brittany, but always within an aura of mystery. The architectural remains are modest and of great austerity. Generally they are humble chapels sometimes topped by a steeple, with a single nave or aisle and a flat chevet or a small demi-cupola apse. They are practically bare of decoration, such as the Madeleine-du-Temple in Clisson, with window/loopholes and massive buttresses, the oratories of Limerzel (Morbihan) and La Nouée, or even the Roman chapel of Saint-Cado near Belz (Morbihan). This last sits in a marvelous site on a small island in the middle of the Étel River and was most likely a dependency of the Templar establishment on Île-aux-Moines, of which nothing remains. Rare decorations can be seen in Brélevenez near Lannion (Côtes-du-Nord) and Merelevenez (Morbihan). The southern porches of both are adorned with masks, flowerets, and broken staves. Of note is that these two toponyms contain the word *levenez*, or "joy," which may not be mere accident. Why did the "red monks," who did not appear to be unpopular during the twelfth and thirteenth centuries, become veritable agents of the devil according to tradition—men who, as punishment for their sins, were compelled after death to wander in pursuit of travelers and sinners, whom they dragged to hell? If there is a Templar mythology, it is definitely in Brittany where one must seek it.

Strange tales are certainly told of the Templars elsewhere, but they appear less diabolical—as in Bézu near Rennes-le-Château (Aude) and in the mysterious Razès region. There is good cause to wonder why the Templars settled in this wild and remote area, far from all roads, on the sides of an impressive peak. What happened after October 13, 1307, in Bézu is also a puzzle. The Templars living there were not arrested, as were the other Templars in France. Was this because they were answerable to the commandery of Mas Deu in Aragon territory?[13] Did they have a special mission to fulfill? Or did they enjoy a special status? While many questions about the Templars of Bézu remain to be answered, this does not prevent legends from proliferating. For instance, above the ruins is a well, and in this well is the silver bell of the Templars:

[O]n the nights of both October 12 and 13, it tolls; and on those nights you will see a long procession of white shades leaving the

---

13. If Mas Deu was subject to Aragon authority, it would not be under jurisdiction of French sovereignty; thus Philip the Fair's orders would not have been binding on local authorities. —*Trans.*

abandoned cemetery to climb toward the ruins. These are the deceased Templars; they are looking for the church, the little church that used to be there, so as to sing the service for the dead. This appears to be a fairly impressive vision.[14]

In other places it is not ancestral folk traditions that prevail, but rather intellectual speculations fueled by intriguing remains. This is the case with the former commandery of Arville near Mondoubleau (Loir-et-Cher). The buildings are almost intact and countless alchemical "symbols" can be found there. According to some authors, if the area is searched thoroughly, even a way leading to the Great Work [the true task of every alchemist, usually referring to the creation of the Philosopher's Stone. — *Trans.*] could be found there. Likewise, the lectern offers a summation of a hermetic message transmitted across the centuries, and an old altar cloth allegedly bears a heraldic pelican in which can be recognized a symbol of the Rosicrucians and the Scottish Freemasons, the Ancient and Accepted Rite. It goes without saying that all of these symbols originate from a time long after the Templars, but demonstrate the persistence of the idea that the Masons are the continuation of the order. It is worth the effort to try to explain Templar wealth with their understanding of alchemy, which is far from a proven fact, but does no harm as food for thought.

It is in the magnificent village of La Couvertoirade where perhaps the most moving and most evocative vestige of the Temple remains. The village is located in the middle of the Causse-du-Larzac, in an area so desolate it makes one wonder why men would settle there. In the twelfth century the counts of Millau gladly welcomed the Templars to their lands, and the order founded a commandery in Sainte-Eulalie on the banks of the Cernon. They would later expand and have two important annexes in this area: one at La Cavalerie, whose name is quite revealing, and the other at La Couvertoirade. It was in 1189 that they settled on the plateau. They had only a simple *mas* [the Occitain word for house or manor

---

14. M. R. Mazières, *Les Templiers de Bézu* (Rennes-le-Château: Philippe Schrauben, 1984), 30.

—*Trans.*], but by the end of the twelfth century they were practically the masters of all Larzac, provoking the envy of—and thus friction with—the lords of Nant and Roquefeuil. This was how La Couvertoirade became an important establishment intended to house the knights who were old, wounded in battle, or ill. Today, the village is girded by a rampart dating from the middle of the fifteenth century and thus not of Templar construction. The oldest monument is some five hundred yards outside the village, the church of Saint-Christol, of which some ruins remain. The nave, dating from the eleventh century, was enlarged by the Templars after they moved in and before they built it into a castle. The current parish church dates from after the suppression of the order.

Overall, La Couvertoirade resembles one of those fantasy villages from the pencil of an artist inspired by the past. In the wind that roars violently across the Causse, you may sometimes hear the moaning of the knights who have yet to find rest in the Other World, where the flames of the pyres are still too much in evidence. If you are wise enough to listen to the voices emerging from memory, you may understand why these strange Templars settled here, in the midst of a hostile environment, between the stony soil and the fierce sun or biting winds from snowcapped mountains. Dream is sometimes closer to reality than the dust-covered documents found in some archive where the smell of mold prevails.

It is said that the Templars guard their mystery. Throughout all the regions of France where they dug roads, they have left here and there, elsewhere and everywhere, shadows that will not be dispelled.

Part 2

Who Were the Templars?

5

The Founding of the Templars

EVEN IF THEIR PRESENCE and activities in Europe excite an unfailing interest in the Templars, it must be acknowledged that their existence as an organized order can be explained and justified only by the Crusades. In short, no Crusades, no Templars—although the opposite may be just as valid: In many ways the Crusades would not have taken place without the Templars. This is where the full scope of the Templars' ambiguous nature is made apparent. The order was founded in Jerusalem, but also in Troyes, and was created to take action in the Middle East, but also in Western Europe. It was a religious order, but it was also a military order, an indispensable element of the official policies of the pope and sovereigns of Europe, but also a parallel militia whose purpose remains unclear. It was an association of knight-monks who declared their Christian faith and died for that faith, but it was also a group of men who—this is incontestable—renounced Jesus. It was a group of believers who proudly and openly wore the red cross, but it was also a bizarre conglomeration of men from every point of the compass who spat on this same symbol. It is true that the Templars' standard, the famous Baucéant or Baucent, was black and white. There could be no better representation of the order's duality or single reality with two faces.

In order to better understand the Order of the Knights Templar, we should examine the circumstances surrounding the birth of the order as well as the apparent motives of its founding fathers.

These circumstances in a nutshell are the Crusades. On November 27, 1095, Pope Urban II, who had just returned from a journey through Occitania to assess the progress of Church reform championed by his predecessor, Gregory VII, preached before a regional council meeting in Clermont. Before an audience of bishops and abbots, among whom could be seen a few scattered secular lords, he violently denounced the clerics who trafficked in Church property. He also cast his lightning bolts at the nobles, such as the king of France, Philip I, who were wallowing in luxury and, contrary to the laws of the Church, were violating God's Peace by fighting like brigands among themselves for material gain or prestige. However, there is no sin without remission and every sinner is capable of finding the road to salvation. With remarkable Machiavellian skill, Urban II indicated what this road was to be: Instead of fighting fellow Christians, instead of murdering their own brothers, these knights—who were fit only for fighting, as was their duty—had only to go to the Holy Land to liberate the tomb of Christ from the hands of the infidels:

> May they henceforth be Knights of Christ, they who were no better than brigands! May they fight in righteousness against the barbarians, they who fought their brothers and relatives! Eternal rewards would they earn, they who had been mercenaries for a few miserable souls![1]

The message of this grandiloquent appeal, which had been prepared following lengthy deliberation, was grasped immediately. During the end of the eleventh century in Europe, and especially in France, the class of minor nobility and knights was particularly numerous and restless. To tell the truth, no one was very sure about what to do with these unruly warriors greedy for booty. Urban II was offering them the means to satisfy their appetites and bellicose enthusiasm at little expense. They would

---

1. Foucher de Chartres, *Historia Hierosolymitana.*

be able to acquire booty and new lands and finally establish themselves on lands they would own. In addition, instead of incurring the wrath of royal justice and the reprobation of the Church, with its parade of anathemas, excommunications, and infernal threats, they would be absolved in advance and guaranteed entrance to paradise.

Urban's methods were hardly new. They have been used numerous times throughout history. Whenever certain individuals become too great a burden on a nation and threaten that nation from within, they are sent outside. Bertrand du Guesclin employed the same strategy with the Grandes Compagnies during the time of Charles V, as did the third French Republic at the most intense moments of the colonization of Africa and Asia. Such means presented a double advantage. First, new territories could be won for the nation; second, whether they lived or died, the men sent elsewhere generally never came back. Good riddance!

The Crusades functioned in precisely the same way—the fact that they were wrapped in spirituality, with the glory of Christ and the salvation of souls placed at the forefront, changes nothing. Later, economic benefits became the residual of the Crusades, despite the fact that Louis IX turned the Crusades into a rule of moral conduct. At the beginning they provided—at least overtly—an answer to the question of how to rid Europe of unwanted knights while at the same time investing in its promising future.

Of course, the Clermont appeal prompted enthusiastic reactions. An eager but undisciplined crowd took to the road, asking at each stopover if this was not Jerusalem. But behind this mob that pillaged and killed the Jews of the Rhine Valley, Hungarian peasants, and the subjects of Byzantium were groups of knights from France, England, Holland, and Norman Italy converging on Constantinople. The emperor, quite disturbed at this, arranged their passage to Asia Minor as quickly and in as orderly a fashion as possible. Let others deal with them! Thus the Turks, who had been the masters of these regions since 1071, were vanquished by the Crusaders in 1097, after which the Crusaders entered Syria from the north, besieged Antioch in 1098, and took Jerusalem on July 13, 1099. Drunk on their own righteousness and their victory, the Crusaders massacred everyone—

Muslims and Jews alike, even Christians who had been unrecognized as such. The capture of Jerusalem was a bloodbath. But it was better that this took place in Jerusalem than in Paris or Provins.

Thus were organized the Latin kingdoms of the Middle East. Godefroy de Bouillon, head of the victors, turned down the crown he was offered and settled for the title Champion of the Holy Sepulcher, but because of his death one year later, his brother Baudoin, count of Édessa, became the first king of Jerusalem in 1118.

Some of the Crusaders, having fulfilled their vows of freeing Christ's tomb and making a pilgrimage to the Holy Land, returned to Europe. After all, the Crusades were a pilgrimage, even though the journey was undertaken with weapons (though pilgrimages in Europe were hardly any more peaceable, given the insecure nature of the roads in the eleventh century).

Other Crusaders remained in Palestine and Syria, where they carved out their own domains. There was also a need for Christians to remain there and organize future pilgrimages. Replacing for Christians the former fervor for liberation of the holy places was a new enthusiasm: to journey to the tomb of Christ to pray. It was thus necessary to organize the arrival, sojourn, and safety of the pilgrims, many of whom were neither warriors nor adventurers. It so happened that the lands occupied by the Christians remained under constant threat from the Muslims, who controlled two strategic points: Tyr and Ascalon. Combat, if not outright war, continued between the two camps and the roads to Jerusalem were never free from danger. The main pilgrimage route from Jaffa through the plain of Ramallah was a permanent battlefield. Furthermore, the influx of pilgrims attracted profiteers—not only merchants of dubious goods, but also brigands and cutpurses. As a matter of course, pilgrims traveled in groups and hired mercenaries to ensure their protection during the journey.

Of course there was an institution in the Holy Land that looked after pilgrims: the Hospital. The origins of this order remain very unclear. An official history written much after the fact claims the institution's roots extended all the way to John the Baptist. What is safe to assume is that the Hospital must have been created around the same time as the kingdom of Jerusalem, in 1099 or 1100. The institution was made up of monks or laymen affiliated with a monastic order (most often the Benedictine Order) who welcomed, sheltered, fed, and cared for travelers in large houses or monasteries. But the function of the Hospitallers was purely civil and humanitarian. They were happy to play the same role long played by the different European monastic orders for pilgrims of all sorts.

However, the Holy Land was dangerous territory, and different methods were required from those employed in Europe. In 1133, Pascal II issued a papal bull establishing an independent order to be called the Hospital of St. John of Jerusalem. This John is not the Baptist or the Evangelist; the patron saint of the Hospitallers was a certain Jean l'Aumônier, who was born in Cyprus to a noble family, married, had numerous children, and, after he became a widower, gave all his worldly goods to the poor and became bishop of Alexandria and a model of exemplary charity. He died in Cyprus in 617. By taking as their patron saint a man who had devoted his life to others, the members of the Hospitaller Order demonstrated their true purpose. Furthermore, in 1113, the date of its official recognition, the order had already opened hospices in Europe, namely Saint-Gilles-du-Gard, Pisa, Bari, and Tarento, all ports of embarkation for the Holy Land—it was purely and simply an international order devoted to charity. And even if the order subsequently evolved to be somewhat more militaristic, it was certainly not relied upon for policing the roads leading to Jerusalem.

This is where a minor noble of Champagne, Hugues de Payns, enters the scene. The following account is from William of Tyre, archbishop and former chancellor of the kingdom of Jerusalem:

> That same year of 1119, certain noble knights, full of devotion toward God and who were religious and God-fearing, entrusted themselves into the hands of the lord patriarch to serve Christ, making a profession of wishing to live permanently according to the custom of canon rules by observing vows of chastity, obedience, and refusing to own property.

Given the fact that William of Tyre was not born until 1130, he did not have personal knowledge of the Templars' beginnings. He spoke of it many years later, based only on what he had heard. Nevertheless, his is still the oldest testimony on the subject. One century later, Jacques de Vitry, bishop of Acre, retold the same events:

> By solemn oaths sworn before the Patriarch of Jerusalem, they committed to defend pilgrims against brigands and marauders, protect the roads, and chivalrously serve the Sovereign King. They observed vows of poverty, chastity, obedience, according to the rules of legitimate canons. Their leaders were two venerable men: Hugues de Payns and Godefroy de Saint-Omer.

This is the first time that the purpose of this new order—ensuring the safety of the pilgrimage roads in the Holy Land—was set down in writing. At the beginning of the twelfth century the Hospitallers were specialists in providing shelter, but were incapable of fulfilling the role of guaranteeing safe passage for Holy Land pilgrims. We must remember, however, that Jacques de Vitry wrote more than a century after the events in question. We do not really have any actual proof that this policing mission was truly the purpose of Hugues de Payns and his first companions.

There has been fierce discussion about whether Hugues de Payns was a native of Champagne or of the Ardèche region, as is claimed by some who base their contention on a fairly suspect document. While his exact place of origin has no bearing whatsoever on his mission, he did own—as a fiefdom—a domain granted him by the count of Champagne in Payns, near that mysterious Orient Forest and not far from Troyes, a city of commerce but also an intellectual city where Jewish kabbalistic circles survived. The illustrious Chrétien de Troyes, most likely a converted Jew, was perhaps one of the most illustrious disciples of these circles. The lord of Montigny, dubbed a knight, also possessed properties in the area of Tonnerre. He was married and is known to have had one son, Thibaud, who later became abbot of the Saint-Colombe Monastery in

Troyes. The lord of Montigny was a man of moderate importance, perhaps a member of a cadet branch of the Champagne family and, through the play of marriage alliance, related to the Montbard family (the family of Bernard de Clairvaux). We know little of his activity prior to 1104, at which time he accompanied the count Hugues de Champagne to the Holy Land. Nor do we know the date of his return from this journey. But we do know that he traveled again with the count of Champagne to Palestine in 1114, and that this time he remained there to found, with several of his companions in 1118 or 1119 (it is impossible to know the exact date), what would become the Order of the Temple. The chronicler Guillaume de Nangis notes in a single phrase in 1120 that "the Temple militia commanded by Hugues its master" was founded at this time.

We should examine more closely these companions of Hugues de Payns. First, there were not very many of them. According to Jacques de Vitry, "in the beginning there were only nine who made such a sacred decision, and for nine years they served in secular habit and lived off only that which the faithful gave to them." The figure nine has been seized upon by a number of commentators, some of whom have viewed it as a symbolic number. The ninth Major Arcana of the Tarot is The Hermit and the ninth house of the zodiac, Cancer, rules over secrets and hidden things. Yet it is hard to believe that the first Templars would have remained so few for nine years while performing a particularly urgent and necessary police mission (if we are to believe the different testimonies from the time) that by all evidence required a large number of participants. How could nine knights, even nine very strong and brave knights, have been sufficient to fulfill that task in such circumstance?

There is another point that fuels discussion: Was the creation of this militia the initiative of Hugues de Payns and his companions as some sort of personal religious commitment, or did the initiative for its inception come from the king of Jerusalem, the military leaders, and the Church hierarchy in Palestine? On this subject nothing is very clear. If we are to go by the word of William of Tyre, the nine simply wished to become monks to serve God and save their souls, and it was later that "their first mission was commanded for the remission of their sins by the Lord Patriarch and the other bishops: that they guard for honest folk the roads and paths against ambushes by thieves and invaders, and this for the great salvation of pilgrims." So it seems that the sole objective of the nine was to embrace a religious vocation. They made their commitment and swore their religious vows with no particular purpose in mind. But should we believe on all points William of Tyre, who hated the Templars?

In any case, according to the words of Jacques de Vitry:

> [T]he king, his knights, and the Lord Patriarch were filled with compassion for these noble men who had sacrificed everything for Christ, and bestowed upon them certain properties and benefits to support both their needs and the souls of the donors. And because they owned no church or dwelling, the king lodged them in his place near the Lord's Temple. The abbot and regular canons of the Temple would give them for their needs use of land not far from the Temple, and for that reason, they were later known as the Templars.

There can be no doubt, then, about this fact: At the moment they were making their decision to form a religious militia, the nine founders were unaware they would be establishing themselves directly in or in immediate proximity to the Temple of Jerusalem, and they had no intention whatsoever to do so. Their name—Templars—is thus accidental and is owed simply to later common usage. This fact enables us to dispense with all esoteric commentary regarding the Temple's significance with respect to the Templars' subsequent conduct and the actual motivations of Hugues de Payns and his companions.

The nine years following the founding of the original order remain very obscure. In 1120 Count Foulques of Anjou, future king of Jersualem, landed in the Holy Land, where he met and lodged with the Templars, donating thirty Angevin pounds to them. And in 1126 Count Hugues de Champagne joined the Knights Templar. It is highly questionable that the Templars remained a company of nine, because these contacts could have come only if the Temple had already acquired a certain notoriety that attracted goodwill. In fact, the donations to their cause began to pour in. Hugues de Payns, accompanied by five of his knights, returned to Europe with the threefold purpose of gaining recognition for his order, winning it official approval from the Western Church, and gathering recruits. This was a decisive turning point for the Order of the Temple.

By all evidence, Hugues de Payns had the benefit of important connections. It was Baudoin II of Jerusalem who encouraged him to go to Europe and furnished him with everything this long journey required. Moreover, Hugues de Payns was a friend of the count of Champagne, one of the most important French barons, and he undoubtedly pointed out to him and others in high places his personal interest in supporting the Templar initiative. In fact, it is almost certain that Hugues de Payns went to Rome and gained an audience with Pope Honorius II, which must have been a determining factor in how the Rule of the new order was drawn up. But the council charged with ruling on the fate of the Temple met in Champagne, in the Troyes cathedral, on January 14, 1128.

The chairmanship of this council was provided by Cardinal Mathieu d'Albano, the papal legate in France. The participants were the archbishops of Sens and Rheims, with their suffragans and several abbots, including Hugues de Macon, abbot of Pontigny; Étienne Harding, abbot of Cîteaux; and Bernard, abbot of Clairvaux, who would later become the famous St. Bernard. There were also several powerful lords such as Thibaud de Blois, count of Champagne, his seneschal André de Baudemot, and the count of Nevers. Hugues de Payns was accompanied by brother knights Godefroy de Saint-Omer, cofounder of the order; Payen de Montdidier, Archambaud de Saint-Armand; Geoffrey Bisol; and someone known only as Roland. After several discussions and the working out of some minor details, the Rule of the order was adopted. Henceforth the Templars officially existed.

It is hard not to see in the happy success of Hugues de Payns and the speed at which all of this happened the profound and decisive imprint of Bernard de Clairvaux, the man "who made popes and kings," and no doubt one of the most remarkable figures of the Church in the twelfth century. Hugues de Payns was connected by marriage to the Montbard family of which the future saint was a member, and Bernard's uncle, André de Montbard, would later join the Templars. The counts of Champagne were also closely connected to the Montbard family and enjoyed the best relations with the abbot of Clairvaux. It has even been claimed that the statutes and Rule of the Templar Order were the work of Bernard. This is certainly not the case, however. It was Hugues de Payns or his immediate advisers who deserve the credit for their redaction. However, Bernard's influence is more than obvious.

This is a very important point because it has often been repeated that the "military orders" were of Benedictine inspiration. The Council of Troyes and the imprint of Bernard show to the contrary that it was the Cistercian influence that predominated in the fashioning of the Templars' Rule. Étienne Harding, abbot of Cîteaux, was present in Troyes. He and Bernard were the masterminds of the Cistercian movement, which was incorporated into the framework of the reform of the Church started by Gregory VII. Bernard went even further with his support when writing his famous letter known as "In Praise of the New Knighthood," in which he lent his sincere and total backing to the new order's objectives.

This brings up some serious questions, because the Church was not, at least originally, a temporal power. Nor was it a military organization; in fact, during Christianity's first centuries it had condemned all warfare, refusing to make even a subtle distinction between just and unjust war. Cracks in this determined stance had appeared by the time the idea of the Crusades emerged. The explanation for this change in ideology was that Christianity was threatened by the Muslims and that faith in the true God was in danger of disappearing if the infidels were allowed to become too powerful. In short, the Church employed the argument of self-defense, though that argument may have appeared somewhat specious. It was justified in Poitiers at the time of Charles Martel, but it had become dubious in the year 1100 when replaced by the necessity of protecting the Holy Land sites against the presence of the infidels, which was considered a defilement. After all, wasn't society organized according to a tripartition at that time? It had been established once and for all that there were those who pray, those who fight, and those who work. The contemporaries of St. Bernard would have been dumbfounded if told that this tripartition was extremely ancient and formed the very structure of all Indo-European societies. It had even had its correspondence in Gallic society, where, according to Caesar, there were Druids, Warriors, and the Others. So it was the duty, then, of the knights to do battle. The clerics had the mission of serving God and Man through prayer.

But this simple division of task was complicated to a great extent when churchmen were led to take up arms. The problem had still not been resolved in the time of Rabelais, if we can believe the story in *Gargantua* in which Brother John of the Hashes vituperates against those monks who are content to drive off their enemies by singing psalms but who also, in his words, grab the processional cross to skewer said enemies. What is generally overlooked is that the creation of soldier-monk orders could not be realized without introducing a deep challenge to the fundamental principles of the Roman Catholic Church. We cannot evade this problem, and it was a concern to the theologians of that era as well.

It seems, in fact, that the creation of military orders was not so appreciated in certain ecclesiastical milieus. For example, in 1128, Grigues, the prior of the Grande Chartreuse, wrote a fairly stern letter to Hugues de Payns in which he clearly expressed his disapprobation. In particular he said:

> [W]e cannot in truth urge you to wage material and visible wars; nor are we anymore apt to inspire you for the struggles of the spirit, our daily concern, but we at least want to warn you from thinking of waging them. It is in fact vain to attack outside enemies if one has not first prevailed over those on the inside. . . . Let's first conquer ourselves, my very dear friends, and then we may safely battle our outside enemies. Purify our souls of their vices, and then we can purge the earth of barbarians.

This diatribe is followed by a reference to St. Paul's message in the Epistle to the Ephesians: "It is not against adversaries of flesh and blood that we must fight, but against Principalities, Powers, the rules of this world of darkness, against evil spirits who dwell in celestial spaces" (Ephesians 6:12).

This is why Hugues de Payns went on the counterattack. He wrote letters or had friends more learned in theology write them (he does not seem to have been very well versed in the subject) in which he said that any recriminations made against the Temple were ill founded and even a ruse of the devil. Finally, running short of arguments, Hugues de Payns appealed to Bernard of Clairvaux, who, after hesitating for a long time, wrote his famous "In Praise of the New Knighthood."

In the first part of this text, Bernard of Clairvaux justifies and describes the mission that has fallen upon the Knights of Christ. To do this, he contrasts the new knighthood, the Templars, with the knighthood of that century, meaning all others without exception.

"Where will this profane militia lead us, rather let's say *malice?*" he asks first, not at all loath to resort to a simple play on words. [This refers to a play between *malice* and *milice*, which is French for militia. *Malice* in French can mean mischievousness as well as spite. — *Trans.*] Then directly addressing that century's knights, he says: "What strange blindness or fury, to spend so much money and take so much trouble to wage a war whose only fruits can be death or sin! You cover your horses in silk; you line your breastplates with long hanging fabrics; you paint your lances, your shields, your saddles; your gold and silver stirrups and bits are set with jewels; and it is in that get-up that you have the impudence of daring death? Can you hope that gold, jewels, and silk will protect you better from the blows of your enemy than iron? But enough of that. I have a more serious grievance against you, one that should terrify your knightly consciences. I am thinking of the frivolity of the motives that lead you to war. Why, in fact, do you take up arms? To satisfy a passing mood, an irrational anger, a desire for glory, or conquest. Do you think your salvation can be found by killing or dying for such motives?[1]

---

1. St. Bernard de Clairvaux, *Textes politiques*, collected and translated by Paul Zumthor (Paris: Bibliothèque médiévale, 1986), 197–98.

Here is a condemnation of war that is completely within the tradition of the Roman Catholic Church since its origin. As a consequence of original sin, war can only be evil and illicit. It is the greatest scourge of humanity. But, of course, this fundamental theory immediately collided with the realities of ordinary life. After all, when a Roman squadron under Pilate's command came to arrest Jesus in the olive garden, the apostle Peter was carrying a sword hidden beneath his robes and he wished to use it. It was surely not by chance that he had this weapon. Furthermore, this little evangelical detail speaks volumes about the band of "outlaws," on constant alert, formed by Jesus and his disciples. Jesus certainly prevented Peter from starting a fight. No doubt this was why nothing came of it.

This passage from the Gospels, which has been spared any lengthy analysis (except for emphasizing Christ's nonviolence), did not escape the notice of the fathers of the Church. It helped to provide a subtler theological position. A war whose purpose is the acquisition of wealth and honor is always illegitimate, but a war whose objective is to defend a right, with the right to live coming first, is permissible, on condition that it is used only as a last resort. St. Augustine even sketched out a theory of the "just war." Those wars are just that "avenge wrongs, when a people or nation, against whom war must be waged, has neglected to punish those among them who have committed evil deeds, or to restore what has been unjustly taken by means of these unjust actions." And the Bishop of Hippo, a former Manichean and great sinner, adds this to the argument: "I do not believe that the soldier who kills an enemy, like the judge and executioner who execute a criminal, is committing a sin, for in acting that way, they are obeying the law." St. Augustine did not specify whether the law in question was divine or human. That is beside the point. What is important is that it leads directly to the words of Bernard of Clairvaux:

> When he kills an evildoer he is not a man killer, but if I may say so, a killer of evil. He avenges Christ on those who do evil; he is the defender of Christians. If he is killed himself, he does not die, but has reached his goal. The death he inflicts is to the profit of Christ; the death he receives is for his own gain.

These words would seem definitive. But their seeming meaning was not exactly what Bernard of Clairvaux had in mind. He was much too prudent and intelligent to fall into such a trap. He could remember perfectly what Isidore of Seville had said in the seventh century: "That war is just that is waged, following a warning, to recover property or repel an enemy." This is why Bernard goes on to say in this address to the Templars:

> There is no doubt that murder is always evil, and I would forbid you to slay these pagans if another means can be found to prevent them from oppressing the faithful. But as things stand, it is better to fight them with arms than to allow them to prevail over the just, for fear that the righteous be delivered into iniquity.[2]

This seems clear enough. For Bernard of Clairvaux, war was a lesser evil that should be engaged as little as possible. Among Christians it could be just only if the unity of the Church, or, in other words, the Christian community, was at stake.[3] Violence against Jews, heretics, and pagans was to be avoided; the truth could not be imposed by force.[4] The duty of the Christian was first to try to convince—and only in the case of failure could Christians resort to war. This was how the Crusades earned total justification. The infidels had been asked to return those holy sites that were Christian property. They did not wish to return them; they did not deign to repair the injustice. Justice would therefore have to be restored by force.

This brings to mind Blaise Pascal's famous aphorism: Incapable of making the just strong, they worked to make the strong just. This takes us directly into the era of test by ordeal and the judgment of God. As someone said later during the sack of Béziers: "Kill them all! God will recognize his own!" In any case, Bernard's thinking on this matter is

---

2. *Textes politiques,* 202.

3. A powerful argument that justified in advance the Crusade against the Albigensians and the massacre of Protestants.

4. Bernard forgot certain examples from the past, in particular how Charlemagne converted the Saxons.

quite precise: The Muslims can always convert to Christianity, where-upon they will be welcomed like brothers, and if they do not wish to do so, well then, too bad for them. No doubt the abbot of Clairvaux recalled that the evangelist Luke attributes to Jesus: "Bring my enemies here that did not wish me as king and slaughter them in my presence" (Luke 19: 27). The Roman Catholic Church, which strove to do everything in its power to present Jesus as a prophet of peace and a "lamb of God," care-fully refrained from commenting on this phrase, although it is to be found in one of its own official texts. It is also overlooked that Jesus said: "Don't think I came to bring peace to the earth. I have come not bearing peace but a sword."

This was Bernard's state of mind when he wrote "In Praise of the New Knighthood," which was his effective contribution to the official founding of the Order of the Temple. There was just one problem: Al-though the possibility of a just war was recognized, this war would be the concern only of the knightly class by virtue of the tripartition of that society. No matter what Bernard said or did, the mission of the clerics would remain prayer. The abbot of Clairvaux was perfectly aware of this, for he was a man who had renounced the world for the monastic life. And although the head of Christianity in that century, he primarily claimed to be a "man of God," a man dedicated to silence, meditation, and prayer. So how to reconcile war and prayer?

Bernard of Clairvaux's position clearly foreshadows the Jesuit casu-istry of the seventeenth century that was repeatedly denounced by Pas-cal. As war is an evil, but a necessary one, and people must wage war, the sole solution is to purify the intention. In this way, the commission of sin is avoided. To wage war for material motives is illicit. To wage war for the glory of Christ becomes legitimate. But as it was out of the question for the existing monastic orders—the Benedictines, the Clunisians, the Cistercians—to leave their monasteries, to which they were absolutely attached by their commitment and mission, it was therefore necessary to turn toward the creation of new religious orders made up of those who would be both monks and soldiers. The Templars made their appear-ance on the scene at just the right moment and St. Bernard immediately made of them that "Militia of Christ" for which the Church had such need. In short, the Templars were, at least from the time of their official recognition by the Council of Troyes, the equivalent of a *secular arm* for the contemplative orders, particularly the Cistercians. It could even be said that the Temple was an extension of Cîteaux, a veritable army of soldiers of Christ at the exclusive disposal of ecclesiastical authorities, headed by the pope. A convergence occurred here between the needs of the moment—in other words, the safety of pilgrims to the Holy Land—and the desire of the Church to have an active and devoted militia at its service. But it should be explicitly said that in 1128 and immediately subsequent years, the Templars' sole mission was the surveillance and protection of the holy sites and pilgrimage routes. They did not engage in offensive or defensive actions against the Muslims until much later. By that time the Temple had evolved from a simple militia guard to an elite corps in the war against Muslims—in truth, the sole group capable of maintaining the Christian presence in the Middle East for as long as it did. This is all to the honor of the Templars. They demonstrated remarkable courage, tenacity, and devotion in withstanding any ordeal, a rare strength of soul, and an unshakable faith. But in so doing, they deviated from their original mission and, in the process, were completely transforming their order.

Thus was the official birth of the Order of the Temple in 1128 at Troyes, with the full approbation of Bernard of Clairvaux, the master thinker of Christianity in that era. The sequence of events that followed is well known. Hugues de Payns made a tour throughout Europe and collected not only enthusiastic support but also the means for successfully fulfilling the mission they had been given. Donations flowed in from all sides. The Temple organized throughout Europe as well as the Holy Land with its Rule and its uniform: The knights wore white robes and cloaks, while the squires and sergeants wore white robes and black cloaks. At first they did not wear the red cross they would later bear on their left shoulders; it was bestowed upon them by Pope Eugene III in 1148.

All were not equal in the Templar Order; there was a very strict and carefully designed hierarchy. First were those who had taken vows—knights, squires, and sergeants—then the rest, consisting of all those who had in one way or another "given" themselves to the Temple, hence the name *donats* that was conferred upon them. *[Donats* is similar to the French *donner,* meaning "to give." —*Trans.]* But these donats, like the serfs and often temporary servitors, were not bound by vows and took little part in the Templar community life. In fact, the internal structure of the Temple was a perfect reflection of the three-tiered class system of feudal society. The knight-monks were those who fought but were not monks. The chaplains were those who prayed, and they were the sole priests of the order. All the others were working brethren, likened to the lay brethren of the monasteries. And, because it was necessary to be of noble birth, unmarried, and free of other attachments to be a knight-monk, as it was to be a knight, another category of combatants was created to fight alongside them: the squires and the sergeants, who, though not among the notables, were a constant presence.

This reality is important to note in order to understand the puzzle of the Templars, their evolution, and the proceedings brought against them: The sole authentic Templars were the knight-monks, who were not priests, and the clergymen who were their chaplains. Again, it needs to be specified that within this upper class there were divisions according to rank and degree of education—because the majority of Templars were illiterate. In fact, those who had a general education were quite rare. The last grand master of the order, Jacques de Molay, who died at the stake, was entirely illiterate. In any event, we need to stick strongly to the point that the knights who became Templars joined the order not to engage in intellectual speculation, but to serve God by fighting. If they had wished to indulge in theological studies, they would have gone elsewhere.

The legends concerning the possible esoteric nature of the Temple have played a small part in altering the image of the Templar reality. It was primarily an order embodied in its century and for very specific purposes. These are again explicitly laid out in a papal bull issued by Pope Innocent II in 1139. As pointed out by Georges Bordonove, this was the "source of all the order's privileges and the obvious demonstration of the wonderful development of the Temple since 1130." What does this mean?

In the beginning the Temple, functioning thanks essentially to the knight-monks who constituted its reason to exist, partially depended on clerics who were strangers to the order, which hence created a more or less subordinate relationship between the Templars and various ecclesiastical authorities. In practice, if clerics—ordained priests—entered the Templar Order, they became *ipso facto* the exclusive chaplains of every member of the order. Following several requests made by the Templars personally, Pope Innocent II agreed to their requests for full autonomy while reserving for himself the role of exclusive supervisor to the order. This papal bull freed the Templars of all episcopal jurisdiction. The decision-making power was entrusted to the order's grand master and his chapter, with the pope reserving the right to intervene in Templar affairs only with serious cause. Furthermore, according to the Rule of the order that was revised on this occasion, the Templars did not have the right to confess to priests who did not belong to the order, except, of course, when at death's door. This revision is of capital importance to the extent that it excludes any possible intervention on the part of clergy outside the order and reinforces the idea of a group acting with complete material and spiritual independence. The Temple's accusers would remember this in 1307 and use it as an effective argument against the "occult" aspect of the Templar Order. We will later see that the obligation to confess only to a priest of the order also addressed deeper issues involving admitting the renunciation of Jesus and spitting on the cross when received into the Temple.

The Temple's autonomy extended to the right to build its own sanctuaries. This was enough to cause resentment among the other religious orders and especially among the lay clergy. It also provided more fuel to active imaginations: If the Templars wanted to worship away from others, perhaps it was because they had something to hide. A good portion of the legends concerning the Templars' esotericism derives from this particular freedom because, as pointed out by Rabelais, who knew where things really stood, the more that is hidden in the monasteries, the greater the tendency of those outside it to imagine that something strange is going on.

There were quite a few other advantageous decrees in Innocent II's bull, in particular the Templars' exemption from paying tithes due the secular clergy for their domains—an exemption the Cistercians had already obtained—and the permission to collect them for their own use. This makes it easy to understand why numerous conflicts caused the Templars to oppose the ecclesiastical authorities of several countries, and also why the order had so few defenders when facing the terrible accusations eventually leveled against it. In short, the lay clergy and the other monastic orders, especially the Dominicans, the Templars' most relentless foes, were delighted by the charges levied against the Templars (charges that the Dominicans had played a large part in imposing). They made out quite well from the proceedings—in full Christian charity, of course, and for the noble motive of defending the True Faith.

Thus the Order of the Temple was launched. By the middle of the twelfth century, though it had not yet attained the summit of its power, it was well on the way to doing so. It had rapidly established itself everywhere, in Palestine and Western Europe alike, and had covered itself with glory in the struggle against Islam. The realization was setting in that the surest guarantor of Christianity in the Holy Land was the Temple. On the European continent the Templars put to work the lands entrusted to them. They provided jobs and thus the means to live to a populace that often had nothing. They organized and protected the roads used by pilgrims. They saw to the efficiency of production in the domains under their control and amassed much money from the sale of their products, which they immediately invested in purchasing additional land, arming their fleet, or procuring indispensable war materials for the Crusades. They saw to the construction of a great number of buildings and sanctuaries, and wove an important web of international commerce and, consequently, diplomatic relations among the different Western nations. The Templars often offered their services as mediators, settling conflicts and negotiating treaties. And most important, one of their primary missions was the transfer of funds from Europe to the Holy Land for the use of pilgrims and Crusaders. Thus, by the very nature of this transaction they became actual bankers. When large sums of money were entrusted to them in London or Rouen, they ensured that these funds would be available in Acre or Jaffa. The Temple provided a sense of security. It was envied, even hated (William of Tyre has left us testimony of that), but it stood in a position of strength: No one could manage without the order, a situation both exceptional and unique in history.

Historically, the Temple emerged from the pious and steadfast will of some knights who wished to provide some useful work that would ensure their eternal salvation. Through the play of events; the blessing of Bernard of Clairvaux, the greatest cleric of his era; the generosity of all the kings and lords of Western Europe; and the support of several popes who succeeded each other to the throne of St. Peter, the Order of the Temple had become one of the greatest political, economic, military, and religious powers in the world in less than fifty years. But is this how things usually happen?

Where the Templars are concerned, there is no need to extrapolate or fantasize or imagine. The historical reality is more than sufficient as it is, laden with shadows. Was the success of the Temple usual? Absolutely not. The very least we can claim is that this success may conceal certain motives that are not at all easy to establish.

The founding of the order remains surrounded by mystery. It appears that Hugues de Payns and his companions did not strictly define their purpose. Furthermore, it now seems clear that the establishment of this militia charged with protecting the roads to Jerusalem had been desired, if not instigated, by the civil and religious authorities of the Holy Land. In this instance, the wishes of the patriarch of Jerusalem and King Baudoin I must have carried some weight in the decision of the nine original Templars, even if the word *temple* was never uttered before Baudoin II granted them the use of a wing of his palace. Therefore, while dismissing the idea of a concerted plan to effectively make these knights Templars in order to benefit from some mystic connection to the Temple and to Solomon the Builder and High Architect, the possessor and keeper of secrets from the past (though in fact, Hiram was the architect), we may well ask if the founding of this group was sought by others who purposely refrained from stepping forward.

Numerous answers have been forthcoming in this regard that rest only on circumstantial evidence or assumptions. It is useful to examine them, though, in order to attempt to shed more light on how the Order of the Templars became a mysterious organization with two faces.

There is, of course, the hypothesis of an order that preceded the Templars and prompted their creation. The famous Priory de Sion, if it were less phantomlike, would be perfectly suited for this role. Baudoin I, the king of Jerusalem, was the brother of Godefroy de Bouillon, so-called founder of the Priory de Sion. Because it appears certain that the decision of Hugues de Payns corresponded to the wishes of Baudoin, it is acceptable to think that Hugues de Payns was given a mandate by the king of Jerusalem, the successor to Godefroy, to set up this militia of Christ. Such an organization would have echoed in that time the secret activities led by the clandestine order to which Baudoin belonged. But, of course, nothing can be proved in this regard, and the goals of this clandestine organization run a strong risk of remaining a mystery forever, all the more so because in the ensuing years the Temple evolved from what it was at the onset. Those advocating this hypothesis dismiss the matter casually by claiming that a rupture occurred in 1188, beneath the Gisors elm, between the clandestine organization and the Templar Order. However, because there is no proof concerning this rupture, we are no further along than we were before.

But there is something connected to the possibility that Hugues de Payns and his companions were "teleguided," or given a mandate. This possibility extends back to a much earlier time—the year 1000, to be precise—when Pope Sylvester II, formerly the famous monk Gerbert d'Aurillac, voiced in a letter his hopes that France would recover the holy places so that a search could be made for the keys to Universal Understanding hidden there. The authenticity of this letter has never been proved, but the idea of some hidden knowledge was not a new one. It had been a long-standing belief in certain Western circles that Solomon's Temple was built following precise rules and in obedience to occult laws and that it concealed incomparable and overwhelming secrets, if only the famous Tablets of the Law that Moses brought out of Egypt. The mirage of the Orient was already at work and it was imagined in good faith that the East had retained certain knowledge lost to the West. But this knowledge, whatever it was, was not to be divulged to all comers. To the contrary, it was well hidden and accessible only to a few "initiates." In reality, it is known that when the first Crusaders conquered Jerusalem, clerics instituted excavations at certain sites in the city, in particular beneath the former Temple of Solomon. It is but a step—one quickly taken in the Middle Ages—from this fact to imagining a mysterious voice encouraging Hugues de Payns to form an elite troop in order to recover these "secrets." The relentless persecution of the Templars after 1307 and the pains taken to interrogate them prove in any case that the henchmen of Philip the Fair and the Inquisition suspected something of this nature. It was not the Templars' material treasure the king was after but possible documents or revelations. It seems he got nothing for his trouble, unless the results of certain interrogations were carefully hidden.

Assuming that Hugues de Payns and his companions were given a mandate to undertake this search for secrets under the official and convenient pretext of watching the roads and protecting pilgrims brings up the question of whether they actually found anything. If they did, they certainly did not tell everyone. In such a case as this they would have revealed their discovery only to those with a right to know. It is at this point that they would have been sent back to Europe to convince the pope and the rulers of Western Europe to give them the means to use the secrets at their disposal. This explanation is both logical and ingenious. Unfortunately, here again we find ourselves in the domain of the most unwarranted kind of hypothesis.

What secrets might the monk Gerbert d'Aurillac have had in mind? He was the student of several Oriental scholars and was an enigmatic character who was suspected of practicing if not magic, then at least the so-called hermetic sciences. It is speculated that the objects of Gerbert's focus may have been the Tablets of the Law—the true tablets and not those divulged to the Hebrew people in the guise of moral precepts. The true Tablets of the Law would be none other than the "secrets of the Great Pyramid," stolen by Moses. This would explain pharaoh's stubborn persistence in first forbidding the Israelites to leave Egypt and then in pursuing them to the shores of the Red Sea. Legends never emerge from whole cloth, and quite often it can be seen how they correspond to certain realities that have been recorded in images and symbolically codified so as to be transmitted down through the generations in a form that is accessible only to those who have attained the degree of initiation allowing them to understand the true meaning of such a code. But in the case of the Tablets of the Law, or the "secrets of the Great Pyramid," people have embellished something about which there is no knowledge. While the Great Pyramid itself offers a digest of Egyptian knowledge concerning not only architecture, but also astronomy, astrology, cosmology, and perhaps even psychology, there is nothing to indicate it concealed tangible or written secrets that Moses could have taken.

It seems true, however, that if Hugues de Payns and his companions had laid hands on such boundless secrets, they would not have been obliged to modestly solicit significant material aid from the pope and the nobles of Europe—aid that they received, moreover, in fairly inexplicable fashion.

Some will respond to this objection by insisting that the Templars had not yet discovered these secrets and required more time and material to attain them, hence the appeal for help to those figures who had been taken into their confidence and officially recognized by the Temple—such as Bernard of Clairvaux, who, having understood the exceptional importance of this search for great secrets, would have done what was necessary to see that the demands for aid were met.

In fact, it is Bernard of Clairvaux himself who poses a problem. In one way or another he is always found at the center of the cyclone in which the Temple took shape and from which it emerged. Either Bernard of Clairvaux was the source of inspiration for Hugues de Payn in 1118 or 1119 or he built upon the enthusiasm of the nine original knights. Objectively it can be concluded that he necessarily recuperated—in the strict sense of the term—Hugues de Payn's vocation, leaving on it his own discreet but profound imprint and making the Temple what we now know, or think we know. Bernard of Clairvaux was a master player. This assertion will not surprise anyone who knows the eminent role he played in the Church of the twelfth century and his influence on the evolution of Western spirituality.

But who was this Bernard of Clairvaux about whom so many legends are spread, making of him a visionary for his sycophants and a hysteric to his detractors? He was the son of a Burgundy lord and belonged to a lineage of knights whose sense of the community formed by one's family and lands was still quite strong. He spent his childhood in the closed world governed by ancestral custom—including the vendetta. When he realized his vocation was calling him to become a monk, he resisted this call until after he had succeeded in convincing all his brothers to join him. You either have the family spirit or you don't—Bernard never did anything half way. At the age of twenty he entered the Abbey of Cîteaux, recently founded by the Clunisian Robert de Molesmes. This man, who had seen in the wealth, comfort, and power of the Benedictines a source of spiritual decadence, wished to return to the original principles of St. Benoît and the Irish Colomba. Bernard was won over to the grand notion of this reform. Like Robert de Molesmes and his successor at Cîteaux Étienne Harding, he preached austerity, poverty, and purity as the *sine qua non* for greatness. Bernard's faith, will, and enthusiasm were of an exceptional caliber, and these were all linked to his exceptional intellect. When, on the counsel of Étienne Harding and by the choice of the monks sent with him, he became the abbot of the monastery of Clairvaux, which the Cistercians had decided to establish, Bernard was the focal point of Christianity, the person whose words were awaited before any decision was made because these words were regarded as coming from God. Few people have such power by virtue of the spirit. But if his power over others was apparent, that which he had—or attempted to have—over himself was no less great.

He understood that man was torn in two, and that this rending was the source of his unhappiness. For him, the return to oneness could be achieved only by following Christ's example. But which Christ—He who died on the Cross or the victorious Christ seen on the porches of some Romanesque churches? The hagiographers of St. Bernard take pains to avoid probing the matter in order to preserve his rank as one of those honorable saints who can be depicted without causing alarm. Nonetheless, much mystery remains surrounding Bernard of Clairvaux.

He has been seen as the heir of Western tradition stemming back to the druids and before. René Guénon went so far as to say he was "the last druid of the Gauls." This is absurd. Bernard of Clairvaux's actions belie this contention on every point. There is no one more Roman than Bernard, no one more centrist or universalist than he, which is, as needs to be said, the exact opposite of the druidic attitude incorporated in Irish and British monachism and filtered by small doses into the Benedictine monachism on the Continent. Rome, in the seventh century, did all it could to destroy Celtic Christianity because its practice did not conform to the model outlined by the popes and their confederates and because it allowed for a different interpretation of the evangelical message.[5] While the issue was raised in the seventh century, there can be no doubt that Bernard of Clairvaux opposed Celtic Christianity with the customary virulence he had used against the proposals of Abelard, which he deemed too rationalist and overly intellectual to be spread where the faithful might hear them.

Convinced he was the guardian of the faith and Church unity, aware that he was participating in an evolution of Christian society and as an instigator of a certain style of monastic living, Bernard was incapable of turning a deaf ear to the solicitations of Hugues de Payns and his companions. For him the idea of the profane was not yet separated from the idea of the sacred. With this conception of the world and governed by a divine law that needs to be grasped and interpreted, man, like the state, is totally engaged in life, which is the ripening of redemption. Whatever changes remained to be made to man or state (which simply addressed organizational issues), the fundamental structures of society—there is only one society and it is Christian—are unshaken, and furthermore

5. Jean Markale, *Le Christianisme celtique et ses survivances populaires* (Paris: Éd. Imago, 1984).

unshakable, and there is no need for them to be overturned. From Heaven to Earth and down into Hell, Christianity forms a large and perfectly coherent organism. This was the ideal of Bernard of Clairvaux and he defended it his entire life. Further, it has nothing at all in common with the flexible and always debatable doctrine of the pre-Christian druids and the bishop-abbots of the Irish monasteries during the high Middle Ages. But it fully justifies the abbot of Clairvaux's interest in the Knights Templar.

In fact, these knights could not fail but please him. Bernard saw in them the possibility of creating under the exclusive authority of the papacy a militia of Christ that could contribute to ensuring the cohesion of the Christian people by eliminating all those who did not want to take part, meaning the infidels and the Muslims. They could also mount an effective watch over large areas of Europe and prevent any possible upheavals. There is good reason to assume that Bernard of Clairvaux wanted the establishment of the Temple as a tight network across Europe because it would guarantee the unity of the Christian world. One leader, the pope; one faith, Christianity; one people, the Christians—this was the ideal of Bernard and the Cistercians. The Templars would supply the necessary arm for this action to take place.

It has been assumed, fairly unwisely, that Bernard knew of the existence of certain documents concerning the early years of Christianity, that he understood these to be stored in a safe location in Jerusalem, and that he sent the Templars on a secret mission to recover them. There is no need whatsoever to resort to this argument to explain the Clairvaux abbot's attitude toward the Templars. It is explained well enough by his grandiose vision of Christianity, in which nothing could be accomplished without the permanent presence of a "tranquil force" composed of "Soldiers of Christ," keepers of public order and guardians of an immutable divine order. The Temple, an international force reliant solely on the papacy—as were the Cistercians, incidentally—would provide, in his view, that incomparable means of cohesion needed by Christianity. So the Templars' mission in the Holy Land was, in Bernard's mind, merely a pretext. The true mission of the Temple should extend into the West. It can never be repeated enough that the first avowed purpose of the militia of Christ was the surveillance and protection of roads. Who controls the roads controls everything else, from a military as well as an economic and political point of view. And a Christian Europe held in respect was ready to assume its role as God's kingdom on Earth. If there is an occult motive behind Bernard of Clairvaux's enthusiasm for the Knights Templar, this is the direction we should definitely be looking for it. "Happy are those who live as travelers and strangers in the middle of this perverse world, and know to guard their purity against defilement; for we have no city here that remains, but we are seeking for the one that will come."[6] The Temple was unquestionably the privileged instrument for this quest.

One of the Temple seals depicts two knights riding on the same horse—a symbol of fraternity, of course, but also of duality, reinforced by the two colors, black and white, of the Baucent standard, which is evidence of the Templars' dual status as monks and soldiers, those who pray and those who fight. It is also a declaration of a dual activity, in Europe and in the Holy Land, and perhaps a symbol of many other double meanings.

In the mysticism of Bernard of Clairvaux, was Jerusalem only in Palestine? Wouldn't that "city that will come" be the "City of God"? And, like God himself, this city is "everywhere and nowhere." Definitely some strange fairies were leaning over the cradle of the young Order of the Temple.

---

6. St. Bernard of Clairvaux, *In Praise of the New Knighthood.*

6

The Evolution of the Temple

IT IS A FAIR TO SAY that two centuries following its founding, the Templar Order was no longer what it had been originally. Every human institution undergoes some degree of evolution, in both its structure and its ideals, and the Temple could not escape this rule, especially as the ambiguity surrounding its founding predisposed it to multiple interpretations and numerous deviations.

The description of the original Templars can be found in the texts of Bernard of Clairvaux. The portrait he draws is quite gripping and he clearly shows the ferocious intent, body and soul, of Hugues de Payns and his companions to serve their cause.

They practice disciplined obedience. Food and clothing are provided them by their leaders; they confine themselves moreover only to what is strictly necessary, and lead a frugal and modest life together without women and children. Following the advice of the Gospels they all dwell beneath the same roof, have no personal possessions, and cultivate oneness in the bond of peace. They seem to possess one heart and one soul, so much has each renounced his individual will to remain blindly submissive to his leader. They are never seen sitting idle, but on those rare occasions when they are not on duty, they are earning their living by repairing their own

133

armor and clothing, or devoting themselves, on orders from their superior, to tending to the ordinary needs of their community. There is no distinction made among persons and it is merit, not noble blood that determines rank. Each shows deference to his fellows and works mutually to carry each other's burdens, thus fulfilling Christ's law. Any arrogant or frivolous speech or immodest laughter or spreading of rumors will entail swift correction. They hold both hunting and gaming to be disreputable. Jugglers, troubadours and their clownish songs they regard with the utmost scorn for they comprehend the vanity and folly of the theater. They crop their hair in accordance with the words of the Apostle, knowing it is shameful for a man to care for his locks. They never comb it and rarely wash, preferring to appear with tousled hair and dirty faces burnt black as their armor.[1]

We may wonder whether St. Bernard actually had an opportunity to witness them in this state, but there can be no doubt that this portrait conforms to reality, even if it clashes to some degree with our contemporary sensibilities. This behavior at least shows a renunciation of the world, intentional austerity, and derision of everything superficial. But it is a portrait of the Templars in the time of Hugues de Payns, who died in 1136. His position of grand master of the order was succeeded by Robert de Craon, which is when everything seems to have changed.

Though a wretched soldier, Robert de Craon was a remarkable administrator and the Temple was radically transformed under his management. The original roughness was replaced by a sort of quest for the beautiful in all its forms, something that conformed to a certain evolution of aristocratic mores. This was the beginning of the courtly era, with Lancelot of the Lake serving as its model knight, thanks to the diffusion of Arthurian legends. Certainly Lancelot is a model of bravery and tenacity who never hesitates to fulfill his duty, but he is also a courtly man, cultivated and well taught, who knows how to behave honorably

---

1. "In Praise of the New Knighthood," *Political Texts*, 202–3.

in society. Adopting some of these values allowed the Templars to be more fully integrated into the society of their time. In fact, the order became its indispensable pivot, and the original humility of Hugues de Payns gave way to a kind of pride: Not just anyone could be a Templar. Consequently, being a Templar assumed its own *aristocratic* value, in the etymological sense of the word. Of course, during the time of Hugues de Payns, no one could become a knight unless he was the son of a lord— hence, of noble blood—but committing to knighthood essentially involved a voluntary renunciation of that noble status through mortification or through the sense of duty to all members of Christian society without exception. Later, however, a knight of the Temple acquired a certain nobility by entering the order. This illustrates a clear deviation from the mind-set that presided at the founding of the order and it was by pursuing this direction that the Templars found themselves branded by infamy a century and a half later.

The decisive point dates from the time of the papal bull *Omne datum optimum,* issued in 1139 by Pope Innocent II, giving the order extravagant privileges while modifying part of the Rule adopted by the Council of Troyes, around which there has always been something of a mystery: In 1128 this Rule was set down in Latin, but in 1139 it reappeared written in French, with part of it no longer corresponding to the Latin text. There can be, however, grounds for thinking that the medieval clergy were incapable of translating Latin texts correctly.

This new Rule, rewritten in French, specifies one capital element: "All the orders spoken and written in this present Rule are at the discretion and regard of the master." This phrase does not appear in the Latin text, and it is easy to understand why. According to the statutes of 1128, the order was subordinate to the authority of the patriarch of Jerusalem. The papal bull freed the Templars of this supervision, thus conferring absolute authority upon the grand master, who in this instance was Robert de Craon. The patriarch was cleanly eliminated from the loop, and with him all lay authority. The French version of the Rule of the order integrated as independent members of the Templars those clergymen previously outside the order, making them brother chaplains who answered only to the exclusive authority of the grand master, once a priest but now a simple monk. The least that can be said is that with the explicit accord of the pope, the Temple became an organization totally independent of the ecclesiastical hierarchy, even going so far as to confer supreme authority on a non-priest. We may ask what actually took place in the religious ceremonies celebrated in the private sanctuaries of the Temple, those ceremonies that were uniquely reserved for members of the order and whose officiants were answerable only to the grand master. Such practices provided grounds for numerous interpretations, even outright lies, which would be brought up during the trial in 1307, in particular the accusation lodged against the priests of the order for omitting the words of the consecration.

But there is more. We know that the Latin Rule called for a novitiate for those wishing to become Templars. It was quite clear that no one could be accepted into the Temple until after the end of this probation. But the French version doesn't even mention this period of time. Should we believe that anyone who expressed a desire to join Christ's militia would be accepted into the order after meeting the necessary conditions? Originally it was required to show proof of nobility and to renounce the privileges associated with that nobility before entering the community; but the French Rule stipulated that it was through entering the order that glory and nobility were acquired. There is something in this reversal that lends weight to the accusation that the Temple had become an initiatic entity.

This important change found in the French Rule relates to Article 12 of the Latin text, concerning the recruitment of new members: "There where you know *non*-excommunicated knights are gathered, we command you to go." The French version, however, erased the negation, thereby making itself the exact opposite of the Latin version: "There where you know excommunicated knights are gathered, we command you to go." This is not simply an error, for the text goes on to say:

And if there is one who wishes to return and join the order of the knighthood of Outremer, you should not only consider the worldly profit you may expect, but also the eternal salvation of his soul. We order you to receive him on condition he presents himself before the bishop of the province and makes known his resolution. And once the bishop has heard and absolved him, if he asks it of the master and the brothers of the Temple, if his life be honest and worthy of their company, and if he seems worthy to the master and the brothers, then he may be received with mercy.

This was certainly in complete accord with Christian charity and testified to the most laudable intentions. But many seized on this lax attitude toward excommunicates as demonstration of the slow corruption that had taken hold of the Temple, thus justifying the reaction the order inspired at the beginning of the fourteenth century. This reaction may not have been entirely unwarranted; it needs to be examined with care. In fact, Articles 11, 12, and 13 of the French version, which correspond to articles 58, 64, and 57 of the earlier Latin Rule, form a consistent whole on the subject of the admission of new members into the order. Article 11, in particular, deals with instances of lay knights or other men who wish "to depart from the road to perdition and abandon this century, and choose a communal life." Acceptance is left up to the assessment of the grand master and the brothers who make up a particular chapter of the order. Article 12 concerns the excommunicated knights who could be accepted into the order as long as they had reconciled with the Church. Article 13 forbids any contact with the excommunicated beyond the case specified in Article 12.

Several murky areas remain, however. If we take the Latin Rule as our basis, it will be noted that Article 58 stipulates that lay knights are to be welcomed directly by the grand master and the chapter, while Article 64 states that non-excommunicated knights cannot be accepted until after an interview with the bishop. But what is the difference between lay knights and non-excommunicated knights? Perhaps Article 64 is correcting an omission concerning the bishop's role in the admission of new members before the independence of the order from the lay hierarchy was recognized. This is not clear, however.

All that can be said for certain is that the new Rule allowed the Templars to recruit wherever they liked, and not always in the best neighborhoods. Carrying the good news to excommunicated knights was clearly a case of "fishing in troubled waters." According to what we know, there were a countless number of knights excommunicated in the twelfth and thirteenth centuries throughout Europe and Palestine for various reasons (church looting, attacking monasteries, adultery, evil lifestyle, felony against a lord, lack of respect for religious authority, and so forth). After all, what king of France wasn't excommunicated, at least briefly? (Louis IX just barely avoided it!) It should also be noted that the excommunicated knights were not necessarily the worst of their lot—far from it.

It must have been recognized that it would be stupid to do without the services of men like these. Accepting them was more in conformance with the original concept of the Temple, solemnly reaffirmed by Bernard of Clairvaux, of leading the sinner knight toward salvation by offering him a novel form of asceticism. This alteration in the Rule simply reinforced the Temple's vocation: Convert and put in service to the whole of Christianity a social class that was indocile by nature and sometimes lost. But this practice was accompanied by an obvious risk. If the Temple turned into a welcoming organization for the marginal members of Christian society, wasn't there a danger of it becoming something of a Foreign Legion? The often repeated reproach to the Templars for having recruited "hot heads" is not completely groundless. As support for this we need only recall certain anecdotes, such as that concerning Geoffroy de Mandeville.

The story takes place in England, during the time of the war waged by Étienne de Blois and Empress Mathilde over the throne. Geoffroy de Mandeville, an Anglo-Norman lord, attempted to recapture three castles that had been previously taken from his family. Thanks to the intervention of Étienne de Blois, he succeeded. But he was also plotting with Mathilde. Arrested in 1143, he had to surrender all his castles in order to regain his freedom. He then became a veritable outlaw, killing and pillaging without restraint, taking possession of Ramsey Abbey and Ely Island.

Fig. 1. The octagonal tower of Gisors Castle, which allegedly housed the Priory of Sion after 1188
Fig. 2. Church of Saint-Gervais-Saint-Protais in Gisors

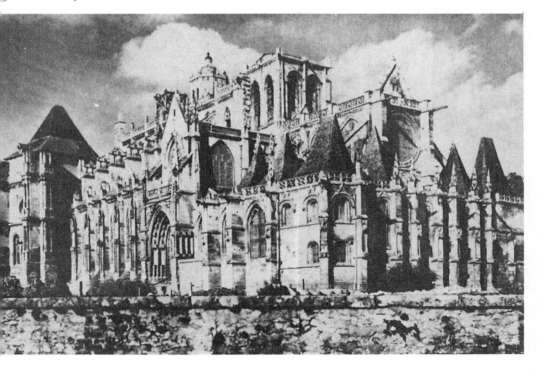

Fig. 3. Templars in battle, from a twelfth-century wall fresco

Fig. 4. *The best-known Templar seal*

Fig. 5. *Templars, from a fourteenth-century manuscript*

TEMPLE·A·PARIS· BASTIMENT· ANCIEN·DES· TEMPLIERS

Montmartre

Fig. 6. The Paris Temple
(Bibliothèque nationale)

Fig. 7. The Temple as it appeared
at the beginning of the fourteenth
century

Fig. 8. Jacques de Molay, grand master of the Temple

Fig. 9. Guillaume Nogaret (Bibliothèque nationale)

Fig. 10. The Church of the Knights Templar in London. Its round nave was consecrated by the patriarch of Jerusalem in 1185.

Fig. 11. Tombstone of a Templar in the Church of the Knights Templar in London

Fig. 12. Pope Clement V (Bibliothèque nationale)

Fig. 13. The execution of the Templars, from a
fourteenth-century manuscript

Wounded by an arrow in the summer of 1144, he died without absolution after several days of agonized lingering. He was therefore cursed and could not be buried in consecrated ground. According to the chronicle of Walden Abbey, however, which he founded and whose monks remained loyal to him, Knights Templar then appeared on the scene, covering the corpse with the Red Cross (this part of the tale is an invention, for this symbol was not attributed to the Templars until after 1148) and taking cover behind their privileges in order to transport the body to London. There they placed it in a coffin, which they hung from a tree in the garden at their house of Old Temple so that the consecrated ground would not be contaminated. Twenty years later, the monks of Walden, having obtained a posthumous pardon for their founder, received authorization to bury him. They then found out that the Templars had already interred him in their cemetery at New Temple.

A strange story. Its details were forged by the Walden monks for the greater needs of the cause, but it does present an obvious connection between Geoffroy de Mandeville and the Templars. But why this interest on the part of the Templars for a particularly odious criminal knight? Did the Knights Templar have a habit of associating with such individuals in flagrant disregard of Article 57 of the Latin Rule, which forbids association with excommunicates?[2]

Logically speaking, the Templars would hardly have been capable of recruiting if they had not turned to excommunicates. We can hold forth endlessly on the high spiritual mission of the Templars, their secret doctrine, and their allegedly heretical beliefs, but we will always stumble against the same truism: An order of soldier-monks has more need of roughneck soldiers than it does of metaphysicians. The mystics and contemplatives could go elsewhere, to the Cistercians, Clunisians, or Benedictines—there was a variety from which to choose. It was a harder kind of man who was drawn to the Temple—not that there could be any doubt about his Christian faith, but simply because the order provided

---

2. The resting place of Geoffroy de Mandeville is still shown in the church of the London Temple, but it is a fake dating from at least fifty years after the alleged burial. Further, the coat of arms that can be see upon it is not that of the Mandevilles.

an honorable exit for swashbucklers of all stripes. Those who would join the order knew that the Templars needed sturdy and aggressive men. And for those who felt completely excluded from Christian society and no longer knew which way to turn to ensure their survival, wouldn't joining the Temple prove a great temptation? In many ways, then, it truly was a "Foreign Legion." Men found with the Templars both the means of meeting their material needs and their salvation in the Other World, no small matter. The Templars took a vow of poverty, of course, but the order was wealthy and would not let its members die of hunger. In return for obedience to the Rule and work suited to his abilities, a poor knight—of which there were many in the twelfth century—lacking both a penny and a purse to put it in saw the possibility, through serving with the Templars, of making ends meet, eating good meals, sleeping in comfortable lodging, and entering paradise when his life was over. This observation may appear revoltingly cynical to the Templars' most ardent supporters, but it corresponds to the reality of the time as it has been revealed to us by various eyewitnesses.

Does this mean that the Templars were thick-headed brutes? Of course not. All kinds entered the order. The fact that the Templar Rule was translated, or rather adapted, into French in 1139 shows that many of the Templars were illiterate. Let's not mistake the meaning of the term *illiterate* as it pertains to medieval times. It strictly meant that someone did not know Latin. But that did not guarantee that the person in question knew how to read French (or any other common tongue or vernacular) or possessed any cultural education or theological training. In principle, a Templar had no need of either culture or theology. He needed only to believe and obey. It is quite certain that being illiterate—in other words, knowing no Latin—especially in the twelfth and thirteenth centuries, would keep someone far removed from real culture and any true understanding of the fundamental religious texts, none of which had been translated. Latin was, after all, still the official language of not only the Church but political institutions as well. The fact that Jacques de Molay, the last Templar grand master, was illiterate speaks volumes about the cultural level of the leaders of the Templar Order—at least the official leaders, those who occupied the foreground. Doubt is allowable as far as this is concerned, and it is not far-fetched to assume that a parallel, occult hierarchy directed the Temple, entrusting to certain known figures the duty of establishing contact with the members of the order and being, on behalf of others, the guarantors responsible for the order. The so-called institution of figureheads is as old as civilization.

That said, the Rule, especially after its translation into French, was intended for diffusion among all the members of the order. It was not changed again after 1139, but it was "finalized" several more times, particularly with the famous revisions, whose composition goes back to the time of the grand master Bertrand de Blanquefort (1156–1169)—the very same man whom certain "secret" documents from the so-called Priory de Sion tried to pass off as a native of Razès, near Rennes-le-Château, and who historical documents irrefutably prove was a member of a noble family in the Bordeaux region. There were other additions in 1230 and 1260 to specify details concerning conventual life, discipline, and sanctions as well as admission into the order. This final Rule and its supplement are known perfectly today.

But what exactly did the Rule mean to the Templars? We know that the basic Rule was read, in a summary form at least, during the ceremony welcoming a new Templar. Article 11, in fact, explicitly states: "Test the spirit to see if it comes from God, but once he has been granted the company of the brothers, may the Rule be read to him." It will be noted that the Rule was communicated to the new knight only after he had been accepted and welcomed into the order and not before, which might seem unusual. The admission ritual of 1260 also stipulates that a summary of the main articles and principal revisions of the Rule be included. At this time the entire set formed a solid collection of some 678 articles; thus it is obvious that it would be possible to give only a summary.

This reading of a summary of the Rule has prompted much comment and has been seen as proof of the Templar Knights' lack of education: Not only had the Rule been translated, along with all the Scriptural quotes it contained, but it was also read aloud. It seems certain that the majority of the soldier-monks did not know how to read, but there were exceptions and they were anticipated in the Rule. In fact it was forbidden for a brother Templar "to possess either revision or Rule, unless given leave to do so by the monastery." In other words, the possession of a copy of the Rule was subject to supervision. Furthermore, the reasons mentioned for this restriction are fairly odd. It seems there was a wish to prevent the Rule from falling into the hands of those who would take unfair advantage of the knowledge it gave them: "Squires sometimes find and read it, and thereby reveal our establishments to people of the country, which can cause harm to our religion. So to avoid that such a thing should come to pass, the monastery establishes that no brother should possess it unless as a bailiff, whose office requires its possession." (Article 326)

If we understand this correctly, the Rule and revisions are not to be divulged to ordinary citizens: maybe to the squires who by law are members of the Temple, but not to others. We find here elements of a profound distrust of anyone not belonging to the Temple, as well as a taste for secrecy that borders on the obsessive. However, the Rule and the various revisions say nothing especially contrary to the ruling orthodoxy. We can react to this distrust only with surprise. If we take this article at its word, the harm "to our religion" caused by divulging the Rule really means harm to the Temple. In this instance and in the 1307 trial, however, it was the Templars' fierce desire for secrecy that was harmful to their "religion." They were reproached for this secrecy and it provided the element of doubt concerning the Templars' true motives.

It is all the more astonishing, then, that the Rule and its revisions seem to have been widely diffused. Every important Templar house had a copy in its possession. During the trial, a brother chaplain of Mas Deu gave the bishop of Elne and the members of the commission "the aforesaid book of the Rule, that he had carried from the house of Mas Deu, and which began as follows in Roman [in other words, Catalan]: *"quam cel proom requer la companya de la Mayso . . ."* A copy of the Rule in French, most likely from the Templar house of Dauges, near Douai (Nord), was found in Baltimore, Maryland, in the vaults of a library. Along with the text of the Rule, a poem in the style of the courtly era's *trouvères* was added. The fact that both were found together does not seem to conform exactly to Templar regulation, but there they were. We may conclude that Templars who felt inspired by the Muse could indulge their inclinations and compose love poems despite their religious vows. This lends weight to certain folk traditions that depict the Templars as womanizers who sought the company of unrepentant women. But it equally proves that access to the Temple Rule book was quite open. Why, then, all the secrecy? Why this fear of the Rule falling into profane hands, to the great harm of "our religion"?

There is no answer unless we assume the existence of a secret Rule. But what we are discussing here is no secret Rule book, but the official Rule diffused everywhere and for which we possess a dozen manuscripts today. Furthermore, this Rule was so widely and officially known outside the order that it exerted a strong influence on the Rules of other military orders. For example, certain details of the Hospitaller Rule, notably those concerning the chaplains, the chapter, and dignitaries, presume a direct influence from the Temple and Cîteaux. Similarly, in 1198 the knights of the hospital of St. Mary of the Teutons, currently known as the Teutonic Knights, an order that was both military and charitable, received a copy of the Rule of their fraternal rival, the Templars, on which they could model their own. So, what was the point of this mania for secrecy?

It did not prevent the order from expanding; its branches extended everywhere. The famous Templar "spider web" firmly attached itself to the western half of the European continent. And the Temple, proportionate to its growth, deviated from the path laid out for it by its founders and Bernard of Clairvaux himself—a deviation that was due essentially to the prodigious wealth that characterized the order.

The Temple had in fact become the supreme financial power of the thirteenth century. Of course, in accordance with original regulations, no Templar could own property for personal use. Grand Master Armand de la Tour Rouge had proudly answered the Muslims holding him for ransom: "All a Templar can offer as ransom are his belt and his fighting knife." The rule of poverty remained in force, but when there is plenty for all, there is necessarily enough for one. After all, the Templars were men like other men, even if they had deliberately chosen a certain marginal position. It has been calculated that at the end of the thirteenth century the Templars owned almost nine thousand establishments, a figure that has been used as a basis to estimate their transferable fortune. A figure of some 130 billion francs [about 20 billion U.S. dollars today — *Trans.*] was what historians have come up with. While there may have been some overestimation (the translation of currency worth from the thirteenth century to our own era is always tricky), it should still be recognized that in a time when poverty was predominant throughout the world, the order had amassed considerable wealth. Further, because the Holy Land had been lost, this fortune no longer served any purpose, at least none in accordance with the vision of its original mission.

Where did this wealth come from? First, there were two centuries' worth of donations and gifts. Donations reached their height at the end of the twelfth century, but were still a source of constant income at the beginning of the reign of Philip the Fair. The Templars were able to manage these properties profitably because the members spent very little on their own needs. In short, the Templars lived completely self-sufficiently; thus, every new acquisition was pure profit.

There was another source of revenue that was rarely spoken of, but was quite considerable: war booty. Like all their contemporaries, the soldier-monks of the Temple practiced pillaging. Furthermore, they were given express authorization to do so by the papal bull of 1139.

Nor should the donations of pilgrims be overlooked. In all times, pilgrimages have been a source of profit. Evidence of this can be seen in the bitter struggle among sanctuaries, churches, and monasteries over the possession of certain relics that could attract a horde of pilgrims—or in the occasional invention of such relics. It is well know that a two-story house could be constructed from all the authentic remnants of the True Cross spread throughout the world. The Templars, like so many others, exploited the good faith of pilgrims.

But it was the Templars' banking operations that were most responsible for providing the order with its fabulous wealth. Profiting from its presence along all the main commercial routes, as well as from its autonomy and prestige, the order had set up a financial organization that was very advanced for its time (and not for the purpose of sneering at modern economists). The order invented the exchange note, the check, and various kinds of credit. It was entrusted with considerable sums of money, which it kept meticulously secured. In fact, the enormous fortress of the Templars in Paris was built for just this purpose. Through the Templars anyone could pay for his purchases in foreign lands. Because it prospered, it is certain that this banking organization answered a real need, but it also contributed to the growth of the Templars' fortune through the fees exacted by the order for each transaction. We might ask, however, if this was really the role of a religious order founded for the protection of pilgrims in the Holy Land.

This brand of activity incited not only hostile criticism at the time but also serious consequences, including interminable conflicts with secular authorities. In France, for example, because the Templars were authorized to sell their wine without charging tax, the wine merchants protested against the Templars' unfair trade practices. The cloth merchants complained that the Templars wrongly charged high rates on certain merchandise, causing them harm. With the ownership of its own private fleet, which thereby diverted the trade of merchants and pilgrims, the Temple also drew the animosity of the sailing companies of Marseilles and the Italian ports. Furthermore, when its own interests were at stake, the order showed proof of a pitiless severity that was hardly in keeping with Christian charity. Firmly convinced of their inherent superiority and used to viewing themselves as the elite warriors of Christianity, the Templars had no compassion for the troubles of their peers, nor even respect for their ideas or feelings. The order had become a huge machine that functioned smoothly but had the defect common to all machines: It was no longer human. When a Templar house quarreled with its neighbors, it no longer recoiled from resorting to murder, pillage, or arson, no matter which feudal lord was the object of its displeasure. It ran little risk of incurring any punishment thanks to the enormous privileges the order had at its disposal and the conspiracy of silence that surrounded certain incidents.

However, people were beginning to ask a certain basic question: Did the order still serve a purpose? Saladin had retaken Jerusalem in 1187 and it was apparent that Christians would never again be masters of the holy city. The Christian kingdom there had been reduced to a small swath of land surrounding Saint John of Acre, and this final bastion collapsed in 1291. There was no longer any Christian kingdom in the Middle East. There were no longer any pilgrims, either, and therefore no more roads to keep watch over in order to ensure their safety. Certainly, the Templars still fought against Muslims—but the battlefield had switched to Spain, which, moreover, created a unique mind-set and set of circumstances in this country. But elsewhere in Western Europe there was an impression that the order had lost all reason for being.

It survived, however, following its transit through Cyprus, and transferred its head house to France, to the enclosed Temple of Paris. It retained its seven provinces—France, Aragon, Portugal, Poitou, England, Pouilles, and Hungary—and continued its financial operations even more adeptly without any other business serving as a distraction. The order also retained the immense privileges conferred upon it by the popes. Under these conditions, is it any wonder that the Templar Order inspired jealousy and, of course, slander?

Against the milieu of the common people, the order was primarily reproached for its wealth, which was scandalous and offensive to those living in misery. Further, its members were criticized for leading a life that bore little resemblance to the monastic ideal. It was during this time that the expression "drink like a Templar" became proverbial. It is true that the willingly anticlerical populace of the Middle Ages ceaselessly mocked the monks of all orders, emphasizing their intemperance and gluttony, but criticism of the Templars took on a more specific meaning. The Templars were soldiers more than they were monks, yet they were exempted from certain abstinences applicable only to monks in other orders. This caused tongues to wag. It was rumored that their mores were not always in keeping with the vow of absolute chastity symbolized by their white cloaks. Even children were advised to avoid the company of Templars and to be especially wary of their kisses. While the

Rule of the Temple forbade the brothers from kissing women—even their mothers or their sisters—it in no way forbade the kissing of children. Thus vague suspicions of pedophilia emerged and it is cause for surprise that these suspicions were not transformed into formal charges in the trial of 1307. Mainly malicious gossip was behind all of these suspicions, but there were a few truths as well.

The Templars were also reproached for their ostentatious luxury, not in the decoration of their churches, which were always of a notable sobriety, but rather on specific occasions when the richness of their dress drew attention. To this they answered that because business dealings were their principal activity, they had to effect an imposing presence.

In their defense, it must be pointed out that the Templars were not the only ones criticized for this by the public. The Hospitallers of St. John were hated for the same reasons. And the Hospitallers were embroiled in some scandals that were even more serious. They often drew the wrath of the papacy for their sexual incontinence, for shielding those who robbed and murdered pilgrims, and for straying into heretical doctrines. These accusations were certainly hurled against the Templars as well, but on each occasion the Temple benefited from a surprising indulgence on the part of the papacy. Only Innocent III, who was still a friend of the Templars, dared address these remonstrations with them at the beginning of the thirteenth century. "The crimes of your brothers," he wrote to the grand master, "pain us profoundly for the scandal they have provoked in the Church. The Templars practice the doctrine of the demon, the habit they wear is hypocrisy." And in 1263, no doubt following some incident involving a woman, Pope Urban IV excommunicated the Temple's marshal, Étienne de Sissey, a protégé of Grand Master Thomas Bérard. The next pope, Clement IV, agreed to lift the excommunication on the condition that the marshal be relieved of his duties, and he made use of the occasion to issue a solemn warning to the entire order: "May the Templars beware that I may lose my patience and oblige the Church to examine more closely the status of certain reprehensible things that have been indulgently tolerated until now, for then there will be no remission." Nothing more than this is known of the matter, but it seems fairly serious. The accusers of 1307 would surely have remembered it.

These reprimands, combined with the permanent conflicts the Templars had with the other military orders (the Hospitallers and the Teutonic Knights), weigh quite heavily on the legitimate and justifiable suspicions with regard to the Temple. According to all evidence, by the end of the thirteenth century the order had changed drastically. But in reality, the Templars were never saints.

There are also some regrettable episodes, which the Templars' most ardent supporters refrain from discussing. In 1187, when Saladin took control of Jerusalem, he offered safe passage to the populace of that city—freedom for the men for ten gold pieces and freedom for women and children for five and two gold pieces, respectively. The rich easily ransomed themselves, but the majority of Christians, who were mainly people of modest means, were incapable of paying and were subsequently reduced to slavery to Saladin. The Temple, which had saved its treasure and had the means to aid these disadvantaged Christians, bluntly refused to ransom the population of Jerusalem. The pretext used was that grand master Gérard de Ridefort, being himself a prisoner and having the sole power to authorize such an expenditure, absolutely forbade the brothers to withdraw anything from the Templar treasury. Thus 16,000 Christians, including women and children, were reduced to slavery.

Louis IX nearly met the same fate. When the sainted king was made prisoner, the Templars refused to contribute to his ransom, though Joinville, who had little love for the order, used a number of ruses to force them to comply. St. Louis, however, would not forget: Later he humiliated Grand Master Renaud de Vichiera by forcing him to kneel before him and make amends.

Another anecdote is even more revealing. We know that Emperor Frederic II of Hohenstauten, a mysterious figure, an apostate (or heretic—it is not known which, for sure), and an excommunicated foe of the pope, had managed to conclude a pact with the Muslims. At the price of some kind of shady deals, no doubt, he had succeeded in obtaining the return of Jerusalem to Christian rule. But in order for this return to be cemented, Frederic II required the guarantee of the Templars. He negotiated with the Templars, promising them a sumptuous gift, but they refused because their house was not included in the proposed restitution. The deal effectively died. This Frederic II never forgot and he subsequently poured his energy into virulent attacks against the Templars.

It can be easily seen that the order, through its involvement in temporal matters, inevitably compromised itself in one way or another. The operations in the Holy Land constituted a diversion that allowed the military orders—including the Hospitallers and the Teutonic Knights—to maintain fallback positions in case of need. After the fall of Saint John of Acre had put an end to the final hopes of Christianity, the military orders reverted to these positions prepared in advance. The Hospitallers chose the sea as their domain. From their bases in Cyprus and later Rhodes, they ensured the safety of the Mediterranean and won renown for their pursuit of Muslim pirates. The Teutonic Knights were already committed, for the most part, to a war of nationalist expansion against the Slavs on behalf of the German empire. Those who had remained in the Holy Land rejoined their brothers in arms to become a veritable German army at the service of the emperors. The Temple, however, apart from those members who continued to fight the Moors in Spain, was the only order that did not find a new sphere of military operations. The Templars retreated to the Continent, where they developed their domains.

It was at this point that Philip the Fair entered the picture. He has been portrayed as an implacable foe of the Templars, but that was not always the case. Certainly in 1295 he withdrew the royal treasure that had been stored at the Temple of Paris and transferred it to the Louvre. Some have tried to view this as the first gesture of hostility against the Templars, but in actuality the king simply hoped to manage the public treasury himself with some skillful financial transactions and thereby contribute to the increase of his own fortune. This plan was a failure, and in 1303 the royal treasure was again entrusted to the Temple. The Templars had shown themselves to be the best financiers of the time and the king of France gave them his complete trust. He also gave the Templars a number of generous gifts and addressed them with warm words: "The works of pity and mercy, the magnificent generosity shown through the entire world and at all times, the Holy Order of the Temple . . . we are determined to extend our liberality upon the order and its knights, and to give marks of our special favor to the order and its knights for whom we have a sincere predilection."[2]

This all seems a bit too good to be true. Philip the Fair was a complex individual—both a politician with a crafty, calculating mind and a somewhat megalomaniacal religious fanatic who, we should not forget, was the grandson of a saint and king. From his ascension to the throne in 1285, he undertook the consolidation of a kingdom larger and better administrated than any the world had ever known. Clearly his purpose was the greatest possible expansion of the power of this embryonic state. In his eyes, this was his sacred duty. Just as St. Louis, he thought that by defending the interests of the state and the dynasty, he was also serving the cause of God and the Christian faith. Endowed with a will of iron and a heart of stone, he never doubted for an instant that he was acting on behalf of God. This fact should be remembered before we issue against him any hasty and impassioned judgments. In his mind it was God who was acting through him. Strengthening the power of the king of France, the country known as "the eldest daughter of the Church," could only be putting divine intentions into practice, even when doing so necessitated battling the pope, for the pope's mission was only spiritual and nontemporal. Furthermore, the example of his grandfather offered him reassurance on this point. On several occasions St. Louis had locked horns with the pope, although he recognized the Holy Father's spiritual primacy. In a word, the king of France was master in his kingdom and responsible to God alone—an early example of the absolute monarch of divine right.

Since the fall of Saint John of Acre, Philip the Fair, who had a keen sense of reality but at the same time indulged chimerical dreams related to the divine mission with which he felt he had been invested, was open-

2. I should point out a particularly spicy little detail. Illustrating the close ties between Jacques de Molay and Philip the Fair, the grand master agreed to be the godfather of the king's son despite the rules prohibiting Templars from assuming such relationships. In fact, during a riot by Parisians in 1306, it was in the enclosure of the Temple that the king of France found refuge.

ing his eyes to new possibilities. Because the Holy Land was lost, he told himself, and impossible to reconquer, at least in the short term, other means must be sought. He found these means in the mystic and somewhat esoteric thought of Ramon Lulle.

The Catalan poet and alchemist Ramon Lulle, who had long been interested in the possibility of converting the people of Islam to the Christian faith, had in 1292 come up with an ambitious plan for conquering the Muslim countries and preaching the Gospel there. His plan was as follows: Missionaries with a solid grounding in the Arab tongue (Lulle himself was an Arabic specialist) would receive the support of a new Crusader army built around a nucleus formed by the Hospitaller and Templar Orders, which would merge into one under a supreme leader whose title would be *bellator rex* and who would assume the position of king of Jerusalem. Ramon Lulle hoped first to convince King Jaime II of Aragon to mount a campaign against Grenada, which was still in Muslim hands, but it was in Paris that his request fell on open ears in the court of the French king.

Philip the Fair understood the full scope of the benefits to be gained by anyone who had the audacity to assume the title and role of bellator rex. He knew the power represented by the military orders. The Hospitallers ruled the Mediterranean and the Templars were the masters of the European continent. To become the supreme leader of both the Templars and the Hospitallers would be a real trump for the king of France, and he could then become a veritable world leader by assuming the title of king of Jerusalem.

Philip's hypothesis was not entirely groundless. He actually formulated a plan and wrote it down in an eighty-point program. We, in fact, possess a manuscript that, while fragmentary, is precise enough to allow us to re-create it in its entirety.[3] These documents show that Philip the Fair was thinking of abdicating in favor of his eldest son in order to

---

3. The few surviving fragments of this ambitious program were integrated into an Aragonese document dating from the beginning of 1308. H. Finke, *Papsttum und Untergang des Temperordens*, vol. 2 (Munster, 1907), 118. Commentary in the same work, 121–22. See also Norman Cohn, *Démonolâtrie et sorcellerie au Moyen Age* (Paris: Payot, 1982), 109.

become the grand master of the combined orders. This new order would take the name of Knights of Jerusalem and its grand master would bear the title of king of Jerusalem. After the death of Philip the Fair, the title would pass down through the generations to the eldest son of the king of France. The revenues owed every prelate, bishop, and archbishop would revert to the grand master for the reconquest of the Holy Land, less only enough to provide each a modest salary. The same would be true for the monastic orders not actively involved in the reconquest. Furthermore, the bellator rex would have a supervisory right over the election of popes. In this way Philip the Fair planned to become more powerful than the emperor, and all for the greater glory of the kingdom of France. The king of France, consecrated one day or another as king of Jerusalem, would rule, as a Roman emperor ruled, over a vast federation of nations, and thus would universal peace be established.

Whether or not Philip the Fair was a megalomaniac, he really did dream of bringing this plan to fruition. He actually achieved several of its points concerning the Templars and his famous "right of supervision" over the election of the popes. Indeed, it is an established fact that Philip the Fair wished to gain control over the Order of the Temple and the Order of the Hospitallers. He knew full well what awesome power they embodied and wished to put it to work for his own interests or, to be fair, for those of the king of France. It was a grandiose idea, certainly, and one that explains the charitable attitude he took toward the Templars.

But when all the attempts of merger had come to naught because of the intransigence of the Templars, who were overconfident about their own strength, Philip the Fair realized that if he could not become master of the Temple, he would have to attack it. The order had grown to be too powerful and thus dangerous, with the risk of being used by a bellator rex other than himself. This is a historical reality. The prosecution mounted against the Templars, while it also belongs to history, resulted from the vengeance of a man who, having witnessed the collapse of his grand plans for world hegemony, could not forgive the Templars their refusal to cooperate with him.

7

The Templars on Trial

IN SEEKING TO UNDERSTAND the inner workings of the charges lodged against the Templars, the torture inflicted on a large number of knight-monks, and the dissolution of the order obtained with great difficulty by Pope Clement V (there was never a condemnation of the Temple), it is a good idea to place everything in its proper context. This context happens to be nothing other than the undying struggle between the king of France and the pope—particularly Pope Boniface VIII. This struggle extended to such lengths that it provided a pretext for a posthumous trial against Boniface VIII. Curiously enough, this trial gave Philip the Fair currency to wrest from Clement V any concessions he wanted, or at least some of them: the abandonment of proceedings against his counselor—and henchman—Guillaume de Nogaret and the annihilation of the Temple.

Let's look at the facts. Following the death of Pope Nicholas IV in 1291, various conclaves were unable to elect a new pontiff. This continued for two years. Weary of the struggle, the conclave sought a pious hermit who would be no threat to their personal interests and forcibly installed him on St. Peter's throne under the name of Celestine V. But saints have never made good popes. Celestine V, a figure of frankness and charitable spirit, began distributing the goods of the Church to the poor. It is easy to imagine the scandal this provoked among the Roman

Curia, and he eventually decided to abdicate when confronted with the growing hostility of the cardinals.

His successor was Benoit Caetani, better known as Boniface VIII, but the issue of his legitimacy was raised immediately. Did Celestine V have the right to resign his pontifical office? Opinions were divided on this point. For those who refused to accept the possibility of abdicating, the election of Boniface VIII was invalid. The question had still not been settled by the time the Templar affair broke out, although Boniface had been dead and buried a long time.

Boniface VIII had all the necessary qualities to make a good pope, but certainly not a saint. Proud and authoritarian, he warred with everyone and thrust his knife into the cardinals of the Colonna family, who were his political adversaries. His disputes with the king of France over the basest financial matters (royal taxes on the clergy) are well known and went back and forth in attacks and counterattacks until Boniface VIII finally threatened to depose Philip the Fair.

This was not something the king would allow. He had reliable allies in Italy, namely in the figures of the Colonna cardinals. The Colonna, who hated the pope, allied themselves with the French king and participated in the defamation campaign against the pope. They even went so far as to suggest that Boniface had performed magical or diabolical ceremonies with the intention of obtaining help from demons. In March 1303, an assembly of bishops and nobles gathered at the Louvre to meet with the king of France. There they heard Guillaume de Nogaret, a formidable orator and excellent jurist specializing in Roman law, denounce the pope as a heretic and call for a meeting of the General Council of the Church to sit in judgment on him.

Boniface retorted by preparing a bull that excommunicated the king of France. Nogaret then traveled to Italy, where he organized a plot to seize the pope and drag him before the council—the famous kidnapping attempt in Anagni, which the Colonna caused to fail. For three days Cardinal Sciarra Colonna tormented and insulted the pope. He also antagonized the inhabitants of Anagni so much that they rose up and freed Boniface. Nogaret was wounded and fled. As for Boniface, broken both physically and mentally, he died within the month.

His successor, Benoit XI, issued a bull excommunicating Nogaret and fifteen of his accomplices, though the actual target was the king of France. Benoit XI had the good fortune of dying the following year after eating, it is said, too many figs. Of course, rumor went around that the figs were poisoned, but how are we to know? Nogaret was quick to exult: "God, more powerful than all the temporal and ecclesiastical princes, struck said Benoit in such a way that it was no longer possible for him to condemn me." The cardinals then elected as pope the archbishop of Bordeaux, Bertrand de Got, who took the name of Clement V.

It has been said repeatedly that Clement V was a man in the pay of Philip the Fair, an assertion predicated on jumping to conclusions. Certainly the king of France and Nogaret plotted to install a pope who would look on them favorably, but it does not seem they went so far as proposing Bertrand de Got for the position. Further, Bertrand was not even present at the conclave. Essentially they accepted the new pope while letting him know that it was in his best interest to cooperate. With the situation in Rome still chaotic, the new pope had to settle for living in Avignon. Because the kingdom of France lay on the other side of the Rhône River, Philip the Fair had every resource for keeping watch over what transpired in the pontiff's territory.

It needs to be explicitly stated at this point that Bertrand de Got had been one of those who refused to participate in the campaign against Boniface VIII. It would be easy to view him as hostile to the French king, but he was an excellent diplomat, expert in the art of vascillation. Most important, he understood the great danger to the Church that declaring a pope a heretic would present—even if the accusation were posthumous. It would amount to a direct challenge to the papal institution itself. Thus Clement V employed all his efforts to have the posthumous trial against Boniface VIII adjourned. To do so he had to make large concessions in other areas, regarding the Templars in particular. To buy time he strove to tame the zeal of the king of France by flattering him.

It should be clearly recognized that the Boniface matter weighed heavily on the scales. The surreptitious accusations were multiplying. It was declared that the deceased pope had been not only a heretic but also a magician and wizard. He was said to have "a private demon whose advice he sought on every matter" (Nogaret). Later it was claimed that he had not one demon familiar but three. One of these demon advisers had been offered by an Italian woman; another, more powerful one by a Hungarian; and the third and most powerful had been given him by a certain Boniface de Vicenze. In addition he was said to carry a "spirit" in a ring on his finger: Numerous clergymen and cardinals noted that this ring sometimes seemed to reflect the image of a man and sometimes that of an animal head. It was further noted that during the election of Celestine V, the future Boniface had been heard conversing with one of his demons while closeted in a room filled with clouds of incense. It was also alleged that he declared he had been saved from the Colonna at Anagni not by divine intervention but through diabolical assistance.

Anecdotes of this nature multiplied, prompted or encouraged by the Colonna and carefully gathered by Guillaume de Nogaret and his men, who made sure to spread detailed versions everywhere. Of course, witnesses were found who could confirm these rumors in every detail. It seems there was also much emphasis placed on an "idol" owned by Boniface, which, it was said, he worshiped. It is not, perhaps, by chance that among the accusations lodged against the Templars, pride of place goes to the famous so-called baphomet, the double, bearded head that has intrigued those weighing in on the matter so strongly.

Another matter similar in kind to the Boniface affair was taking place simultaneously with it. Guichard, the bishop of Troyes, was also accused of various evil spells, collusion with demons, and diabolical practices. Guillaume de Nogaret took advantage of these accusations and amplified them considerably, even so far as to bait Clement V: According to the logic of the system, the pope, by not defending the Church against heresy—that of Boniface, the bishop of Troyes, and the Templars—was himself guilty of a crime against Christianity. Guichard was imprisoned and his trial dragged on interminably. After the Templar affair was concluded, his innocence was finally and entirely recognized. That accusations of magic and commerce with demons, the first of their kind in the

Middle Ages, should have been affairs of state reveals to what extent Philip the Fair and his advisers profited from these situations to manipulate public opinion for the purpose of reaching objectives they had set their sights on. Even if there had been no actual accusations of the practice of demonic magic levied against the Templars, all of this focus and talk would nevertheless have contributed to reinforcing the suspicions and doubts people would have about them.

Moreover, the Templar affair had its origins in the same mechanism: the exploitation of vicious rumors and depositions by witnesses who were more or less in the pay of Nogaret. It began innocuously enough in Agen in 1305. A Templar, guilty of some misdeed—things like this do happen—was on his deathbed in prison. For lack of a formal confessor, he confessed his "errors of faith and criminal acts" to another prisoner, a bourgeois from Béziers named Esquieu de Floyac, who was possibly himself a Templar renegade. Horrified by these revelations, and perhaps also seeking to turn them to his personal advantage, Esquieu de Floyac, once freed, gave an account of them to King Jaime of Aragon. Jaime, little wishing to be dragged into such a murky business, got rid of Esquieu by sending him to the king of France. After all, as the seat of the order was in France, it was in actuality the concern of the French authorities.

Philip the Fair was subsequently made aware of Esquieu de Floyac's revelations. At that time he already knew it would be impossible to attain the union of the Templars and the Hospitallers and for him to become the grand master of this new, combined order. He also recognized that the Temple constituted a permanent danger to the authority of the French king. He would have to either gain control of the Temple or see to its disappearance. Because the first solution was impossible to achieve, he resolved to see to the second, deciding that any means would be justified to gain this end.

Seizing this windfall information from Esquieu, Philip launched an official inquiry in Corbeil, an area close to the Temple. There was certainly no difficulty in finding, here and there, renegade members of the order, even brothers who had been dismissed for misconduct, and these marginal figures, who sometimes found themselves in embarrassing situations, were ready to confess all in return for amnesty or favors. In any case, Esquieu de Floyac's statements were confirmed and Philip the Fair seems to have decided to push things as far as possible. He contacted the new pope, Clement V, whom he had met at his coronation ceremonies in November 1305 in Lyon.

Clement V reacted immediately. He saw clearly the danger lurking before him. The papacy was dead set against a public trial that might allow glimpses behind the closed doors of an order that was already mysterious and that likely would reveal state secrets affecting both the official Church and the kingdoms of Europe. Neither did Philip the Fair desire a trial that could threaten to revive certain matters from the archives that had been long forgotten. Nevertheless, he played on the threat of a trial in order to wrest from the pope if not a condemnation of the order, then at least its supervision. After all, we cannot forget that it was the pope and only the pope who was, after the grand master, the omnipotent leader of the order. Philip then began to indulge in veritable blackmail: Who stood to be most harmed by the affair, the king of France—who had no role in it—or the sovereign pontiff, supreme leader of the Templars?

Philip's maneuvering was skillful and Clement V did not delude himself. Wanting to neatly bury the matter, he summoned Grand Master Jacques de Molay and, using the plans of his predecessors, proposed the merger of the Templars and Hospitallers into one new order. He believed he could thereby disarm the trap and satisfy the king of France while keeping his own hands free to hold the reins of the new entity created. Of course, he knew full well that this plan was simply a way of buying time, that the problem would crop up again, even more acutely, when it came time to decide on the grand master for the new order. It was, nonetheless, the last chance to save the Templars.

However, Jacques de Molay stubbornly refused to consider any idea of the Templars merging with the Hospitallers. This gesture has been subject to varying degrees of scrutiny, revealing not only de Molay's position but also that of the entire chapter of the order. There have been many questions and many obscurities surrounding Jacques de Molay, a person who some consider a martyr and others an imbecile. Not much is known about him, but his behavior appears so inglorious and so far removed from the gravity imposed by the responsibilities of his office that the most common reaction to his selection as leader of the Templars is one of surprise. Was he only a figurehead? If so, who was hiding behind him? Jacques de Molay was one of the veterans of Palestine, in contrast with many of the new members of the order who had not lived in the East—we must note that the order recruited constantly, even following the fall of Saint John of Acre.

Elected grand master in 1295, Jacques de Molay held his main mission to be overseeing the retreat of the order into the West. At the time of his arrest he was sixty-four years old and yet, surprisingingly, he presented himself before the commission as a poor, illiterate knight. That a grand master of such an important order did not know Latin and might even have been illiterate in the modern sense of the word is truly disconcerting. What kinds of intrigue were behind his election?

For his part, Philip continued to encourage action against the Templars. His attitude has been explained as being motivated by his desire to possess the wealth of the order. It is a known fact that he struggled constantly throughout his reign with financial problems. At the time of his ascent to the throne, the kingdom was on the verge of bankruptcy and Philip was forced to resort to a number of expedient measures. In 1294 and 1296 he imposed tithes on the Church of France, which set off a bitter struggle with the pope. This hostility was exacerbated in 1296, when he banned the exportation of gold from the kingdom, including the normal contributions destined for the Holy See. Other measures were pursued as well: He commandeered silver and gold plateware from his wealthiest subjects for only a fraction of its worth and had it melted down to be minted into coins; he created a new tax on commerce and property that was higher than any previous tax; and he devalued the currency on several occasions, earning him the nickname of the Counterfeiter. It should be noted that he was only a pioneer in this field; others have simply improved on his methods. But the fact remains that all these actions eventually succeeded in causing his subjects to rise up against him. Following a particularly significant—and singularly dishonest—currency devaluation, the people of Paris rose up in revolt and Philip was forced to seek refuge—oh the irony of fate!—in the Templars' castle. Once the storm had abated, he saw to it, as a show of authority, that a few bourgeois subjects were hanged. Then he proceeded to attack the Jews. In the course of a single day, July 22, 1306, every Jew in France was arrested and imprisoned. Their money was confiscated by the royal treasury, their goods were sold at bargain rates for the enrichment of the crown, and their business affairs were transferred to Italian banks, which enjoyed the complete confidence of the king. The Jews themselves, those who had the good fortune to survive, were banished from the kingdom. It is known that many of them found shelter in Avignon, through special protection of the pope, where they established themselves and then spread throughout Provence, a realm of the Holy Roman Empire at that time. This expulsion was presented by the crown as a great victory by Christ over his tormentors. The idea of the *pogrom* is not new . . .

Subsequently, Philip allegedly saw all the benefits he could gain from the wealth of the Temple, which explains his relentless drive to destroy the order so that he could take possession of all that it owned. This argument, however, does not stand up to analysis. It is simply a convenient explanation for history textbooks, and one that is satisfying to all the fans of the Templars, who are quite numerous in our time. Certainly attributing to Philip IV the dark design of stealing the Templars' wealth is not in conflict with what we know about him. But the king of France was far too intelligent to have any illusions about the concrete reality of the Templar treasure. He knew full well that the fortune of the Templars did not consist of a collection of gold coins or objects, a fact confirmed by his spies. If the Templar vaults were filled with coins, including those of the royal treasury, these coins were merely deposits; none of them actually belonged to the Templars. Their Rule itself specified that the brothers were forbidden to own wealth of any sort. There can be no doubt that objects made of gold were extremely rare in Templar establishments. Furthermore, the agents of the king had never found a single such object in any of their searches. No, it is naïve to believe that the wealth of the order consisted solely of gold and silver coins and precious objects. Rather, the wealth of the Temple was primarily the enormous web it had spun over Europe and all the potential it held. The Temple owned a fortune in property, but this was merely real estate. All in all, we would be taking Philip the Fair for an imbecile if we were to claim that he undertook this relentless struggle against the Temple simply to bail out the royal treasury. In contrast with the Jews, who possessed gold, the Templars owned nothing but potential.

But this potential was formidable—so much so that it had to be either controlled or destroyed. Having resolved to oversee its destruction, Philip the Fair put everything at his disposal to work to reach a rapid conclusion. In the ensuing drama, the director was obviously Guillaume de Nogaret, without whom Philip would have been incapable of realizing the "base works" that later permitted him to achieve by himself the "high works."

On September 11, 1307, the king of France met with Clement V in Poitiers. Philip revealed to the pope everything he had learned concerning the Templars. Clement V took the king's accusations quite seriously and wrote him a letter to confirm that he would lead a personal inquiry into the matter. "You have not forgotten that you spoke to us several times about the Templars, in Poitiers. We could not decide to believe what we were told in this regard, as it seemed so impossible. However, we are forced to doubt and inquire further with a great deal of pain at heart." This letter is important in that it reveals the extent to which Clement V was shaken by the king's revelations. But the pope strategized to gain time: While he displayed his willingness to launch an inquiry, he did not order one. No doubt he had his reasons—he knew full well that the allegations against the Templars were true and was in no great hurry to have them brought out in the open, where they would threaten to tarnish the papacy. Clement V necessarily adopted a course of vacillating, waiting, and allowing the matter to drag on.

Philip the Fair understood his adversary quite well. He likewise knew the truth of the allegations, but had nothing to fear from their publication. To the contrary, it would ensure for him the best role and at the same time assist him in reducing the power of the papal institution, which was a considerable restraint on the king's freedom. Clearly, what Philip was aiming at was to create a scandal, for a scandal could not help but weaken the papacy. Let us not forget that he was the first sovereign who dared to openly attack the traditional institutions of the Roman Catholic Church.

But he knew he had to act quickly. The king was not unaware that the pope had warned Jacques de Molay and that the entire order was informed of the threats looming ahead of it. It would be silly to think that the Templars had not taken certain precautions. In the depositions, Brother Géraud de Causse explicitly stated that at this time the grand master took away all copies of the Rule in the possession of the brothers in order to burn them. Of course, he did not find all of them, for the Rule—at least its official version—has survived to the present day in the form of several manuscripts. This burning, however, explains why the Templar archives have never been found. Might they really have had something to hide?

On September 14, 1307, the decision to arrest all the Templars was made, on the advice of the king. Only the archbishop of Narbonne, chancellor of the kingdom, dared oppose this decision. He resigned his post, which was immediately entrusted to Guillaume de Nogaret. But the actual arrest of the Templars did not take place until October 13. Thus an entire month went by between the decision to arrest and the execution of that decision. We cannot deny, then, that some may have fled. The Templars were certainly forewarned of what lay in store for them—indeed, some brothers, at the time of their interrogations, acknowledged it without the need of torture, particularly the brother Jean de Vaubellant, sergeant of the Soissons house. However, overall very few Templars sought to flee and the majority allowed themselves to be taken into custody peacefully. Just another mystery to add to the Templar ledger.

The month delay between the announcement of intent to arrest and the arrest itself is explained quite well by the difficulty of the operation. It had to take place at the same hour on the same day, simultaneously. The king wrote down his instructions, which were placed in sealed envelopes that were not to be opened before October 13 and were sent to all the officers of the crown. These well-known instructions include the arrest warrant for all the Templars and an order for an immediate inquiry while awaiting the judgment of the Church. The king's prudence will be noted: "while awaiting the judgment of the Church." The king knew full well that the trial would bear on questions of faith, and he was not claiming to take the place of the ecclesiastical authorities, who were the only ones qualified to judge in this matter. He was satisfied simply with locking up the accused and launching an inquiry. Finally, Philip's text skillfully justified his actions. The words seem to have been meticulously chosen so as to reject the Templars as being beyond the borders of humanity:

A bitter thing, a deplorable thing, a thing horrible to think upon and to hear, a detestable crime, an execrable evil act, an abominable work, a frightful infamy, a thing wholly inhuman, and worse, foreign to all humanity has, thanks to the reports of several trustworthy persons, reached our ears, striking us with a great stupefaction and causing us to shiver in violent horror; and, as we weigh its gravity, an immense pain rises in us, all the more cruelly because it is beyond all doubt that the enormity of the crime overflows to the point of being an offense against the divine majesty, a shame for humanity, a pernicious example of evil, and a universal scandal . . . This race [the Templars] is like beasts of burden who lack all understanding; even worse, they surpass the folly of animals with their astonishing bestiality, they expose themselves to every crime so supremely abominable that even unthinking beasts know to abhor and flee . . . Not only by their acts and their detestable works, but by their hasty speech they soil the earth with their filth, suppress the benefits of the dew, corrupt the purity of the air, and ensure the confusion of our faith.

A great example of dialectics. No doubt the hand of Nogaret's men could be seen at work here, all chosen for their judicial and oratorical skills. As for the signatory, he seems to have forgotten that his most cherished desire once was to become the grand master of these corrupt men whom he now denounced so vigorously. But the die had been cast: The Templars did not want him and would thus be destroyed through application of the word allegedly of Jesus in the Gospels (Luke 19:27): "Bring my enemies here who did not wish me as their king, and kill them in my presence." Never has a quote from the Gospels been more appropriate to the circumstances. Who could maintain that Philip the Fair, king of France, did not act as a good Christian respectful of Holy Scripture?

But this was not all. The royal missive listed the crimes the Templars allegedly committed, which can be summarized in five key charges:

1. *The denial of Jesus.* During the order's induction ceremony for new members, following the normal ritual that was in conformance with the Rule, the commander brought the new member aside and commanded him to spit three times upon the Cross and deny Our Savior Jesus Christ three times.

2. *Obscene kisses.* The newly inducted knight stripped off his clothing so that the person welcoming him could kiss him at the base of the spine, under the waist, then on the navel, then on the mouth.

3. *Homosexuality.* The new brother was told that while it was forbidden to have sexual relations with women, in instances of lust a brother of the order was expected to lie carnally with another brother if asked to do so.

4. *Idolatry.* Each brother had to wear a cord that had been previously placed around the neck of an idol that had taken the form of a bearded man's head, a head that was the object of worship in secret chapters.

5. *Non-consecration.* The priests of the order left out the words of consecration when they performed Mass.

The royal missive specified to the officers that they were commanded to send as quickly as possible "the copy of the deposition of those who confessed said errors, or principally the denial of Our Savior Jesus Christ." This indicated that the question of denial was the strongest part of the case against the Templars. The missive then ended with permission for the use of torture if the accused were recalcitrant.

Until the end of the nineteenth century, historians, while satisfied to declare that Philip the Fair had exaggerated the key charges against the Templars in order to benefit from the situation, had generally accepted these charges as bona fide. However, within the last one hundred years, curiously enough, they have adopted an attitude diametrically opposed to that held by their predecessors. The majority now asserts that everything the Templars were charged with was invented. Some have even gone so far as to suggest that these accusations were only fantasies comparable to those that prevailed in the famous witch hunts of the sixteenth and seventeenth centuries.[1] The esotericists, on the other hand, are more likely to believe in the validity of the charges, but in their more symbolic form.

It is well known that the royal officers did not abstain from torturing their Templar prisoners and that it is, of course, impossible to place any faith in confessions obtained under torture. Those who were tortured merely confessed to whatever their accusers wished them to say. But some confessed without any provocation. Jacques de Molay and three other high-ranking members of the order (Hugues de Pairaud, visitor of France; Geoffroy de Cernay, preceptor of Normandy; and Geoffroy de Gonneville, preceptor of Aquitaine and Poitou) freely admitted denying Christ. Here is Jacques de Molay's confession:

> The ruse of humanity's enemy . . . had led the Templars to a perdition so blind that for a long time those who entered the order denied Christ at the peril of their soul, spit on the cross shown to them, and on that occasion committed other enormities.

---

1. This is the theory of Heinrich Finke in particular, at the beginning of the century, and of Norman Cohn in his work *Europe's Inner Demons*.

Jacques de Molay repeated this confession later that same year, on October 24, 1307:

> It has been forty-two years since I entered the order at Beaune. Brother Humbert placed before me a steel cross bearing the image of the Crucifixion, and enjoined me to deny Christ, who was pictured thereon. Maliciously, I did so. He then ordered me to spit upon the cross, but I spat on the ground a single time.

And yet another document testifies to a consultation at the University of Paris concerning Jacques de Molay:

> It is a constant that the said Master spontaneously confessed immediately his errors to the inquisitor in the presence of several other good people; subsequently, over a period of several days, in the presence of the same inquisitor and several clergymen, at the University of Paris, he tearfully confessed his error and that of his order, publicly in the form of speech. . . . While weeping for his human shame, he asked one day to be tortured so his brothers could not claim he had freely caused their downfall.

This document is a sad one, for not only was Jacques de Molay neither tortured nor threatened with torture, but he actually requested to be tortured in order to hide his free admission from his brother Templars, a request that was denied. Further, it is distressing and alarming to imagine this high dignitary, a man who carried the responsibility for a powerful order, weeping publicly and confessing in this way. Jacques de Molay's confession is no unwarranted hypothesis but is instead a historical fact that took place in front of witnesses. The document goes on to say: "The vain image of suffering could not have induced a man to make such consistent confession . . . And it would be impossible for the Master of the Order himself to be unaware of such things."

And as if this were not enough, there is the confession of Hugues de Pairaud, the second most powerful man in the order:

He who received me led me before an altar and showed me a cross
upon which was the image of Christ crucified. He commanded me
to deny him whose image was depicted there and to spit upon the
cross. In spite of myself, I denied Jesus Christ with my mouth but
not my heart. But the order I was given notwithstanding, I did not
spit upon the cross.

And the confession of Geoffroy de Cernay was also obtained without the use of torture:

After having received me and clasped the cloak around my neck, a
cross was brought before me upon which was the image of Jesus
Christ, and the same brother told me not to believe in he who was
pictured there because he was a false prophet and not God. He made
me renounce Jesus Christ three times, by mouth and not by the
heart.

We must note that in these confessions, as in many others recounted
in documents of that time, there is one constant: None of those who
confess seems to understand why he was made to deny Jesus and spit on
the cross. Unless they pretended not to understand, we are forced to
conclude that the Templar leaders were complete imbeciles. They never
questioned this bizarre ritual, but rather accepted it, however begrudg-
ingly—and most important, when they attained positions of power in
the Templar hierarchy, they did nothing to put an end to it. Do the un-
conditional supporters of the Templars' innocence take us for naïfs? And
what is the explanation for the detail acknowledged by Geoffroy de Cernay
concerning "a false prophet who is not God"? His assertion is not listed
in the accusation; only denial is mentioned. So what are we to make of
this part of his confession?

Logically, we must realize that Philip the Fair was well informed.
The key charges were not established by chance and cannot be confused
with the fantasies projected into accusations against witches. In the accusations against the Templars, everything is clear and precise. Of the

one hundred and thirty-eight Templars arrested and interrogated without torture, all except three confessed the denial of Christ and the obscene kisses. As for the other key charges, homosexuality and non-consecrations, these were denied by all. The cord and idol were acknowledged by some, but with so many conflicting details that it is hard to come to a clear conclusion. Yet the denial of Christ, *or rather Jesus,* is a constant.

Furthermore, it was to the detail concerning the denial of Christ that Philip the Fair had drawn the attention of the royal officers and inquisitors. It seems he knew what to hang his case on. No doubt this denial is where the great secret of the Temple resides, maybe its only secret. The rest is only a smoke screen. And while this secret has given birth to much commentary, it is far from being elucidated.

Whatever the truth may be, Philip the Fair's orders were carried out to the letter throughout the kingdom. In other countries the Templars were not immediately disturbed, and when they were, it was in very modest fashion, generally without resorting to torture. In Spain and Portugal the Templars emerged unscathed by forming new orders. In England they found a safe haven. Persecution was nonexistent in Scotland, which is one of the reasons that Freemasonry, of Scottish origin, claims to be the heir of the Templars.

But what role did the pope play in all of this? He could not remain outside the affair. In a bull issued on November 17, 1307, he commanded the arrest of all the Templars in Europe. Then he asked Philip the Fair to turn over all prisoners to him. Because he could not do otherwise, the king of France agreed to the pope's demand and handed over some of his prisoners to papal envoys. But because the ecclesiastical prisons were not large enough to hold all of them, the majority of Templars were forced to remain in civil prisons. However, with a drastic decision made at the beginning of 1308, Clement V stripped the inquisitors of all their powers. The pope, it seemed, wanted everything to return to basics, a decision in conformance with Church law. The inquisitors' power was derived from that of the sovereign pontiff. In fact, Clement V was again sought to stall. He combed through the entire court dossier before starting a public trial, something he still wanted to avoid at all costs.

The king was furious. Were the Templars going to escape from him? The people, full of hate for the Templars, whom they knew as rich and arrogant and who had been portrayed as monsters, began to murmur that the pope had allowed himself to be bought off by them. Petitions were addressed to the king demanding death for the guilty. Public opinion was visibly in favor of Philip and against the Templars.

However, the king was indecisive. The ground over which he was walking was quite unstable. Fortunately, he was very well advised by his legal experts. He consulted the University of Paris on the extent of their powers. By virtue of the privileges granted it since its founding, the Order of the Temple was answerable only to the pope. It was independent of all temporal authority, but the fact that its members were now recognized heretics might alter the earlier judicial situation. Did the king have the right to continue proceedings against the Templars? This was the question of canonical law submitted to the university, which responded on March 2, 1308. Its advice was unfavorable toward the royal action:

> The authority of the secular judge does not extend so far as trying for heresy any person who has not been surrendered by the Church. By very reason of the nature of the crime, everything touching on this crime belongs to the Church, no matter who the individual involved is.

Certainly this advice from the University of Paris was not binding. But if Philip stepped beyond it, he would risk incurring the wrath of the entire Church, and this time in complete agreement. He confined himself then to pushing what we would call today a "press campaign." Nogaret's henchmen were unleashed throughout the kingdom and beyond, accusing the pope of cowardice and demanding the king take the place of this "devil's son," or, in other words, Clement V. With the ground prepared in advance in this way, the king convoked the General Estates at Tours, May 11–20, 1308, with the purpose of being recognized himself as defender of the faith. This is actually what happened: In a plebiscite of sorts, Philip the Fair was voted defender of the faith by the clergy as well as the nobles and the bourgeoisie.

But the king had to move cautiously. He knew full well that he could not permit another Anagni raid. He thus decided to find the pope, who resided more often in Poitiers than in Avignon (because it was closer to his mistress, the countess de la Marche), in order to share with him the decision, made by the General Estates, to force Clement to expedite prosecution of the Templars. But Clement V retorted that the decisions of a civil assemply were not binding on a pope. The two men argued bitterly and the pope, whom people too often considered a lackey of the king, fiercely stood up to him. Because the situation was becoming explosive and neither could find a solution, they arrived at a compromise: the convocation of a consistory—an ecclesiastical assembly—which the king would be allowed to attend both as witness and to plead his case.

The consistory was held on May 29, 1398. One of the king's counselors, Guillaume de Plaisans, gave an indictment, declaring that the facts against the Templars were "well-known, indubitable, and clearer than the light of noon," and he pleaded with the pope to ensure the defense of the faith. Among the participants were the archbishops of Bourges and Narbonne, who had been skeptical of the charges but now declared themselves convinced otherwise by the proof that had been provided. But Clement V launched into a long, wily speech. He confessed to having once loved the Templars, but that now he could only hate them if they were truly as they had been depicted. This restraint is present throughout his speech. Furthermore, the pope said, the irregularities concerning their arrests meant that they were legally flawed. In addition, he alluded to the torture inflicted to gain some confessions. Certainly ruthless measures have their place, Clement V concluded, but only after mature reflection. This speech had the overall effect of irritating the king and his counselors. On June 14, Guillaume de Plaisans took the floor again and sharply attacked the solemn pontiff while casting a sober warning: If the pope did not want to take action, according to his role and duty, then "all those affected by the matter would be called upon to defend the faith."

Clement V studied the matter once more and postponed his decision. But because he knew the king would never admit defeat, he sought to give the Templars one last chance. He summoned before himself and his three closest collaborators seventy-two incarcerated Templars, withholding any threats of torture. In the pope's mind, now was the time to reveal the truth. Yet with no outside pressure—this is confirmed fact—the seventy-two Templars repeated all their previous confessions.

This event is of capital importance to our understanding of the whole affair. After this incident, there were no longer any grounds for maintaining that the Templars had done nothing for which they could reproach themselves or that they were the victims of an arbitrary use of authority. They may, in fact, have done nothing for which to reproach themselves—*except with respect to orthodox Catholicism,* and this they could not deny. As for knowing what their behavior was hiding in reality, that is an entirely different question:

> We do not have the minutes for these hearings, they are in the Vatican Archives. But they are known thanks to . . . Napoleon who, fascinated by the Templar affair, saw to it that the secret archives in Rome were seized. Thus they were available for reading and Raynouard analyzed them before they were returned. No major new discoveries were made, much less finding the key to the Templar enigma,[2] but at least we know that these documents largely confirm the earlier hearings.[3]

The pope then made public his decision with the bull of August 12, 1308. He declared that the fate of the order did not rest with him alone and that it was too serious to be ruled on immediately. He thus called for a commission at whose head he placed the archbishop of Narbonne, known for his integrity (he had refused to support the arrest of the Templars), assisted by three bishops and by competent clergy. This commission was

---

2. Even less a so-called secret Rule that would be published later.

3. Guy Fau, *L'Affaire des Templiers* (Paris: Le Pavillon, 1972), 61.

to present its findings in two years. Then, dissociating himself from the order, whose power derived from him, and its members, he placed the latter into the hands of the Inquisition, reserving for himself only the cases of the four highest-ranking leaders, over whose fate he reserved the right to rule on later.

The majority of French bishops detested the Templars, as did the other religious orders, the Dominicans being the most virulent. This hatred was motivated not by spiritual reasons but by the much more prosaic reason that the Templars had often diverted large profits that would otherwise have gone to them. It is known that in many dioceses the Templars were somewhat mistreated, even being subjected to torture and burned, as in Paris and Sens, where the archbishop, the brother of Enguerrand de Marigny, was a minion of Philip the Fair. The commission could thereby easily obtain other confessions, sometimes considerably inflated and circumstantial, but the majority of which had not been extorted. The same was not true in other countries.

Portugal's sovereign purely and simply refused to authorize the arrest of the Templars. An investigation was opened in Castille, but nothing came of it. In Aragon the bishops led an inquest but remained very discreet about the guilt of the Templar knights. In England a face-saving compromise was arranged and the majority of Templars were left undisturbed. In Germany they were almost all acquitted. Those who were condemned were condemned for their individual offenses, and the same was true in Cyprus. The guilt of the Templars was definitely and primarily a French matter; in the other countries of Europe, the order was not as powerful, nor had it succeeded in creating as dense a network. With their dangerous potential decreased, the hostility against the Templars was necessarily less violent.

There were several attempts made at defending the order, but these were the work of the Templars themselves. This defense, though sometimes courageous, was extremely clumsy. Despite a certain Pierre de Boulogne, who, incidentally, vanished into the night before the end of the trial, the various defenders were forced to renounce their task. There were only a handful of brothers who, recanting their confessions, denied all guilt and persisted in that attitude. This was not the case with Jacques de Molay.

He was interrogated on November 26, 1309, by the papal commission, under the most objective conditions that included every possible guarantee: The commission answered only to the pope and not to the king or local bishops. He was asked to defend the order, logically enough, as its grand master. His response was pitiful: "I am not as learned as necessary . . . I am ready to defend it to the best of my abilities . . . but this appears to be a very difficult task. How to defend it appropriately? I am a prisoner of the pope and the king of France, and do not even have four *deniers* to spend for this defense."

The confessions he had made before three cardinals were then read and he was asked to explain himself on the point of each. He demanded two days to consider it, which were granted him with the explicit invitation to take more time if he wanted.

He thus appeared on a second occasion, on November 28, 1309. From the first, he refused to defend the order—"I am only a poor, illiterate knight." His attitude was, frankly, incomprehensible, unless he was hiding something. Who was Jacques de Molay trying to protect with his silence? He declared that as the pope had reserved the right to rule on his fate, he would wait on the pope's pleasure. The charge was brought up again and he was again asked if he would consent to defending the order. He was content to simply give vague praise for its brilliant material results and the knights' courage in combat. He was answered that none of that sufficed if the true faith was lacking. He then consented to make a profession of Christian faith, swearing that he believed in God and the Trinity. But he did not utter the name of Jesus Christ. And he added these somewhat sibylline words: "When the soul has left the body, it will be seen who had been good or evil, and the truth will be known about those things presently in question." If we understand his words correctly, this was a pure and simple refusal to reveal certain things. But he uttered not a word concerning the suffering of his brothers, not a comment about his prior confessions. He asked only to hear Mass, which request was granted.

Jacques de Molay's third hearing took place before the commission three months later, on March 2, 1310. This was an even greater disappointment. He confined himself to repeating that as the pope would be his judge, he would await the pontiff's judgment. The commission explained to him clearly that its mission was not to sit in judgment upon him but simply to proceed with its inquiry. Still Molay remained mute. The order did not appear to interest him; his only concern seemed to be the pope's personal judgment. Not another word could be pulled out of him. The same seems to have been the case with another high-ranking Templar, Geoffroy de Gonneville, who appeared to have lost all interest in the order while waiting for the pope to rule on his personal fate.

No one understands why. The least that can be said is that the Templar Order was not defended by those who should have done so. At this stage, the attitude of Jacques de Molay and his principal colleagues is of the purest egotism, even stupidity. What did they expect from the pope? Were they hoping to gain time? If so, from whom did they expect assistance? In any case, they completely abandoned their brothers. There are no answers to all the questions that can be raised concerning their appearances before the commission.

Meanwhile, the council convened again in Vienne, an empire town near both France and Avignon, on October 13, 1311. The affair had been dragging on for four years. It was time that it ended.

The commission this time examined the reports of the papal commission in charge of the inquest. They then separated to allow the various smaller commissions created for this purpose to work on their reports. The arrival of the king of France was expected, but he seemed in no hurry to explain himself. Things were dragging on in this way when nine knights of the order presented themselves and asked to be heard by the council for the purpose of defending the Templars. A rumor circulated that in the vicinity of the town an army of two thousand Knights Templar stood ready to mount an assault. It was false, of course, but to quell disorder, Clement V had the nine arrivals imprisoned. He was criticized for this, but this was, in fact, the sole means of protecting them.

Philip the Fair arrived in Vienne during the month of March 1312. He was, reasonably enough, accompanied by members of his court, but also by a large and well-armed troop. He was seeking to make a strong visual impression on the council, and Clement V feared the worst. He knew that the accusations against the Templars were in large part well founded and that any public debate ran a good risk of causing the Church considerable harm. Skilled manipulator that he was, he found a solution.

On March 22 he called a consistory that was granted the right of settling the issue itself with no debate of any kind. Then, when the council sessions reopened on Monday, April 5, 1312, the pope read out loud the text of the bull *Vox Clementis,* which future historians will obviously turn into the *Vox Clementis.* This bull ordered the dissolution of the Order of the Templars and the devolving of its property to the Order of the Hospitallers of St. John. Its members were meanwhile remanded to the competent ecclesiastical authorities. The text of this bull is a masterpiece of ambiguity, but there should be nothing surprising about this in a matter where everything is ambiguous. The "considerings" are particularly revealing:

Considering the evil reputation of the Templars, the suspicions and accusations of which they are the object; considering the mysterious manner and fashion in which one is welcomed into this order, the evil and anti-Christian behavior of many of its members; considering especially the oath demanded of each of them to never reveal anything about this admission and to never leave the order; considering the peril threatening the faith and souls, as well as the horrible infamies of a great number of the members of the order . . . we abolish, not without bitterness and personal sorrow . . . the said Order of the Templars with all of its institutions.

It will be noted that the Order of the Temple was not condemned but simply abolished. There is more than one nuance to this. Furthermore, not a single individual was to be condemned; only certain members of the order were accused of "infamies," a matter on which no one dwelled at the time.

If there was a winner in all of this, it was Clement V and Clement V alone. It cannot be said that Philip the Fair succeeded. His dream of obtaining for himself and his descendants the title of hereditary grand master of a new order of Crusaders had evaporated. He did not even succeed in gaining possession of the Templar property, which instead devolved onto the Hospitallers. Certainly, having these properties and goods in his possession, he took steps to ensure their restitution as late as possible, after realizing substantial profits for himself. But this was not what he had hoped for. The king of France had been greatly disturbed and greatly compromised during the trial against the Templars, whereas his adversary, Clement V, came out of the affair with his honor intact by avoiding any public debate. The king had to be satisfied with simply the dissolution of the order.

But that may have been Philip the Fair's secret objective all along. With nothing either very clear or definitive in this entire history, it can certainly be assumed. The king of France had, in any case, effectively contributed to the elimination of an enormous machine, the Temple, which had always been, for him as for his successors, a sword of Damocles suspended above the throne. Once the power of the Temple had been beaten down and the Temple itself had been discredited, the pope would be stripped of one of his most faithful supports and the king of France could hope to govern the world alone. Whatever his deepest motivations may have been, Philip the Fair did succeed in placing the pope in a difficult position and tarnishing the image of the Church. The Temple, after all, was absolutely part of the Church.

Historians are very divided on these questions, and will long remain so. Everything depends on the point of view that is being defended, in which case it is difficult not to be swept away by our more passionate feelings.

One thing is sure, however: The order was dissolved but not condemned. For the men who were the Templars, this made quite a difference. Many of them ended up being burned at the stake. Others died in prison. The four high-ranking officials of the order were judged in Paris on December 22, 1313. Once again, they admitted everything: the denial of Jesus, spitting on the cross. During the trial, which lasted until March 18, 1314, they had all the time in the world to explain themselves. Finally the verdict was handed down on March 18. Jacques de Molay, Geoffroy de Charnay, Hugues de Pairaud, and Geoffroy de Gonneville, the four highest authorities of the dissolved order, were condemned to life in prison.

Then a theatrical development occurred: Jacques de Molay and Geoffroy de Charnay publicly retracted and refuted all their earlier confessions, though Pairaud and Gonneville stood by their earlier words. Retracting a confession in matters of faith earned both Molay and Charnay the death sentence. Declared relapsed heretics, they were condemned to be burned alive in the presence of Philip the Fair. It is claimed that the grand master then cast a curse upon Pope Clement and King Philip. With the death of these two shortly thereafter, quite a few legends were fueled. However, it is more likely that Jacques de Molay uttered these simple and somewhat disillusioned words: "Our bodies belong to the king of France but our souls belong to God." This would be more in keeping with an individual claiming his innocence at the last moment.

But what could be the reason behind his very late about-face? It is the sole courageous gesture ever made by Jacques de Molay and had a great influence on the Templars' partisans. But this explains nothing and does not erase his earlier confessions made, we should remember, without the the threat of torture. If Charnay and Molay had adopted this courageous stance at the time of their arrest, they would have earned glory and their denials would have been credible. But coming after so many confessions of "turpitude," their retractions ring false.

So what are we left to believe?

There is no exit from this dilemma: Either Molay lied out of cowardice for seven years, allowing the condemnation of his brothers by supporting their confessions with his own, and thus causing the ruin of the order he headed; or else he had spoken the truth for

seven years but could not stomach the thought of endless imprisonment and, given his age, preferred the panache of a glorious end.[4]

And the latter case was certainly a form of suicide. The questions
persist. Was the order guilty, yes or no, of the horrible infamies of which
it was accused?

------

4. Guy Fau, *L'Affaire des Templiers*, 143.

Part 3

The Mystery of the Templars

8

The Secret Rule of the Temple

WHAT IS PARTICULARLY IRRITATING when we pore over the Templar dossier and examine all its data is that we stumble headfirst into much uncertainty, and this uncertainty is due in large part to the Templars themselves. The papal bull of 1312, which abolished the order, did not shy away from noting "the mysterious manner in which one is received into the order" or "the oath demanded of each of them to never reveal anything about their admission." There is a strong impression that the Templars, since the founding of the order, did all they could to encourage the doubt and mystery hovering over their activities, and this became even more pronounced as the order expanded. The well-known official Rule specified certain cases in which secrecy was obligatory—for example, the interdiction on divulging the deliberations of the chapter. It is certainly easy to see why it would not be useful to let the whole world know how the Temple was organized internally. Any government, when it meets to make decisions, takes pains not to do so publicly, remaining content to publish a communiqué saying only what its authors want it to say. There is nothing out of the ordinary about this. However, suspicions were raised when the Templars insisted that chapter meetings be held in a secret location and that none would be granted admittance unless he was among the small, closed circle of higher-ups. This fierce desire for secrecy obviously excited curiosity and left them open to all kinds of criticism.

But this interdiction against revealing chapter deliberations was justifiable, even if it became the source of so many fabrications. It is legitimate, however, to wonder why it was forbidden to possess a copy of the official Rule without special authorization and why it was feared that the Rule might fall into the hands of outsiders and possibly put the order at risk. This is difficult to fathom, for the statutes of the Rule are clear, precise, and contain nothing that lends itself to questionable interpretation. Even more troubling is the interdiction against all Templars confessing to priests other than chaplains of the order, or, in other words, the insistence that members confess only to priests belonging to the order and bound to it by the same obligations of secrecy. Wasn't the secrecy of confessions a general law throughout the Roman Catholic Church? In answer to this question there is one of two possibilities: Either the Templars doubted the integrity of Roman Catholic priests or the particulars of their confessions might be insupportable to any priest not belonging to the order.

At first sight, this interdiction can only seem surprising. A priest is still a priest, whether a member of the Templars or not, and while at that time the high and mighty had personal appointed confessors, the institution of spiritual advisers had not yet arrived, with its insinuations and intimidating manipulations. In fact, this interdiction could not help but cast suspicion on what was really transpiring within the order. How did it come about that only a priest connected to the order could give absolution to a Templar? While this practice could be found in other monastic orders, it existed as custom rather than absolute obligation. The Temple's accusers in 1307 did not fail to focus on a practice that was so open to criticism.

Another prohibition of the order that was difficult to comprehend and perceived negatively was that forbidding brothers to leave the order. When one entered the Templars, it was for life. Of course a person could be expelled or rejected for a serious dereliction, but these were cases of punishment, the famous "loss of the habit" inflicted on those found unworthy of belonging to the community. All societies practice expulsion, monastic orders included. In addition to expulsion, there was also imprisonment for extreme dereliction of duty. In short, to enter the Templars was to give yourself to the Temple; you were no longer your own man after being accepted into the community. While this is a distinguishing feature of any religious commitment, what was unusual about the order was the deep distrust it attached to those who wished to leave it. The bull of abolition made mention of this expectation: "the oath demands . . . to never leave the order." The conclusion is clear: If a brother is forbidden to quit the order, it is for the purpose of preventing him from telling others of what was conducted within it. Ironically, it was from Templar renegades that Philip the Fair's men received their information, whether false or authentic. But it is the distinguishing feature of any initiatory society—including contemporary ones—to forbid its members to leave. An individual generally can leave only under the express condition of never revealing anything that might cause harm to the society in question. Such a practice is not usually subject to scandal. Under these conditions we must accept the shadowy side of the order—that the Order of the Knights Templar was actually an initiatory order, despite the fact that some historians resolutely deny it, and even if this initiation, whatever it may have been, seemed to have been conferred on only some of its members. This leads us to consider also that the Temple was an elitist, or rather double-faced, organization, that another, secret order existed that was different from the one on display to the world. Once we have acknowledged, then, that the Temple constituted a more or less secret organization, all hypotheses can be advanced.

Likewise, we must consider the existence of a secret Rule—one that would have been known only to certain members—parallel to the official Rule that was summarized for each new Templar on his admittance into the order. Based on certain declarations made by the Templars themselves, it is possible to give credence to the existence of such a secret set of statutes consisting of a recasting of the original Rule.

During his first interrogation, without any threat of torture, Geoffroy de Gonneville, preceptor of the Temple for Aquitaine and Poitou, uttered these cryptic words: "There are those who claim that [the denial of Jesus] was one of the evil and perverse introductions of Master Roncelin into the statutes of the order." This phrase was heavy with consequence: One of the highest dignitaries of the order was presuming knowledge of a parallel Rule. This did not prevent Gonneville from reporting it as an anonymous remark, as if he himself were not in the know. What is surprising is that this "Master Roncelin" does not appear anywhere in the lists we have of the Templar grand masters. Despite that, we have no reason to believe these lists to be either fragmentary or falsified. However, there is a Roncelin du Fos, provincial knight, who was accepted into the order in 1281 by Grand Master Guillaume de Beaujeu. Is this the person to which Gonneville refers? Regardless, it appears that he never rose very high in the order's hierarchy. But if this Roncelin is truly the one who introduced "evil and perverse" things into the statutes of the order, it lends credit to the hypothesis of a second, parallel and secret hierarchy.

Other pieces of evidence presented themselves. At the time of the trial, the lawyer Raoul de Presles claimed to have received the following confidence from a Templar, Brother Gervais de Beauvais: "There is a regulation in the order that is so extraordinary, and over which such great secrecy must be guarded, that any member would rather lose his head to the axe than reveal it." If this were true, it would be easier to understand why Jacques de Molay said not a word about it and why so many Templars went to the stake respecting the law of silence.

However, according to this same Raoul de Presles, Brother Gervais "owned a booklet of the statutes of the order that he willingly showed anyone, but he possessed another more secret one that he would not show anyone for all the gold in the world." This detail smells like a fabrication, as if the witness wanted to show off his knowledge of such confidences. We know that before October 13, 1307, Jacques de Molay was busy destroying copies of the Rule. Which Rule was it—the official one known to the world at large or the secret one mentioned by the witness?

Other declarations also suggest the existence of two parallel orders. For example, among the testimonies collected in England, which are little suspected of having been extorted by force, this declaration by three English brothers can be singled out: "In reality there are two kinds of reception in the Temple. The first is reserved for admittance and takes place with no reprehensible ceremony. The second, which takes place only after several years, is granted only to a few and is kept very secret." This testimony, however, is not entirely convincing because the three Templars in question did not take part in this second, secret admittance; they were satisfied to affirm merely that they had heard it said that it occurred. Yet this testimony does verify that rumors circulated concerning the existence of a parallel hierarchy, giving credence to the possibility that there was a second Rule governing those who were granted admission to a higher degree. Such a Rule can be found in any so-called initiatory society; the existence of the secret Rule within the Templars, while not proved, is at least possible.

It was thought at one time that a copy of this secret Rule had been discovered. In 1877, a certain Mersdorf published the secret statutes of the Temple, supposedly taken from a Vatican manuscript. The publisher explained, without providing the slightest bit of evidence, that this document figured among those kept in the Vatican's secret archives and was stolen in 1780 by a Copenhagen bishop. This particular theft explained fairly neatly why the document in question was not found in those Vatican archives that were taken and later returned by Napoleon. Apparently the document was stolen from the bishop himself under mysterious circumstances, including the lurking shadows of secret societies of all stripes. Thus all trace of this precious piece of evidence was lost until its chance discovery in Hamburg in 1877. Currently this Rule is carefully concealed in the cellars of the Vatican, and the papacy especially desires it not to be revealed for fear of being tainted by scandal. It seems the cellars of the Vatican are definitely an inexhaustible mine for great discoverers of secrets! And it so happens there is always a mysterious priest or bishop with few scruples to find a copy of a secret document and certify its faithfulness to the original. The only problem is that we never quite see the color of the original in this type of scenario.

It is interesting, though, in several respects, to examine this manifestly fake document of secret Templar statutes fabricated entirely from trial proceedings and intended to prove that the lineage of the Freemasons extends back to the Temple to the Freemasons.[1] The document is entitled *Here Begins the Book of the Baptism of Fire and the Secret Statutes Set Down by the Master Roncelin.* At the end can be read: "Signed by the copyist Robert de Samfort, procurer of the Order of the Temple in England, in 1240." But here is something altogether astounding: If the Master Roncelin who set down this text is indeed Roncelin du Fos, accepted into the Temple in 1241, how was it that forty years earlier someone could make a copy of what he had not yet written? In truth, Roncelin du Fos may not even have been born in 1240. But we can be reassured knowing that official history often lies—a well-known fact—with the purpose of masking the Truth that only the occultists, hermeticists, and other keepers of the Tradition have the privilege of knowing.

The document proposed as being the secret Rule of the order begins by making a subtle distinction between the regular members of the Temple and those called the consoled brothers, who would be the true keepers of the message. This appears to be an obvious borrowing from the Cathars. In fact it is known that among the Cathars, the perfects, meaning those who have received the *consolamentum,* thus the "consoled brothers," form a very separate category unto themselves and may be considered as the sole and unique "pures" already in contact with the divine and ready to rejoin the kingdom of light from which they had been driven following the revolt of the angels. This lends credence to the hypothesis that the secret Rule could be known only by the consoled ones—in other words, those initiated to a higher degree.

Specifically, the first article emphasizes the preeminent Cathar theme, that of light: "The people who walk in darkness saw a great light and those who were in the shadow of death saw this light." This is no doubt a commonplace in all religions, most particularly those claiming to be keepers of an esoteric tradition. The light in question is not physical light but that of the spirit, the light that is acquired only after achieving an inner quest, or *illumination.* And, of course, only those who adhere to

---

1. This has been shown by H. de Curzon in *La Régle du Temple* (Paris: 1886), xv. See also L. Dailliez, *Les Templiers et les régles de l'Ordre du Temple* (Paris: Belfond, 1972).

a specific belief are illuminated, a state ordinary mortals do not know. But this first article goes further: The light involved is commingled with a God whose uniqueness is forcefully asserted. "One alone is our God and his spirit gives to ours the assurance that we are sons of God." Here again is nothing new—Hebrew theology does not make the distinction of the Trinity at all and emphasizes the fact that we are all the sons of God. In one sense the declaration of Jesus Christ that he was the son of God had no particular value for the Jews in that each of them could make the same assertion. In this first article there can already be felt a deliberate intention of reducing, if not denying, the Roman Catholic concept of Jesus Christ as the only son of God. Here in the first article there is already heresy.

The second article paraphrases the Gospels: "One must have eyes to see and ears to hear." But it is accompanied by a forthright attack on the official Church. "Realize that kings, popes, bishops, abbots, and masters have wished to see and hear what you hear and see, but they have not seen, nor have they heard, and they will never know." This is the pure and simple refusal of official doctrine colored by an anticlerical attitude that is still strongly imprinted in Catharism. Flattery is always useful with adherents of a doctrine, even a heretical one, in that it suggests that they alone benefit from the truth. It offers the believers reassurance.

Article 3 is more important in that it refers to a notion that upholds the historical activity of the Templar Order: "The time has come where the Father is no longer worshiped, neither in Jerusalem or in Rome. The spirit is God and if you are of God, you will worship him in spirit and in truth." We know, for example, that a sect of neo-Templars—one among many!—meets every March 18, the anniversary of Jacques de Molay's torture, and during the course of the ceremony, the famous appeal is made: "Who now will defend the Holy Temple? Who now will liberate the tomb of Christ?" This steps straight out of a legend concerning the Gavarnie Circus in the Pyrenees. This legend claims that precisely every March 18 the ghost of a Templar appears, wearing the famous white cloak with the red cross, and makes a heartrending appeal. Then, six Templars who have been laid to rest in a nearby chapel rise and respond:

"No one! No one! No one! The Temple is destroyed!" This beautiful and moving story is connected to the phrase in Article 3. One may ask if the Templars, at least those who were among the initiates, did not believe that Christ's tomb was *symbolically* everywhere and that consequently it served no purpose to hold or reconquer Jerusalem.

The following remarks in the third article are explicit: "Realize that everything Jesus has said by the true Christ is the spirit and life in God. It is the spirit of God that gives life, *the flesh of Jesus can no longer serve any purpose.*" Under these conditions, why take the trouble to conquer the tomb of Jesus in Jerusalem? This is a challenge to the veracity of the material and historical figure of Jesus, which would explain the denial and spitting on the cross. But I repeat: The text containing these articles is a nineteenth-century fabrication. It merely adapts certain concepts attributed to the Templars in order to put them in accord with the doctrine of Freemasonry. Consequently, this would also justify the omission of the words of consecration during the Mass, as the *hoc est corpus meum* has thereby lost all meaning.

Article 4 delves further into the secret that only the blessed consoled ones know and which "remains hidden from the children of the New Babylon, which will be reduced to ashes and dust by the humble servants of God." Assuredly, if we are to take this secret Rule at its word, the purpose of the Temple is not the protection of pilgrims on the roads to Jerusalem, but the conquest of the world and the establishment of a united kingdom over which the Great Monarch will rule. Philip the Fair had good reason to seek to become the order's grand master, and it is easy to understand why, not being able to ensure the mastery of this formidable brotherhood of "humble servants of God," he preferred to destroy it. This was preferable to risking the possibility of it falling into other hands. But the same article explicitly states that no prince of this time, or any high priest, has known the Truth. "If they had known it, they would not have worshiped the wooden cross and burned those who possessed the true spirit of the true Christ." This is a clear vindication of Catharism and an allusion to the pyre of Montségur (or a premonitory vision of Jacques de Molay's). The Cathars certainly had a very negative attitude toward the Cross and the Crucifixion. They recognized Christ only in his ethereal form, not his physical form, and they refused to worship a murder victim. Were the Templars' belief and practice similar? The question has been raised and never answered. Nevertheless, the requisite denial and spitting upon the cross in the initiation ceremony seem to show it.

Article 5, the subject of which is taken up again in Article 8, is a veritable plea for universal brotherhood, fully in tune with Freemasonry: "Know that God sees no differences between people, Christians, Saracens, Jews, Greeks, Romans, French, Bulgarians, because every man who prays to God is saved." This is a strongly heretical statement and is completely contrary to the doctrine that says, "[O]utside the Church there can be no salvation." Note the presence of Bulgarians on the list of equal peoples. These would be the Bogomils, ancestors of the Cathars. Article 8 revisits this theme by specifying certain heretics: "the Good Men of Toulouse; the Poor Men of Lyon; the Albigensians, those from the area of Verona and Bergamo; the Bajolis of Galicia and Tuscany; the Beguins; and the Bulgarians" —in short, everyone with a bone to pick with the Inquisition. But it is also a call for recruitment: "By underground paths you will go to your chapters and to those who imagine certain fears, you will confer the consolamentum in the chapters before three witnesses." The terminology is almost exclusively Cathar. It is true that a clear Cathar influence upon the Temple has often been suggested, especially from around the mid-thirteenth century. It wasn't Guillaume de Nogaret, called a "son of Patarin" by Boniface VIII, who could have made a case against this, he who sought to obscure the fact that he was actually descended from a Cathar family!

We must also note that the Saracens are included on the list of "sons of God." This may appear surprising for an order that was founded specifically against the Muslims and which gave such a hard time to all the Saracens of the Holy Land under sometimes perilous conditions and with bravery and even recklessness. The Saracens are mentioned again in Article 9: "The consoled ones of Spain and Cyprus will fraternally welcome the Saracens, the Druze, and those who dwell in Lebanon."

This brings us to the problem posed by the relationship between the

Temple and the Islamic world. It has been repeated far too often that the Templars were an equivalent of the Assassins, or Hashshashin, the faithful fanatics who served the Old Man of the Mountain, a somewhat mysterious sect to which has been imputed—foolishly—esoteric doctrines that have been lost, seemingly by chance, This, of course, is quite convenient for those who are essentially guessing that these doctrines existed. It has also been repeated too often that the Muslims contaminated the Templars and that the origin of their heresy was to be found in the integration of certain Islamic beliefs and customs into their own doctrine. These hypotheses are based on only vague analogies, but an objective study shows that there was never a worse enemy of Islam in all its forms, including heretical sects, either on the battlefield or ideologically, than the Knights Templar. It is also absurd to believe that the Templars hoped to form a large kingdom in the Holy Land that would create a synthesis of the Muslim and Christian mentalities. All the documentation refutes this. Finally, while there are elements in the Temple that can be defined as heretical, it is not in Islam that we should be looking for their origins.[2]

Article 11 displays a great amount of anticlerical venom. Never did a medieval text attack clerics in such a direct and open manner. When the authors of the Middle Ages wished to express anticlerical sentiments, they were far more shrewd—and their shots carried farther. In reading this we might almost feel we are in the era of "little Father Combes," who, being a former seminarian, at least knew where to confine his remarks.[3] The text of this article is quite eloquent: "It is expressly recommended

---

2. With all due respect to the so-called Guénonian school, which relentlessly seeks out similarities between Western Christian traditions and certain heresies of Islam. There are, of course, numerous similarities between Christianity and Islam, for the two traditions—and the Jewish tradition—have all been issued from the same original mold—to wit, the first books of the Bible. But Christianity and Islam had large spans of time to grow apart, and each of the two traditions has incorporated other neighboring and closer traditions that have changed it considerably and consistently. Synthesis is an excellent thing, but syncretism, which consists of artificially gluing together disparate ideas, has never resulted in anything but distressing vagaries.

3. Little Father Combes was the nickname given to former seminarian and theologian Emile Combes (1835–1921), who became a radical politician particularly despised by the right-wing press and the church establishment, primarily for his success in helping draft the law separating church and state in 1905. —*Trans.*

to surround oneself with the greatest precautions with regard to monks,[4] priests, bishops, abbots, and doctors of science, for they act in an underhanded fashion all the better to roll more freely in the mud of their crimes." Even more surprising is the recommendation that these be accepted into the order anyway, with the warning "to reveal nothing of the statutes or customs of the order to them." Article 18 emphasizes these "[t]hings which must be strictly concealed from the ecclesiastics accepted into the order." It begs the question: In 1139 why would the Templars have so strongly demanded the authority to have their own chaplains, or, in other words, priests admitted to the order if all ecclesiastics more or less "roll in the mud of their crimes"? We must believe that any true secret Rule would not have contained such an obvious contradiction.

Article 13 deals with admission procedures and includes a phrase that reveals the ideology that inspired the writing of this Rule. The receiver of the new Templar, after having absolved him, "frees him of all the commandments of the Church in the name of the God, who was not engendered nor does he engender, in the name of the true Christ who is not dead and who cannot die." Once again, this is in keeping with the denial of Jesus and spitting on the cross. But in none of the existing trial documents can such a precise naming of Jesus as "the son of God" be found. Where could this fact have come from?

The explanation is provided in Articles 14 through 18, concerning the prayers and gestures to be performed during the admission ceremony of a new member. In these statutes we are in the presence of an incredible muddle of Gnostic concepts poorly digested by a nineteenth-century occultist who had yet to learn the alphabet. Here, with no need to resort to more scholarly deductions, is proof positive that the Rule attributed to Roncelin du Fos and translated forty years before the said Roncelin could have written it is a fake.

However, this secret Rule, provided it isn't mistaken for genuine currency, is interesting insofar as it suggests an interpretation of the Templars' heresy. It represents only a simple working hypothesis, which is how it

---

4. Did the author of these lines forget that the Templars were monks?

should be taken, that attempts to find a logical explanation for the somewhat deplorable attitude of the grand master Jacques de Molay. Article 20 says, in fact, that "it is strictly forbidden to choose a Consoled Brother for grand master." It is legitimate to wonder why, for the consoled brother, by definition, had attained perfect consciousness and illumination. It is reassuring, then, to learn that Jacques de Molay was not a consoled brother; he knew nothing, hence his disappointing conduct. But this also implies that he was not the true leader of the Templar Order and that a secret, parallel hierarchy did indeed exist, which various testimony collected during the trial indicates was more than a probability.

For all that, other testimony attributes the introduction of the "perverse rite" and consequently the writing of a secret Rule to Thomas Bérard (labeled for the occasion as the "evil master"), who was the grand master of the order from 1256 to 1272. According to all these revelations, it seems that all the Templars were aware of the fact that a secret Rule of the Temple existed, but that none of them knew exactly its date of origin. Furthermore, none of them had ever seen or read this Rule, or at least claimed to have done so. In this area, it is better to take everything and everybody with a large grain of salt. Words spoken by the accused, even without the aid of torture, should always be interpreted with caution; each of the Templars could have been responding evasively or even playing the fool. This makes a convincing case for the possibility that when Geoffroy de Gonneville, preceptor of Aquitaine and Poitou, attributed the introduction of "perverse rites" to "Master" Roncelin during his first interrogation, he simply was trying to send off his interrogators on a false scent. How else can we explain that he allowed such a secret to escape so easily, then guarded his silence for seven years, saying nothing more about the matter?

Let me repeat: This text published in 1877 is a fake. This conclusion is further cemented by its codicil presenting a bizarre prayer to Allah and informing us that the cry of *Yah Allah* must be shouted in any case of danger. This is quite simply syncretism. Finally, and oddly, this secret Rule self-destructs when it states: "The secret statutes will never be translated into the common tongue nor ever placed in the hands of the brothers." Yet this piece from the Vatican archives is written in French—a common tongue.

That this document is false, however, does not imply that there was never a secret Rule known only to a few brothers who were selected for such knowledge no doubt on the basis of their capabilities and were perhaps charged with responsibilities on an occult level. This would be nothing out of the ordinary for a so-called initiatory society and an order of knighthood. Obviously the existence of a hierarchy inspires an emulation that may be of benefit to the entire community. Furthermore, the majority of the brothers were likely incapable of comprehending abstract concepts. We must remember that the Temple was a combat order that had no place for metaphysicians and gentle dreamers. However, these soldier-monks required leaders, and those charged with this responsibility necessarily possessed a greater degree of education, not to mention intelligence.

So we have a properly vexing question that may never be resolved: knowing whether or not a parallel hierarchy really existed. The example of Jacques de Molay, obviously incompetent, lends credit to this hypothesis. It is simply inconceivable that such a worthless figure could have been chosen to direct the destiny of such an important order. In any event, his attitude in refusing the merger with the Hospitallers, followed by his deplorable confessions, led the order to disaster. We are truly tempted to think he was only a straw man, that above him, known only to a few, there was a real grand master who worked in the shadows and that Jacques de Molay and the other dignitaries—this would be their only real merit—never denounced him, preferring ignominy, the stake, or prison. If this were the truth, Jacques de Molay would emerge from the purgatory of history singularly larger in stature.

But, then, if there was an occult grand master and, of course, a no less occult chapter (the grand master could act only with the consent of his chapter)—thus what has been called the parallel hierarchy—why did it not intervene during any part of the trial, if only in an occult fashion, of course? According to what we know, no one truly defended the order, except for a few isolated individuals who themselves did so quite timidly. This leads us to believe that the Temple was indefensible. Those convinced of the actual existence of this parallel hierarchy attribute this lack of intervention to the Templars' single-minded concern for spiriting away the treasure and the archives. After which the hierarchy would also have disappeared without a trace—except, of course, to reappear today in the neo-Templar or related orders, who all claim, despite their divergences, to be the sole true heirs of the white-cloaked knights.

Before launching ourselves into explanations that smack more of a serialized novel than of history, we should ask if this occult grand master ever really existed. But the circumstances under which the Templars were brought to trial; the doubts, uncertainties, and ambiguities that can be detected among the players; the harsh and definitive judgment made against Philip the Fair and Clement V; and Jacques de Molay's famous, much debated (and rightfully so) curse—all add to the confusion.

There is, however, a key figure who appeared throughout this affair. He was directly in the foreground and yet seems to have attracted no attention from anyone. He is, quite simply, the pope. This hypothesis may be astonishing, but is no more absurd than all the others that have been proposed on this subject. It was in fact the pope who, in accordance with the statutes—hence legally—was the supreme leader of the Templar Order. This fact was made abundantly clear at the time of the official founding of the Temple, and was repeated by Clement V himself, who, let us not forget, was the only one to definitively rule on the fate of the order. Furthermore, if we analyze the events of the Templars' trial, it will be seen that the sole person, at least among all the high and mighty of the world, to truly defend the Temple was Clement V. He did all he could to snuff out the matter and to counter Philip the Fair's actions. He learned all he could of what truly went on within the Temple and did all he could to rescue the Templars from the king's justice. He tried to gain time by causing the trial to drag on and gave Jacques de Molay and the other high officials their last chance at salvation. It was they who did not follow the pope's itinerary. Unless . . . It can just as easily be claimed that bound by oath to the pope, their supreme leader, the four officials blindly obeyed what Clement V demanded they do.

While the Temple, especially in France, formed a state within a state, a political, economic, and military power that escaped the king's control, the pope, always more or less in conflict with kings and most particularly with the king of France, had at his disposal this formidable militia to force the retreat of his adversaries. Why didn't Clement take advantage of his authority to set the Templars in motion and force Philip the Fair to listen to reason?

Excellent arguments can be made to explain the pope's lack of intervention on this level. In full retreat to Europe from Jerusalem, the Temple was in a period of fluctuation and the number of knight combatants was not very large. The specific contingents of men belonging to the Temple— valets, serfs, free peasants, and various artisans—were more significant. While the Temple did, in fact, constitute a formidable force, it was a *potential* force. It would have required quite a bit more time to make it operational.

Coupled with this, the papacy appeared to be quite weak at the beginning of the fourteenth century. The Agnani incident and the Boniface VIII affair had delivered a very rude blow to its prestige. Rome was a theater of constant infighting among rival factions and the Church was terribly divided. The fact that Clement V was obliged to settle in Avignon and could not even visit Rome appeared to be a significant illustration of the papacy's state of decline. But this does not explain why the pope abstained from using his principal strength, the one that had remained faithful to him above all others—the Templars.

In truth, the Temple was also weakened and in search of a new equilibrium as the pretext of the Crusades dimmed as a justification for its existence. This is no doubt why Clement V proposed the merger of the Templars and the Hospitallers. But, as is known, the Templars turned down what may have been their order's last chance, and the pope's last chance as well. It is therefore reasonable that Clement V, in abandoning the Temple, in reality lost an instrument that had become ineffective, outdated, and even undisciplined. Was he truly the grand master on the practical level?

This is only a theory, adding still more to the obscurity that has accumulated ceaselessly around the Templar Order with every futile attempt to see its history a little more clearly. By dint of asking questions that remain without answer, we only inspire more questions that also, in turn, remain unanswered. Was there a secret grand master? It is likely, but who filled this role? We do not know. Was there a secret Rule? Yes, definitely. But what did it contain? Where is it to be found? Again we do not know.

Perhaps it lies in the underground tunnels beneath Gisors. Who knows?

9

The Mysterious Head

AMONG THE KEY CHARGES lodged against the Templars, the most intriguing—and the one that gives free rein to the imagination—is certainly the accusation of idolatry. It was obviously a convenient means for denouncing the Knights Templar as heretics who practiced pagan rituals. In itself, there is nothing original about the charge; it was filed against the majority of heretics, the accusers seeming unaware of the fact that certain Catholic devotions could be considered, by ill-informed observers, as veritable idolatrous acts. The worship of relics and even the presence of statues in a church are examples of such standards. This necessarily horrified the Muslims, for they did not tolerate the depiction of God in their sanctuaries. And of the different objects of piety, we can say to those who are ignorant of Christian doctrine that there are definitely many idolatrous elements in the ceremonies performed by the Roman Catholic Church. To be fair, it is fitting to recall that Catholic ceremonies borrowed much from the so-called pagan religious worship of antiquity and the high Middle Ages. All of this is to say that it is appropriate to examine quite cautiously the accusations launched by Philip the Fair's henchmen regarding the subject of the Templars' idolatrous practices.

We should first refer to the various testimonies gathered during the trial. Here is what Hugues de Pairaud, the second in command of the Temple, said without being tortured:

I saw, held, and touched this human head at a chapter house in Montpellier, and I worshiped it just as did all the other brothers present, but it was from my mouth and in pretense, not from my heart.

This is a strange confession, unless Pairaud's words are a pretense intended to steer the inquisitors onto a false trail. It involves a head, or rather the representation of a head, that was said to be kept in each commandery and was sometimes brought out during a chapter meeting in a secret and enclosed location. Those in attendance, it seemed, were to worship this head. As for what it really represented, that's another question, but opinions vary wildly. According to Brother Raynier de Larchant, it was a bearded head that he acknowledged having seen a dozen times. Further, he specified that the brothers present "worshiped it, kissed it, and called it their Savior." If this is true, then the Templars were, in fact, idolaters.

But there is more testimony, this from Guillaume d'Herblay, the king's chaplain:

As for the head, I saw it at two chapters, both times held by brother Hugues de Pairaud, visitor of France. I saw the brothers worship it, but never with their hearts. I believe it was made of wood that was silver-plated and gilded on the outside . . . It seems to me that it had a beard, or a kind of beard.

And here is testimony from another brother, Hugue de Bure: "It was not made of wood, but of silver perhaps, or even gold or copper. It resembled a human head, with a face and a long beard."

To Brother Barthélémy Boucher, "it resembled a Templar's head wearing a hat and a long white beard." But for Hugues de Pairaud, in another declaration, "this head had four feet, two in front and two behind," which rather gives the impression that the high visitor of France was pulling the legs of his interrogators.

Then there is Guillaume d'Herblay's statement in which this head takes on a legendary appearance: "I heard say that it was the head of one of the eleven thousand Virgins.[1] But I now believe it was an idol. It had two faces of a terrible appearance. Its beard was made of silver."

Brother Raoul de Gisy, collector of Champagne, emphasizes the terrifying aspect:

> I saw this head at seven chapters. It was presented and everyone prostrated himself, lifted his hood, and worshiped it. It had a terrible face; it seemed to me the face of a demon, a *maufé*.[2] Each time I saw it, such a great terror would invade me that I could hardly look upon it, and all my limbs were quaking.

Someone then noted to the brother that worshiping an idol was a very villainous act. He answered: "Much worse had been done in denying Jesus, so worshiping the head was easier now."

The brothers clearly did not comprehend much of this ritual they were obliged to attend, and while it was clear that something must have taken place in these famous secret chapter houses, none of those in attendance was capable of explaining exactly what it was.

There were many other descriptions of this nature that figure in the depositions. Let's look at one more, which Brother Bartholomée Rocherii gave on April 19, 1311:

> I was received in the large chapel of the Temple of Paris. After being dubbed, I was made to enter a small chapel. I was alone with an official who showed me a head near the tabernacle. He told me to invoke it in the event of peril. This head was covered by a piece of fine linen. I do not know whether it was made of ivory, metal, or wood. I only saw it one time.

At times this head took on a fantastic appearance. For example, Brother Bernard de Selgues declared that in Montpellier, where the head

---

1. Famous relics preserved in Cologne. According to legend they are the relics of St. Ursula and 10,999 consecrated virgins who were killed by the Huns for refusing to surrender their maidenhood to them.

2. *Mauvais fé*—in other words, "evil spirit."

was guarded, the devil was one with it and he appeared in the form of a cat speaking in a human tongue. According to Brother Jean de Nériton, this satanic tomcat promised its worshipers abundant harvests, plenty of gold, and good health. He claimed even to have heard a chaplain say: "*Istud caput vester Deus est, et vester Mahumet,*" or, "Here is your God and your Múhammád." The reference to Muhammad when speaking of an idol, however, really needs to be taken with a grain of salt! It brings to mind the famous passage in *The Song of Roland* depicting the emir Baligant and the king Marsile, two good Saracens, in an underground sanctuary worshiping three idols, Apollo, Muhammad, and Tervagant—the latter being the bull of the three cranes worshiped by the Celts.

Head, devil, cat, monster—here we can recognize the familiar cast of second-rate sorcery. The least that can be said is that the head is a presence from folklore.

Yet this famous baphomet has been responsible for a generous flow of ink and veritable torrents of learned commentary. Just what is it? For John Charpentier, who is a notable expert on the Templar question, one hypothesis pushes itself forward: that a secret agreement between East and West existed, worked out by the Templars and symbolized by a double-faced head. This hypothesis, shared by Victor-Émile Michelet and picked up again by Julius Evola and René Guénon, suggests that the Templars, or at least some of them belonging to a circle of initiates, wished to join in a kind of *transecumenicalism,* a joining of the wisdom of the East and the West, Islam and Christianity. The baphomet would be a symbolic image of this. Here we find an example of the famed Guénonian syncretism. But why not? It could also be assumed that the Templars were crypto-Muslims—Sufis, for example. Historical events strictly oppose this hypothesis, but let us carry it further. "Western scholars have assumed that bafomet [or baphomet] might be a corruption of the Arabic *abufihamat* (or *bufihimat*), which can be translated as "father of understanding." In Sufi terminology, *ral-el-fahmat* (head of knowledge) refers to the mental process of the initiate."[3] Here is an explanation that deserves another.

---

3. Idries Shah, *Les Soufis et l'ésotérisme* (Paris: Payot, 1972).

The meaning of the word *baphomet* has been the object of much study. At the beginning of the nineteenth century, the Arab expert Sylvestre de Sacy maintained that it was an altered form of the name Muhammad, a claim that obviously unleashed a storm of protest. Most critics found the idea of an anthropomorphic representation in Islamic worship inconceivable, although Sacy had found in an eighteenth-century dictionary the word *bahommerid,* meaning "mosque." The German Orientalist Hammer-Purstall claimed that *baphomet* came from the Arab word *bahoumid,* meaning "calf." He concluded from this that the Templars' head is a reference to the worship of the golden calf—a colorful interpretation when we recall that the Templars were the greatest bankers in Europe.

But as the word *baphomet* was not to be found in any lexicon, Hammer-Purstall quickly changed his theory, declaring that the word was of Gnostic origin and resulted from the coupling of two Greek words: *baphe* (baptism) and *meteos* (initiation). According to him, this indicated an initiation by fire. This opinion was not shared by the occultist Victor-Émile Michelet, who believed the term involved an abbreviation of the phrase *Templi Omnium Omnium Pacis Abbas*—in other words, TEMOHPAB—which was to be read kabbalistically, from right to left, and retaining only certain letters (we may well ask why). On the same principle, John Charpentier, starting from the baseless belief that St. John the Baptist was the Temple's patron saint, suggested that *baphomet* derived from a combination of Baptiste-Mahomet [Baptist-Muhammad], from which was erased a number of letters after the first three, equal to the sacred number of seven. As can be seen, we are drowning in vagaries!

Albert Ollivier took a completely different approach. He proposed a kinship of *baphomet* to Bapho, which is the name of the Cyprus port where the Templars were long established. He assumed there may have been a possible relationship between the worship of Astarte, who had a temple in Bapho during ancient times, and the Virgin Mary, whom the Templars particularly honored. "It is not impossible that the order brought back from Cyprus a head or bones—equally capable of being Christian or pagan—that the judges sought to connect to the worship of Astarte."[4]

---

4. Albert Ollivier, *Les Templiers* (Paris: Le Seuil, 1958), 76.

This assumes that the judges and inquisitors had an extensive education in and profound knowledge of the cults of antiquity, which is far from being proved. That said, the hypothesis is interesting insofar as it is known that there was surely regular contact between the Templars and Eastern Christians, notably the Copts.[5] But it seems that there is little comparison between the bearded idol described during the interrogations and a depiction of Astarte, even if she was considered as the goddess of Bapho.

However, it can be definitively stated that the word *baphomet* was never uttered by either the Templars or their accusers, at least at the beginning of the inquest. Historians and occultists are responsible for the incredible diffusion of this word. The reality is much simpler and can be found in the interrogation of a sergeant from Montpezat near Montauban, who was accused of having worshiped a baphometic image. This sergeant gave his testimony in Occitan, the language of his region, but the inquisitors, who were from the north, did not quite grasp what he was saying. In Occitan the word *baphomet* was the popular deformation of Muhammad. This is proved by a poem from a troubadour we know under the name of Olivier the Templar, who wrote in 1265: "[The Turks] know that each day they humble us, because God is sleeping, who once watched over us, and Baphomet manifests his power and causes the Sultan of Egypt to shine."[6] Accordingly, a *baphometic* image is, quite simply, a Muhammadan image. The sergeant was certainly unaware that the Muslim religion forbids all human representation, as were, incidentally, the author of *The Song of Roland* and a good number of medieval writers speaking on the Saracens.[7] For the sergeant an image to be

---

5. More can be read on this subject in the excellent book by Jean Tourniac, *De la Chevalerie au secret du Temple* (Paris: Éd. du Prisme, 1975), in which the author makes a good case for the possible convergence of Eastern Christian doctrines in the occult doctrine of the Templars.

6. Quoted by A. Ollivier, *Les Templiers,* 120.

7. In countless *Chansons de Geste* written during the twelfth and thirteenth centuries, we are often shown Saracens swearing by Muhammad, Apollo, and Tervagant and indulging in the worship of idols. There was an obvious incomprehension of the Muslim religion in Western Europe and the famous Saracens gathered together everything that was not Christian, including the Roman religion and the druidic religion as well as the folk survivals of these belief systems in the countryside. In the same way, the Saracens depicted in the *Chansons de Geste* are sometimes sorcerers and even devils.

considered as both bizarre and non-Christian could only be a *mahomerie,* as such things were sometimes called during the twelfth and thirteenth centuries, an era when linguistic precision was not strongly sought. In the *Chansons de Geste,* everything that is not Christian is Saracen. It is this error of interpretation that has caused people to believe they have seen a Muslim influence upon the secret beliefs of the Templars and it is upon this error that so many ingenious theories have been constructed! The baphomet does not exist; it is an invention of scholars.

But if there is no baphomet, properly speaking, it does seem that there was a head because so many declarations attest to its existence. *Well, actually, no, there is no head either.* On May 11, 1311, the papal inquiry commission, intrigued by the conflicting testimony about this head, asked the administrator of the impounded Templar property if a head made of wood or metal was among the objects seized. The administrator, Guillaume Pidoye, presented "a large handsome head, plated with silver, that had the face of a woman and contained a skull bone wrapped in folds of stitched white linen and another reddish-colored cloth. Pidoye declared he had found nothing else in the house of the Temple." It should be explicitly stated that this head bore an inscription: "Caput LVIII m," which has been responsible for a generous flow of ink, but is probably nothing more than a simple classification label. There is certainly nothing to indicate it should be regarded as a secret code. In any event, the witnesses did not recognize the female head, when it was presented to them, as that same head they had seen at the mysterious ceremonies. In the course of all the searches made in every Templar house, no head was ever found, a fact that is itself cause for surprise.

We now know full well what this "Caput LVIII m" idol is: a reliquary in the form of a bust of a woman, differing in no way from all the other reliquaries of this type used in the perfectly orthodox worship of a saint or martyr.[8] And no mystery can be contrived from this statement.

We should also recall a strange passage from the prologue of *Gargantua,* by Rabelais, regarding Silenus:

---

8. See Probst-Biraben and Maitrot de la Motte-Capron, "Les Idoles des chevaliers du Temple," in *Mercure de France,* vol. 294 (1939): 569–90.

Now a silenus, in ancient days, was a little box of the kind we see today in apothecaries' shops, painted on the outside with such gay, comical figures as harpies, satyrs, bridled geese, horned hares, saddled ducks, flying goats, stags in harness, and other devices of that sort lightheartedly invented for the purpose of mirth, as was Silenus himself, the master of good old Bacchus. But inside these boxes were kept rare drugs, such as balm, ambergris, cardamom, musk, civet, mineral essences, and other precious things.[9]

Rabelais wishes to show through this example and that of Socrates, who, though grotesque and ugly, was to Rabelais the greatest sage of the world, that it is often necessary to distrust appearances. So what could the hideous and grotesque idol of the Templars have been hiding? What would have been the exact nature of the relics enclosed within this kind of box adorned with a grotesque head?

All of this is symbolic and refers to folk traditions common to numerous countries in both the East and the West. Rabelais' description of the figures on a silenus offers a surprising analogy to the description of the mysterious head in the Templar testimony. It is likely that Rabelais, who was very aware of the Templar affair and who often alluded to it in his work, remembered this and used it to demonstrate that ugliness often conceals beauty and that reality is not strictly what is apparent. This is actually philosophy and has nothing to do with an idolatrous cult.

Another testimony given during the trial extended the debate into the realm of folk traditions. This was the deposition made by the Italian notary Antonio Sicci de Verceil, who served the Templars of Syria for forty years. Here is what he said on March 1, 1311:

Several times the story of something that happed in the city of Sidon was related to me. A certain nobleman of that city had been enamored of a certain Armenian noblewoman. He never knew her while

---

9. Rabelais, *Gargantua and Pantagruel,* translated by J. M. Cohen (Hammondsworth, England: Penguin, 1955), 37.

she was alive, but, when she died, he secretly violated her in her tomb on the very night she had been laid to rest. Once the deed was done, he heard a voice saying to him: "Return when the time of childbirth has come, for you will then find a head, the daughter of your works." Once this time had come, the knight returned to the tomb and found a human head between the legs of the shrouded woman. He heard the voice again, and this time it told him: "Guard this head well, for all your prosperity will come to you from it." At the time I heard this story, the preceptor of this place (Sidon) was Brother Mathieu, called the Sarnage, a native of Picardy. He had become brother to the *soudan* [sultan] in Babylon [Cairo] who was ruling then because each had drunk of the other's blood, which caused them to be regarded as brothers.[10]

This story of necrophilia is well known. Two other depositions attest to it, with variations. The story could already be found a century earlier in the curious works of Gervais de Tilbury and Gautier Mapp, which shows that it involves a mythological theme that has passed into the repertoire of traditional storytelling. Its themes are easily recognized: the magical head of a dead person that gives wealth to its owner, the forbidden but magically effective copulation of a living individual with a dead person, and the idea of the evil eye. A reference to the Templars has been added with the insinuation that one of them, having become the ritual blood brother of a Muslim leader, had inherited this magical head. It would not take much more than this to give the so-called baphomet all its magical and symbolic value.

In fact, as shown by Salomon Reinach, the story of the Templars' head belongs to a series of legends constructed out of the traditions concerning Perseus and Medusa. A century before the trial, the legend of Perseus had enjoyed a sudden new burst of popularity. But instead of being a figure of antiquity, Perseus had become, in conformance with the medieval custom

---

10. Salomon Reinach, "La Tête magique des Templiers," *Revue de l'histoire des religions,* no. 63 (1911), 25–39. Reinach devoted his efforts to a compelling inquiry into the mythological origins of this famous head.

of transforming a hero of the past into a contemporary figure, a knight like Lancelot of the Lake. Now, what was the familiar image of the knight in the Middle East at that time? Why, the Templars, of course. Perseus was thus transformed into a Templar. People of the East had heard rumors that knights hid a magical head (the head of Medusa) and determined these knights could only be Templars. Further, because the knights accomplished bizarre things with this head, it was certain they had secretly converted to Islam and that they worshiped the head like an idol, a mahomerie.

From here opinion went to considering this head as initiatory and a connection was made between the idol and the cord worn by the Templars. According to the trial depositions, this cord was placed on the new knight after having been passed over the neck of the idol. Here is what Brother Huguet de Bune recounted: "The brother pulled a head out of a cupboard and set it on the altar. He then made the motions of cinching it and gave me back the cord whilst enjoining me to wear it above my belt."

It is certain that by taking common devotional acts as a basis here, the intention was to blacken the Templars and connect them with idolatrous customs. In fact, this cord is well known and all monks wear similar ones. It is the reminder of the mandatory chastity that no monk must forget. Using the head to make the cord magical simply meant, in fact, that the cord was blessed, which is not at all a malefic act. The head must, then, be a reliquary. Another brother, Guy Dauphin, relates moreover how his cord had been touched to the Column of Annunciation in Nazareth. It was probably customary among the Templars to place the cord in contact with a sacred object in order to give it more power or meaning. Some may find this superstitious, but it is nevertheless a perfectly orthodox Christian gesture.

Numerous witnesses had, in fact, told of the order's ownership of relics, notably those of St. Polycarpe and St. Euphemia. This famous head, which has fueled so many theories as well as fantasies, would seem to be, in the last analysis, merely a reliquary, just like the one seized at the Temple of Paris and shown to the members of the pontiff's commission. It's nothing to make a fuss about.

Now that we have taken care of that, the satanic nature of the idol, which was seemingly hammered home in a series of confessions, had appeared in company with our old acquaintance the satanic cat. This cat, it seemed, showed up alongside the idol in a sort of cloud, lingered there throughout the ceremony, and then disappeared, never to be seen again. None could explain it except by saying that it came from the devil or was itself the devil. The Templars present at the ceremony revered it, removing their hats, bowing low before it, and, finally, kissing it beneath the tail. Its appearance, however, was as variable as that of the idol in that some saw it as black, some as gray, some as brindled, and some as red.

After all this, it comes as no surprise to learn, from some of the confessions, that the idol was anointed with the fat of roasted infants and that the bodies of deceased Templars were burnt and their ashes mixed into a powder, which was administered to newcomers as a magical potion to make them hold fast to their abominable ways. Nor are we surprised to hear that the worship of the idol and the cat was sometimes attended by demons in the form of beautiful young girls whose arrival was all the more remarkable because every window and crevice in the place was sealed, yet the assembled Templars were quite happy to make love with them.[11] This, of course, should have absolved them from the alleged obligatory practice of homosexuality . . . We are drowning in complete delirium.

It is useless to try to make distinctions between myth and reality. They are too tightly blended to be individually recognized. The Templars' accusers used—it is obvious—all the resources of folklore at their disposal to condemn the ex–Poor Knights of Christ. All the standard witch trial claptrap can be found here. And if the cat, which is a truly mediumistic animal, comes to their aid by being identified with the devil, it is because it strikes the imagination to consider it so. Their accusers eventually convinced the Templars that they had seen certain things or taken part in certain ceremonies. But it remains true that the whole affair rested on two or three quite real elements that Philip the Fair's minions exploited and amplified with a skill that can be labeled—and this time the word is totally appropriate—demonic.

There probably were, at certain Templar chapter houses, more or

---

11. Norman Cohn, *Europe's Inner Demons* (New York: Basic Books, 1975), 88.

less secret ceremonies whose meaning the participants no longer exactly understood. These ceremonies had become routine, emptied of their original substance. All that survived were certain symbolic gestures or evocations.The mysterious head probably never existed physically, but people talked about it and described it, and thus it necessarily appeared in a symbolic form. This is a hard point to refute.

But believing in the reality of these bizarre rituals is something else entirely. All the descriptions we have conform to what we know of that era's superstitions about demonology and sorcery. It was uniquely these fantasies that convinced the inquisitors, and eventually the accused themselves, that the Templars were the witnesses of such things. The same phenomenon held true in all the witch trials. The result was a series of typical images with insignificant variations, ceaselessly repeated and shared in good faith by both the accused and the accuser, and all deriving from easily referenced mythological outlines. In a word, myth, as a mental structure, is stronger than the reality of events.

As far as the mysterious ceremonial head is concerned, its sources are well known in European tradition, extending back to the dawn of time and forming part of the Celtic memory bank with analogous borrowings from Eastern traditions. It is by the light of these sources that we need to examine the "myth" of the head actually experienced by the Templars in one manner or another and, as if through a funhouse mirror, the image of this same myth *dreamed* by their accusers as embodied by contemporary events.

The reference point we will use is a Welsh text contained in a twelfth-century manuscript, which is a copy of an older tale, *Peredur, Son of Evrawg*. This text—at least the original version used by Chrétien de Troyes as a model for his *Perceval, or The Story of the Grail*—is the Welsh and Celtic translation of the quest for the Grail. When the hero finds himself in the Grail Castle, home of the mysterious Fisher King, he witnesses an extraordinary procession:

> He had begun to converse with his uncle when he saw, entering the
> hall and entering a chamber, two men carrying an enormous lance

that had three streams of blood flowing from its socket onto the ground. All those in attendance began to cry and moan at this sight. . . . After a brief interval of silence, two maidens entered bearing a large platter upon which was a man's head bathed in blood. The company gave forth such cries that it was wearying to be in the same hall with them.[12]

We can note immediately that Chrétien de Troyes replaced this man's head on the platter with a grail, whose contents he did not reveal. In fact, the above text represents the sole version of the quest for the Grail that presents the mysterious Grail in this fashion. But this story of the severed head is not an isolated one in Welsh tradition. In another Welsh tale, the hero Bran the Blessed, after an unlucky expedition to Ireland during which he was wounded by a poisoned spear, asks his companions to cut off his head and take it with them to place on the White Hill in London. After doing so, they take part there in an authentic feast of immortality presided over by this severed head,[13] after which they bury the head in the hill. In this way, as long as the head is not disinterred, the country will be protected against any invasion. It is certain that the theme dealt with here is related to that of Perseus and Medusa. The sacred head provides protection against enemies. This reference should be kept in mind before indulging in esoteric explanations for the so-called baphomet.

In the French tale *Perlesvaux,* a text from the end of the twelfth century that was strongly influenced by the Clunisians but relates to the original Celtic legend of the Grail, Lancelot of the Lake is compelled to cut off the head of a giant to save his own life—but on the condition that he return in a year to offer his neck to the giant in return. After the two agree upon this condition, the giant picks up his severed head and disappears. The same story can be found in a much earlier Irish tale, *The*

---

12. J. Loth, *Les Mabinogion,* new edition (Paris: Les Presses d'aujourd'hui, 1979), 203. See also Jean Markale, *The Grail* (Rochester, Vt.: Inner Traditions, 1999), 35.

13. Ibid., 39–41. See also Jean Markale, *L'Épopée celtique en Bretagne,* 3rd edition (Paris: Payot, 1984), 43–52.

Feast of Bricriu, the hero of which is the renowned warrior Cuchulainn.[14] This decapitation game, as it is called, ending with the hero enduring only a simulated decapitation, refers to a well-known theme of Christian hagiography: cephalophoric saints (saints who carry their own heads after being attacked) such as St. Denis in France, St. Tremeur and St. Tryfine in Brittany, and St. Mitre in Provence.

These tales come from the tradition attributed to the ancient Gauls. According to Titus-Livy, the Gauls cut off the heads of their enemies and, after treating them, hung them from the chests of their horses (Titus-Livy, X, 26). Diodorus Siculus (V, 29) and Strabo (IV, 4) say close to the same thing, while specifying that they attached their trophies to the doors of their houses. Titus-Livy (XXIII, 24) further elaborates, somewhat indulgently, on the fate reserved for the skull of the consul Postumius, which, coated in gold, served as a ritual vessel in druid ceremonies. Archaeology confirms these texts: In the ruins of the cities of Glanum (Saint-Rémy-de-Provence), Saint-Blaise (near Istres), and Entremont (near Aix-en-Provence), as well as in the Borély Museum of Marseilles, we can see pillars that served as these "skull hangers," complete with their fastening nails. In the Borély Museum as well as in the Granet Museum of Aix-en-Provence and the Calvet Museum of Avignon, we can also see a certain number of severed heads carved in stone. These depictions can also often be found on the capitals of Romanesque churches, for Romanesque art inherited a great deal from Gallic statuary.

Irish tradition likewise stands witness to this custom. In the fortress of King Conchobar in Ulster, there was a room reserved for war trophies, chiefly severed heads. In one strange story, the hero, Conall Cernach, cuts off the head of King Mesgegra. He then places the head on a stone next to a ford: "A drop of blood fell from the neck and went all the way through the rock until it reached the ground. He then placed the head on another stone and the head passed through the stone."[15] If we understand this correctly, the head is corrosive. The same detail can be found regarding the head of the hero Cuchulainn:

14. See Jean Markale, *Celtic Epics of Ireland* (Rochester, Vt.: Inner Traditions, 2000), 102–8.

15. *Revue celtique* 8, 48 ff.

"His head had caused the stone to melt and passed through it."[16] We can thereby see that the mysterious head of the Templars did not pop out of the inquisitors' imagination by chance. It belonged to a solidly established Western tradition. And need we recall the legend concerning the head of St. John the Baptist, whom some have tried to make the patron saint of the Temple?

But the accusations against the order stretched farther. We know that the Templars were suspected of practicing alchemy, though not with any proof. This would, after all, explain the origin of their wealth, which consequentially reinforced the idea of the existence of a hidden treasure, whether material or in the form of documents concerning the transmutation of metals. The audacious souls seeking to pierce the secret of Gisors' underground tunnels should be ranked with those who believe in the existence of such alchemical documents.

But again, these accusations did not materialize from a vacuum. In the tale concerning the Welsh hero Bran the Blessed, we are told that Bran's head is buried in the White Hill in London. It should be realized that in Welsh and Breton, Bran means "raven." We can then understand that the head of the raven must be buried in the White Hill. In alchemical texts, the head of the raven is a symbol used to label one of the phases of an operation called the Great Work. "Our mercury," said the alchemist and saint Albertus Magnus (*The Composite of Composites,* V), "will remain at the bottom . . . changed into a blackish earth." The poet-alchemist Ramon Lulle, whose grandiose fantasies inspired Philip the Fair, after describing the delicate operations for purifying the Primal Matter necessary for creating the Philosopher's Stone, writes (*The Claivicule,* VIII): "You will then have the Raven's Head so ardently sought by the Philosophers, without which the Magister cannot exist."

But there is more. The famous Nicolas Flamel, in his *Treatise on the Hieroglyphic Figures,* wrote the following: "Regard that man in the shape of a St. Paul . . . He wished to take up the naked blade either to cut off the

16. *Ogam* 18, 352.

head or do something else to the man kneeling at his feet . . . But would you like to know what this man who takes the sword is teaching? It means to cut off the head of the Raven, in other words that man . . . who is on his knees. To take off the head of this black man, the head of the raven, which, when removed, becomes the color white." We know that "the head of the raven" is a phrase of the Great Work in which the stone is "at black." One must get rid of this blackness and cut off the raven's head, which allows reaching the following phase, the stone "at white," from which it is capable of transforming lead into silver.

Oddly enough, we cannot help but think of the Templars' seal depicting two knights on the same horse, an obvious symbol of the alchemists' mercury and sulfur. The union of these, which can be obtained only by the secret fire (represented by the horse), is necessary for creating the Philosopher's Stone. We can recall the Templars' standard, Baucéant (or Baucent or Baussant), which is black and white. It is impossible that there would be no connection between this standard and the mysterious head. And did you know that the name of the wild boar in the *Roman de Renard* is Baucent? Did you know that in the Welsh language the word for *boar* is *baoddan,* which sounds almost like Baucent? Did you know that the wild boar was, in Celtic society, the symbol of the sacerdotal class of the druids? Did you know that in numerous artistic representations, such as the famous Gundestrup Cauldron, the Celtic warriors are wearing a likeness of a boar on their helmets? It is rather odd to find soldiers wearing a sacerdotal emblem. In fact, it is completely contrary to the medieval law of the three classes, which is strictly the same as that held by the Indo-Europeans, thus the Celts. The trifunctional division is clear-cut: There are priests, warriors, and producers. But weren't the Templars, as both monks and soldiers, participating in two divisions, warrior and sacerdotal? In any case, their standard proves it, just as the mysterious head does—the head that is the head of the raven, which must be severed, thus sacrificed, in order to reveal the whiteness, thus the light.

These are alchemical concepts, but alchemy, before becoming a banal matter of transmutation of metals, was first and primarily a philosophical system that claimed to reveal Awareness by virtue of a work on Matter (the Black) and Spirit (the White), the physical and the mental, the body and the soul. But we will never understand the exact role of the mysterious head in the ceremonies described in the confessions if we separate the question of the head from that posed by what are described as the "obscene kisses."

Among the key charges figure practices deemed shameful: "[D]uring the ceremony of reception, the brothers sometimes kiss each other on the mouth, on the navel, or on the naked belly, as well as on the anus or the spinal column." We could almost believe that the accusers borrowed the folklore vocabulary of the Sabbath characterized by obscene gestures, particularly the one that consists of kissing the devil, who has taken the form of a goat, beneath the tail. It is also believable that these shameless kisses formed part of another key charge—that of sodomy. Let's specify straight off that *sodomy* did not have the restrictive sense in the Middle Ages that it does today; the term as understood by the people of that era referred to any homosexual practice, which could be the case for the obscene kisses. But the Templars, almost to a man, rejected the accusation of *obligatory* sodomy, and the inquisitors did not insist on this point, satisfied merely to bring up individual cases. The fact is that homosexuality has always existed and was all the more common in communities of men forbidden the company of women. This does not pose any particular problem.

But the obscene kisses for which the Templars were criticized were part of a ritual that those who took part in seemed not to comprehend in the slightest. The depositions are explicit: "I took them aside and made them give me a kiss at the base of the spine, on the navel, and on the mouth" (Hugues de Pairaud). "I kissed him first at the base of the spine, then on the navel, and finally upon the lips" (Raynier de Larchant). "Still on his command, I kissed him at the bottom of the spine, the navel, and upon the lips" (Pierre de Torteville). "Brother Jean then kissed me three times, first at the base of the spine, then on the navel, finally on the mouth" (Jean de Tour, treasurer of the Temple of Paris). "I kissed the preceptor on the lips, on the navel, and the obscene parts below. I saw him receive Brother Artus, who was with me, in the same manner, and then several others afterward" (Pierre de Boulogne). "The brother who received me crudely told me to kiss his ass" (Nicholas d'Amiens, known as Lulli). "I heard it mentioned five hundred times or more; it was public knowledge that they received kisses on the ass, unless it was the opposite. This was the reason, they said, that the reception was held secretly behind closed doors" (Guichard de Machiaco).

The quotations go on and on. They are remarkably consistent. Except for Pierre de Boulogne, who must have mistaken their order, it involved three kisses, beginning with the anus, continuing with the belly, and finishing with the mouth. This surely implies something, though the regular commentators on the Templar affair pass rapidly over these repugnant proceedings, or are satisfied to laugh about them discreetly in passing, or react in shock (there are some things that just are not talked about!). These try to dispose of the matter with a transparent evasion: They are childish games or hazings such as would be found in private schools or similar types of institutions, or even among soldiers, who, as everybody knows, are fairly crude and not very refined. This is easy enough to say, but before trying to shed more light on the subject, it would be a good idea to look once more for assistance from Rabelais, that crafty old devil who knew so much about traditions handed down from previous centuries. We may recall that the name given by the squire Gymnaste (whose name means "someone who is naked") in *Gargantua* was Kiss My Ass; that in *Pantagruel* there is an impassioned debate—which is completely incomprehensible on the surface because its verbal alchemy is so rich in allusions and symbols—between the Lord of Humevesne [Suckfizzle] and the Lord of Baisecul [Kissmyass]; that the favorite weapon of Brother John of the Hashes—who would have made an excellent Templar—is a bizarre phallic object with the name of Malchus (Evil Ass with a play of words on King Malek). Throughout Rabelais' work there is a deliberate intention to emphasize breath, particularly the breath from "down below." Sensitive souls will judge this as scatology, but they should be aware of the symbolic meaning of "breaths from below" that come from the "underground world." In other words, this is the mining of the Primal Matter of the Philosophers, which through a series of operations and transformations will become the Philosopher's Stone—the pure light of the mind. And the mind is traditionally found in the head.

There you have it. The obscene kisses of the Templars are all that remain—or all that we were intended to hear—of a very ancient initiatory ritual. It is a matter of starting from the ass—that is to say the mining that collects the breaths of raw matter that has not been worked but is rich in potential—then passing through the belly, the site of transformation (this brings to mind Messer Gaster!),[17] where it is worked and purified, and finally reaching the mouth, in the head, the highest point, where the purified breath becomes the divine voice.

Furthermore, this conforms perfectly with the Eastern tradition of *kundalini,* the energy that is birthed at the base of the spine between the anus and genitals and then, in the symbolic form of a serpent, climbs through the body, innervating the various chakras that are the varied centers of human activity before finally reaching the last chakra in the head, which is the chakra of illumination. There is no cause for doubt about this initiatory ritual. It is so well described in the Templar depositions, even though the participants did not understand, that it is impossible to deny. Thus these obscene kisses were not an indecent schoolboy joke, but the remnants of an initiatory ritual with the purpose of making the new knight aware that he must start from the bottom to reach the top and not claim to have already reached the top to go back down. The best thing is that this ritual can be entirely justified by St. Bernard de Clairvaux:

We are carnal beings born of the concupiscence of the flesh, so it is necessary that our love begin in the flesh. Rightly guided by God's grace through the degrees, it will find its consummation in the flesh. That which in us is spiritual cannot precede that which is animal, but the spiritual will blossom later; we must bear the image of earthly man before we can bear the image of celestial man. Man begins by

---

17. Messer Gaster (Lord Belly) is a philosopher and apologist for the stomach who appears in the work of Rabelais. French fabulist Jean de la Fontaine also made use of him. —*Trans.*

loving himself for his own sake, then loving God, but still for self-ish reasons, not for God's sake . . . and when he has tasted for himself the sweetness of God, he ascends to the third degree wherein he loves God for the sake of God. There he must rest, for I do not know if a man in this life has ever attained the fourth degree, which is to love himself for the sake of God.[18]

It is all said here in this text by the abbot of Clairvaux, founder of the Templar Order. But were the Templars capable of understanding these words and drawing practical lessons from them?

The baphomet—that monstrous head we've heard described—is a myth. But myths are realities that are much more powerful than material objects or even human beings. We must raise ourselves quite high to comprehend what is incomprehensible. The mysterious head of the Templars is a symbol of an essential goal to be won: the love of oneself for the sake of God. All the rest is only cheap fiction from imaginations overcharged by legendary stories that are no longer understood by those who need to understand them.[19]

There is, however, a lesson to be learned from the head of the Templars and all the obscure elements that surround it like a halo. When we wish to discover something, it requires patience and avoiding starting the journey with the goal we have set for ourselves. The head is the goal, but the quest must begin in the obscure nether regions. It is perhaps through careful exploration of the underground passageways, those of Gisors as well as of our minds, that we will discover the wells that open on to the light, there where the head is found, freed of its body, with its eyes turned toward the infinite.

---

18. *Textes politiques,* 78–79.

19. Such as the tenacious legend claiming that Pope Sylvester II, the famous monk Gerbert d'Aurillac who was very well versed in the secret sciences, would have crafted a steel talking head; and that the saint-alchemist Albertus Magnus would have also spent thirty years fashioning a similar head. But, the story goes, Thomas Aquinas, founder of rationalism within the Church, allegedly broke this head because it talked too much. The symbolism of this legend is quite clear.

10

The Denial

OF ALL THE ACCUSATIONS brought against the Temple, the most serious was the one concerning the denial of Jesus required during the reception of a new brother. This accusation, the most well founded of all, was put first by all the enemies of the Templars and was the reason that Pope Clement V officially dissolved the order. Its truth is absolutely incontestable; to deny it would be to oppose every single testimony. And yet it is the accusation that remains the most mysterious, inexplicable, and strange.

All the confessions are in explicit and overwhelming agreement on the denial. When the confessions made under torture have been eliminated (they should not be retained in any case), enough remain to shed sufficient light on the reality of this fact. First are the confessions of Jacques de Molay and the three other top officials before the University and Inquisitor of Paris. These confessions were reiterated at Chinon in the presence of three cardinals hastily sent there for that purpose by the pope. Then there are the confessions obtained by the pope himself in private audience with seventy-two Templars. Added to this are the various declarations recorded in England and Germany and the depositions taken by the papal commission in Sens, April 11–May 13, 1310. These depositions are quite significant for their detail, as exemplified by the deathbed declaration made by Brother Jean de Saint-Benoît:

I was received forty years ago in La Rochelle by Brother Paul de Legion. During my reception he told me that I must deny Our Savior. I don't remember if he named Jesus, the Christ, or the Crucified; he told me they were one and the same. I denied with my mouth but not my heart.

Obviously this brother on the brink of death had nothing to lose, so why would he have lied? Then we have the word of Jean l'Anglais:

I was received in La Rochelle in Saintonge by Brother Pierre de Madit . . . He led me behind the altar and told me to deny Jesus three times and to spit on the cross he showed me. On his order I denied Jesus three times, with my mouth and not my heart, and I spit upon the cross.

The description given by Brother Jean Taillefer from the diocese of Langres is remarkably similar. In this case, we note that it is a priest ordering the denial:

On the day of my reception, on the command of the chaplain who received me, I denied Christ, only one time: I did it by my mouth and not my heart. I was then urged to spit upon the cross; I spat but one time and to the side.

As the following testimonies prove, other witnesses alluded to this regulation of the order. What is notable about the last of the following statements is that sergeants, rather than knights or a chaplain, are ordering the denial.

The brother brought out a cross and told me to spit upon it and to tread on it with my feet while denying Jesus three times. I was stupefied by his request and refused. Then the brother told me that it was the Rule of the Order of the Temple. (Hugue de Bure, diocese of Langres)

Brother Jean gave me the order, before placing the cloak upon me, to deny Jesus three times. I am sure of this. Three times I denied him saying: I deny Jesus, I deny Jesus, I deny Jesus. After which the receptor had a cross brought forth and asked me to spit on it. I spit to the side and refused to spit upon it. He told me that it was the Rule, which he would explain to me, but he never explained it to me. (Geoffroy de Thatan, diocese of Tours)

The brother Pierre de Braelle, preceptor of Sommereux, led me into another room where, behind closed doors, he told me to deny God. Terrified, I refused. He replied that I must lest misfortune befall me. I was struck with fear . . . I denied God as he had asked me, but with my mouth and not my heart, and that only once. (Baudoin de Saint-Just, diocese of Amiens)

The brother Raoul urged me to deny Our Lord who hangs from the wooden cross. I was loath to do so, as you may well imagine, but feared they might kill me as they had a large sword unsheathed. I eventually denied Christ, saying three times with my mouth and not in my heart: I deny Our Lord because you wish me to. Brother Raoul then told me to trample with my feet a silver cross holding the image of the Crucifixion and to spit upon it. It was placed on the ground. Three times I stepped on it, to be precise on the feet of the Crucified, and I spat next to it, not on it. (Jacques de Troyes, diocese of Troyes)

Four or five brother sergeants of the order closed the door to the room with a bar or a knot, and displayed a cross that was the length of a hand and a half. There was no image of the crucified One on the cross. They told us, when showing us the cross: Deny God! Terrified and stupefied, we of course refused. You must, they said, unsheathing their swords. Then, under the prodding of terror, we who bore no weapons denied God. I said it with my mouth but not my heart. The other two did the same, I think. Spit upon the cross,

the sergeants then ordered. As we refused they said they would let
it go, on condition we kept our silence and did not denounce them.
(Géraud de Causse, diocese of Rodez)

We possess several hundred pieces of testimony of this nature. All
but approximately fifteen of the accused acknowledged having practiced,
undergone, or imposed this ritual on new Templars. The ritual apparently included certain variants, but its essential structure remained un-
changed. Most often the cross to be denied included an image of the
Crucifixion, but at times it was unadorned or simply the cross on a cloak.
The denial was always to be directed at Jesus, whatever title he was given.
Even those declaring they denied God fully understood that it was Christ
on the cross they were denying. And the majority of the accused, who
appear to have comprehended nothing of this ritual, declared they performed the denial "with the mouth and not the heart." In certain cases it
is probable that the newly inducted Templar was threatened with the use
of force if he refused to utter the denial.

What is striking is that not a single witness seemed to have understood the meaning of what he was asked to do. This bizarre ceremony
was never preceded by any kind of warning or explanation and all the
witnesses claimed to have been surprised by what was demanded of them.
It is clear that it was totally unexpected. It was a secret about which no
one ever spoke, and the secrecy was furthered by the fact that the ritual
took place in a separate room or a corner of the church or sometimes in
a sealed room inside.

Some brothers, but not all, demanded an explanation at their reception, which appears quite surprising. None ever received one, however.
"Shut up. We will instruct you later on the statutes of the order!" Brother
Renaud of the Orléans Temple was heard to respond, but nothing ever
came of it. It should be noted in passing that there is a clear allusion here
to a secret Rule of the order. What is odd is that this ritual appears to be
a rite specific only to the reception ceremony. It was never talked of
subsequently. Some brothers stated that, troubled by the memory, they
never dared bring it up.

Once, however, Brother Bosco de Masualier from the diocese of Limoges asked for an explanation from the preceptor of Bourges: "Brother Pierre told me not to be curious because I would incur the anger of the brothers and the superiors of the order. Go eat, he told me. It involves a prophet but it would take too long to explain." Here, then, is something significant: Within the order were those who did know.

Logically these would have to have been the high officials, but they showed great discretion on this subject. Jacques de Molay knew nothing, preferring to evoke "the ruse of the enemy of humanity" who "led the Templars to blind perdition." Geoffroy de Gonneville entrenched himself behind history, claiming that at his reception it had been explained to him as a custom of the order introduced "by the promise of an evil master of the order, prisoner of the Sultan, who obtained his freedom only by swearing he would impose it on the brothers." We recall immediately Gérard de Ridefort, who was known as the "evil genius of the Temple." But if this claim were true, the pope would not have failed to relieve the grand master and the entire order of this promise made under duress. Gonneville's claim appears totally unlikely; it seems he put his inquisitors onto a false trail.

Hugues de Pairaud, who appears to have been the most knowledgeable of the four officials, gave no explanation. It was Geoffroy de Charnay, ultimately the one to share Jacques de Molay's fate on the pyre, who went farthest with his explanation: "Brother Amaury told me not to believe in the man whose image was painted there, because he was a false prophet, he was not God." The word *prophet* was obviously singled out by the inquisitors to imply an Islamic influence, which is not at all obvious, especially as the Muslims recognize Jesus as a prophet. Charnay adds, "I had taken note that the manner in which I was received was an impious profanation, contrary to the Catholic faith." Apparently it had not bothered him too much—but what a confession! We can say without too much fear of error that the officials certainly knew what this denial of Jesus was about—but said nothing.

The same cannot be said about the majority of the Templars, however. Certainly some of them may have obeyed the law of silence and pretended to know nothing of this ritual, but the naïveté apparent in some of the testimony is quite revealing. It is clear that only some officials and some mysterious elect knew the secret. The others, satisfied to obey, had taken a vow to do so.

This ritual must have been troubling to many pious brothers of good faith. And here is where we find a particularly stupefying piece of the puzzle. Jean d'Aumône, sergeant from the diocese of Paris, after spitting to the side of the cross while shivering in fear, was commanded by the Templar receiving him: "Cretin! Go confess at once!" Another brother, Pierre de Modies, refused to deny Jesus. The preceptor told him it was the Rule, then added, "Go ahead. The chaplain can certainly absolve you!" We may be surprised that the confessors were not alerted by such comments from their superiors. But we must remember that a Templar could confess only to priests who were members of the order—that, in fact, they were under oath to do so. It seems, then, that the entire practice was orchestrated to occur behind closed doors, organized to ensure that no word of the ritual would reach the outside world, where it would surely arouse the wrath of the orthodox clergy. All the chaplains who were the priests of the order were no doubt fully aware of this ritual that was little in keeping with the Catholic faith, and perhaps aware of other things about which we know nothing. If, by some chance, all of the confessors' words were meant as a parodic mockery of confession, this would be regarded just as seriously by the orthodoxy.

Accusations of the denial of Jesus and spitting on the Crucifix logically should have been linked to another key charge that, truthfully speaking, was hardly developed: the charge that the words of consecration were omitted from the Templar Mass. We know that there were very few priests in the order, but four chaplains did speak of this matter. Gautier de Bure and Étienne de Dijon, heard by the papal commission on December 21, 1310, revealed that they were asked to leave out the *hoc est corpus meum* when saying Mass, but they assured the commission that they did not heed this request. Two other priests, Bertrand de Villiers from the diocese of Limoges and Jean de Branles of the Saulx-sur-Yonne Temple, made identical statements. All the Templars interrogated were unanimous in saying they knew nothing of this omission; they believed that the priest said the standard Mass.

The testimonies of these four priests are revealing, though. We can perceive why, from the moment the brothers were asked to deny the man on the cross because he was a false prophet, a Templar priest would no longer continue to say the ritual words "this is my body," which, according to the dogma of the Eucharist, change bread into the body of Christ. Such an omission would only be logical. But where has there been any logic in the entire affair?

All the Templars declared themselves to be Christians and died as Christians, demanded to hear Mass, to make confession, to receive communion and extreme unction. Yet these are the same men who knowingly—even if it was by their mouth and not their heart—denied Jesus. This seems entirely inexplicable. One theory speculates on the possibility of Cathar influence. It is a sensible hypothesis, for the Templars' trial took place a mere sixty-three years after the pyre of Montségur. We also know that the Templars had some reservations about the Crusade against the Cathars and that some of them even aided the Good Folk. Without assuming a general collusion between the Templars and the Cathars, a certain leniency and even alliances must be acknowledged. In the Razès in particular, property owners suspected of Catharism entrusted their possessions to the Templars out of fear their goods would be seized by the king's agents. It also may well be that following the Cathar debacle a certain number of *patarins,* as they were ironically called, entered the Temple as a refuge.[1] We should not overlook this Foreign Legion aspect of the Templars, especially as it existed at the end of the thirteenth century. These Cathars-turned-Templars actually could have influenced the Temple doctrine—but the Temple had no doctrine, at least officially.

These purely historical remarks are not enough to negate this theory of possible Templar-Cathar adhesion, which must be examined on another level. First, the omission of the words of consecration: According to confessions obtained by the Inquisition, this omission was also prac-

---

1. *Patarins* was the term used to describe the Cathars in Lombardy. —*Trans.*

ticed by certain priests who had secretly been won over by Cathar beliefs. No doubt, there were not many of these, and overall the Templar priests do not appear to have heeded the request to omit the sacramental words.

Next, there is the denial of Jesus, which brings to mind the Cathar rejection of the cross as a symbol because it was the instrument of a God's suffering. It is said nowhere, however, that the Cathars denied Jesus or spat upon the cross. Far from denying him, the Cathars worshiped him as a heavenly being and in no way renounced his embodiment or degradation into flesh. They believed he was the one who showed the path to re-ascension to the kingdom of light. The Templars, if we understand it correctly, denied the God in Jesus and not the man; it was the God-man they rejected. Any analogy between this conception and that of the Cathars is far from convincing.

Next, there was no general initiation procedure to become an exoteric member of the order. If there was an initiation—which is quite probable—it concerned only select members and did not take place until well after reception into the order. Especially significant is that there was no private teaching in the Temple as there was among the Cathars. Nor was there, as among all the heretics, an indoctrination that was sometimes practiced on a large scale.

Then, of course, the Cathars and Templars observed completely different rules by which to live. In the first place, the Cathars refused to fight and spill blood, whereas the Templars were monk-combatants. This seems an irreconcilable difference. Then, of course, the Cathars lived a life of privation, which was not the case with the Templars, who, though they swore an oath of individual poverty, lacked for nothing and were rather wealthy. Third, the Cathars abstained as much as possible from taking part in the ceremonies of the Christian church. If they did so at times, it was simply for the purpose of allaying suspicion. The Templar attitude was exactly opposite this: Even in prison they clamored to attend Mass and to receive the sacraments. It is known that the Cathars abstained from all sacraments and recognized only one, the famous *consolamentum*. Fourth, there was a fundamental difference between the attitudes of Cathars and Templars when facing death. Few among the Cathars renounced their belief, even if it meant being burned at the stake. While there were some "repentant" Cathars who returned to the bosom of the Church, it must be acknowledged that the majority preferred death to the renouncement of their faith. The Templars, however, while denouncing the "evil practices" that had infiltrated the order, in fact only sought to save their own skins. Beginning with the top officials, they were hardly disposed to risk their lives defending the "enormities" mentioned by Jacques de Molay.

Finally, the inquisitors at the beginning of the fourteenth century were very well informed about Cathar doctrine and practices; it was the most current object of their attention. If they had found any concordance between the new heresy they were discovering and the one that was so familiar to them, they would not have failed to say so. The same can be said about Philip the Fair's henchmen. It would have given them great joy to add to their accusations such decisive elements toward convicting the Templars of an abominable heresy. No, it is impossible to claim any Cathar influence upon the Templars. They held two different conceptions of the world that were strictly opposite.

Another hypothesis proposed is that of a Muslim influence, but this too runs into countless contradictions. On a purely material plane concerning the founding and structure of the order, an obvious parallel can be found between the Temple and the Muslim institution of the *ribat,* which were military and religious centers installed on the frontiers of the Muslim world. Voluntary and temporary service with the ribat was an act of asceticism and was considered one of the aspects of duty in the *jihad,* or holy war of Islam. The ribat were particularly numerous in Spain. Thus the analogy between the Temple and Islam remains on the level of structural similarity with regard to the institution of the ribat.

There also have been analogies suggested between the Temple and the famous sect of the Hashshashins, or Assassins, whose existence was revealed only by the book written by Marco Polo after the Hashshashins had disappeared. At the same time the Templar order was founded, a certain Hassan settled in the Caucasus and founded a religious sect of

Shiite inspiration. A branch of this sect was next established in the mountains of Syria. The Old Man of the Mountain, a leader with great authority, directed this mystic community, whose purest and most reliable members, the *fidai,* were called Hashshashins allegedly because they used the drug hashish before undertaking certain operations. Another explanation attributes their name to the word *assassin,* deriving from the Arabic word *assas,* which means "guard." The supporters of the Old Man of the Mountain actually claimed to be the "guardians of the Holy Land," just like the Templars. The word *assassin* passed into contemporary language with its current meaning because the favored method of action of the Old Man and his faithful was terrorist assassination. In any case, it has been established that the Templars had contact, even temporary alliances, with the Old Man's sect on several occasions. The two sides were not always at war in the Holy Land; there were periods of truce when not only material goods but also ideas were exchanged. At times the Christians, seeking to exploit divisions in the Muslim world, would ally with one faction against another. This does not imply there was cultural infusion into the Templars from the Assassins. The Assassins' goal was probably the founding of a vast Ismalian state in Iran with extensions throughout the Middle East. It was the Mongols who burned down their fortresses in 1265 and killed the last Old Man of the Mountain.

It has been claimed that the Assassins followed a mystical doctrine and that they had an extremely well-stocked library in their lair. But because their fortresses were destroyed, it is impossible to advance any kind of supposition. All that is known for certain is that the Old Man's sect was connected to the Ismalian movement, which itself extended from Shiitism. The sect espoused both a kind of neo-Platonism and messianism, rejecting the letter of the Koran in favor of a symbolic interpretation. It's possible this could be considered analogous to the Templars' denial of Jesus as they claimed to be perfect Christians, for in this they were refusing to take the Gospel literally in order to view it as a symbolic text. As for knowing whether or not the Assassins had a direct influence upon the Templars, it is impossible to say. We do know that while there were teaching, discussion of texts, and a fairly long initiation among the

Ismalians, we have discovered no similarities between them and the official, exoteric Temple. No matter how we interpret the denial of Jesus and spitting on the cross, these hardly appear to conform to the Muslim mind-set. Certainly the Muslim world of the time was divided into numerous spiritual families, each with its own interpretation of the texts and its own brand of mysticism. Still, without absolutely rejecting all influence of esoteric Islamic thought on the Templars, we must conclude that we do not know very much on this subject.

Basing their belief on the Templars' war cry, "Long Live God, Holy Love," some have arrived at the conclusion that there were possible contributions to the Templar doctrine from the Christian East, where numerous parallel Christian sects survived, some of which were clearly Gnostic in essence. This hypothesis appears to be the most likely. At this time it was in Cyprus, not in the Holy Land, where the Temple had been, if not invaded, at least influenced by Gnostic ideas. The acceptance of Jesus as a man and not God is specifically Gnostic. At that time, Cyprus was the crucible in which were melted all the Eastern doctrines and legends, including that of the famous "Prester John," Solomon's successor and the perfect model of the priest-king. Didn't the Templars, by virtue of their double-faced nature and membership in two classes (both sacerdotal and warrior, from which the king is drawn), have the long-term goal of creating a universal empire headed by a priest-king, the famous Great Monarch that Philip the Fair dreamed of becoming in his fantasies?

In this area we are forced to resort to conjectures. It is acceptable to believe that the Templars' long sojourn in Cyprus put them in contact with the representatives of numerous more or less secret fraternities that shared in both Eastern Christianity and the Gnostic tradition. But it is impossible to come to any conclusions from this. We should remember that the Temple seems not to have had any doctrine specific to the order. There were merely common practices that the overwhelming majority of the participants did not even understand. Unless we return to the idea of a double Temple with a parallel hierarchy, there are no grounds for talking about a Templar esotericism.

But the question of the denial of Jesus still remains. Even though the majority of the Templar brothers did not understand it, it was incontestably the sole authentic entry into the Temple. In their interrogations the top officials never refuted this—but neither did they say anything on the subject, and in some cases it seems that they died to guard its secret. Was the explanation of this secret too shameful to speak about?

The question or secret obviously concerned Jesus Christ the individual, an extremely delicate subject because, if revealed in a way that disturbed good consciences, it risked becoming a challenge to the entire Roman Catholic Church, its official and exoteric doctrine as well as its structures. The Church, as well as everyone it supported—meaning kings, and especially French kings—was not ready at the beginning of the fourteenth century to see its structures shaken. There were too many material interests at stake. The Roman Catholic Church, with the help of the Capetian monarchy, had broken and crushed Catharism because by its very doctrine as well as its way of life, it had caused the Catholic hierarchy to teeter, along with all its attached material interests. It was thus unthinkable that the top officials of the Temple, who were part of the Catholic hierarchy, could contribute to the destruction of that organization that had brought them wealth and power. The Templars never left the Church and always claimed to be among its most faithful supporters, which is probably true. Hence the ambiguity that surrounds the Temple; hence the law of silence; and hence the total lack of information about the figure of Jesus Christ the individual man, the stumbling block within the entire system. All that survived was an incomprehensible ritual, and likely the Templars were workng with whatever remained of it.

Coptic art rejects any depiction of Christ on the cross. This is a concrete translation of a theological belief found in numerous unclassifiable sects, but that is predominanty influenced by Gnosticism. We also know that early Christianity worshiped only a shining, glorious cross, symbol of eternal perfection, and not the instrument of the torture inflicted on Jesus, King of the Jews, who was condemned to death by the Romans for sedition against the established order. Might this be the reason why all the crucifixes in Catholic churches are covered with a veil on Good Friday? The meaning of this ritual is no longer known or has been given a false interpretation (that it is a sign of mourning). Might it mean that it is not the cross of torture that is worshiped but a symbolic cross, and consequently on the day the event of tortured death is commemorated, its purely historical elements should be hidden?

This would explain why the Templar soldiers considered the denial ceremony and spitting on the cross as a simple dishonorable sacrilege—this group of soldier-monks, truthfully more soldier than monk and necessarily more warrior than theologian, confused the physical nonrepresentation of Christ with this simple rejection of the cross. Recall the words of one of the accused, Gérard du Passage, who declared before the papal commission on April 28, 1310, "This is nothing more than a piece of wood. Our Lord is in Heaven."

If we want a way out of the impasse that is the contradiction between the Templars' clear affirmations of Christianity and their ritual denying of Jesus, this is the only possible solution: The Templars (at least those who formed part of the Templar elite) did not believe in the physical existence of a Jesus, King of the Jews, crucified as the leader of an anti-Roman organization, but instead believed in the permanence of a Christ, a universal and timeless messiah or anointed one, the symbolic Son of God who was the image of what all men (sons of God) should become.

It is easy to see why it would hardly be advisable to spread this idea among the great masses of the faithful. They were probably not capable of understanding this subtle ontological proposition. They were ensnared in the fables of a Gospel taken literally, a Gospel from which the spirit had long been absent. This is why the Templars who knew were so brutally killed. This is why Philip the Fair, who wished to have this secret at his disposal alone, persecuted the Templars so relentlessly. This is why the pope, mindful of preserving the structure of the Church, dropped the Templars.

There is no need to revisit the various theories that have been skillfully crafted concerning the historicity of Jesus Christ. Some say that Jesus was not crucified but that an anonymous condemned prisoner was substituted. This is a familiar tune and the widespread opinion of people as far ranging as Adolf Hitler and Joan of Arc. Some theories suggest that Jesus did not resurrect but that his body was skillfully pilfered from the tomb by his disciples in order to provide grounds for the belief that he had walked from his grave. Sometimes we are told that Jesus had a twin brother and that it was his twin brother whom the disciples saw after Easter, wearing something like tattoos of the stigmata in order to convince doubting Thomas.

All these theories bring out the countless internal contradictions that can be found in the Gospels. In the best cases the Gospels are clumsy compilations. In the worst they are truncated and altered versions that were literally trafficked to justify the prevailing Roman ideology. Taking into account the variations between the text attributed to John and those improperly called Synoptic, the Gospels are, to an objective observer, a tissue of fables that contradict each other. There is no more truth in the Gospels than in any other mythological text, whether Irish, Greek, or Patagonian. But what people generally forget to mention is that there are many truths to be found. It is up to us to discover them.

The issue is not to prove whether or not Jesus existed, or whether or not he was several individuals combined into one. The problem is finding agreement on the definition to be given the Christ. To the large majority of Catholics, the word *Christ* is indissolubly linked to the word *cross*. They are completely surprised to learn that the word *Christ* has no connection whatsoever with *crux*. For them, Christ means "crucified." The source of this belief is solely the Roman Catholic Church. It allowed a fundamental error to establish itself in the minds of the faithful and profits from it greatly by prattling idiotically about it all day long through catechism and sermons so laden with platitudes that no one listens to them anymore. Rustics of earlier times responded to this by leaving the church during the sermon and going to a nearby bar. This was a healthy reaction to the mind-destroying stupefaction offered by so many priests despite the incomparable mission with which they were entrusted. The betrayal by the clergy is not exactly what we might think it is. It is made up of believing that the majority of people could be satisfied with fables when what they need are revelations. This little diatribe is not gratuitous;

it only emphasizes what was going on at the time of the Templar affair.

Already within the Temple the simple knights, squires, and sergeants were regarded as oath-bound slaves who ensured the physical life of the order and its external operations. Behind it was another Temple, more discreet and more occult, but jealous of keeping for its own the metaphysical convictions it possessed. This explains the lack of concern in the higher officials for their brothers who were subjected to torture and threatened with death at the stake. If they had applied the doctrine of brotherhood and enlightenment for which they were the keepers, their actions would have been quite different. But instead they did not wish to speak. They did not want to say why Jesus should not be confused with Christ.

It is customary now in Western spiritual centers (or in those claiming to be) to divide Christ into the historic Christ, the cosmic Christ, and the mystic Christ. But Christ is by himself one and indivisible. At a given historical moment, he was able to appear as a man, whether it was as Jesus or someone else. As such he was the ideal man, the absolute but symbolic model of what every human being should be able to become. He was visible and within the reach of everyone. But the Word he was carrying and that he spread around him went beyond the human condition and into the divine, toward a higher plane that is valid at all times and throughout the whole world. This is the cosmic Christ. Our main task is to integrate him into the self, to recognize him as Being—according to the ontological definition, to consciously assimilate ourselves into this Being, and this is where the mystic Christ appears. All of this is contained in nothing more or less than a phrase repeated ceaselessly by the Church, but one which it definitely refrains from explaining and putting into practice: *Live in Christ.*

Instead the Church incarcerates the faithful in a straitjacket of concrete realities or, in other words, appearances, leading the faithful to worship Jesus Christ the man, even whimpering over his misfortunes and imitating them with self-imposed privations and absurd torments—imprisoning themselves within that humanness. The preachers go one better. They declare Christ came to earth to save mankind, but let's not be naïve. If Christ had saved the world in the *mechanist* way (a term borrowed from the rationalist philosophy of the nineteenth century), the way accepted by the majority of the Catholic faithful, and if these same faithful were actually saved, they would no longer be living as they do—that is, in a manner that is absolutely contrary to the spirit of Christ's teachings. The Catholic faithful ceaselessly repeat the sacrifice of the cross, a shameful capital execution. The Catholic faithful mope and practice acts of mortification with dubious masochistic connotations that are detrimental to the ascent of the Spirit. Yet everything still remains to be done. Man is not yet saved and Christ is the model of the salvation that all men should realize. But this Christ is not the Jesus who died on the cross; he is a Christ who was never born and never died because he can only be born through the Spirit. The faith of the first Christians was clearly diverted, the better to subjugate them.[2] Instead of being shown the path of salvation, they were shown the wooden cross and steps were taken to make them kneel before its ill-shaped debris, the origin of which is more than suspect. Who is really idolatrous: the Templars before their so-called baphomet or the faithful of the Roman Catholic Church who worship a piece of wood from who knows where?

The founders of the Temple and their successors, those who had access to a certain secret Rule, were probably aware of all this. For them the Christ was timeless and the Tomb of Christ existed everywhere and nowhere. Hence the ritual of the denial of Jesus—as a crucified man—and the spitting on the cross. Unfortunately, those who knew refrained from explaining to the others, no doubt the better to dominate them, starting with their own brother Templars. This parallel hierarchy of the Temple, whose existence behind appearances seems incontestable, had a mission to fulfill, but this mission was diverted to material ends, betraying both the brothers of the Temple and all Christian people, including Bernard of Clairvaux. It finally met the fate it deserved, but it dragged many innocent people along with it into the pyres of the Inquisition.

---

2. See Jacques Ellul, *La Subversion de Christianisme* (Paris: Le Seuil, 1984). This work by a Calvinist theologian casts light on the mechanisms that led to the complete alteration of the Christic message.

11

The Symbolism of the Templars

EVERY INITIATORY SOCIETY—that is, one based on certain knowledge transmitted to its members in an elitist or hierarchical manner—uses specific signs and various symbols that crystallize certain doctrinal points or that detail in coded form the necessary means for advancement.

One question immediately arises in regard to this subject and the Order of the Templars: Was the Temple an initiatory society? Apparently not, as nothing in its organization seems to have rested on any preparatory teaching, trials, or degrees of knowledge, except for the famous secrecy demanded on the operation of the chapter houses and the insistence on confession only to the chaplains of the order. There were revelations made over the course of the trial that suggested a parallel hierarchy that hid its particular knowledge from the other members of the order. If we accept the reality of this hierarchy and the existence of an initiatory knowledge, we then must discover the coded language of the Temple, the symbolic lexicon that was reserved for the specific use of only those capable of understanding it.

The first potential source of symbolism that comes to mind is Templar architecture. From the time of Violet le Duc and Prosper Merimée, it has been acknowledged that traces of hermetic symbolism can be found in Templar churches, especially those with a polygonal central rotunda. Countless studies have been written on this topic, each striving to prove that this or that church reveals a meaning hidden from the vulgar, the key for which, of course, they are quite determined to provide. But we must tread carefully in this area. As has been shown by Elie Lambert,[1] not only were the majority of churches classified as Templar not, in fact, built by the Templars—or even for them—but many of the chapels, houses, fortresses, and even certain churches they did actually build were generally constructed by merely adopting the style specific to their time. Accordingly, both Gothic and Romanesque Templar sanctuaries can be found, which does not allow us to draw any conclusions. All that can be said is that the Templars appear to have favored and encouraged the appearance of Gothic art. But the masterpieces of Gothic art have no deeper a connection with the Templars than those of Romanesque art.

In fact, the churches built around a central square or rotunda are the exception among the religious constructions of the Templars and, furthermore, are not specific to the order. The few known examples are the very carefully kept buildings in the most important commanderies. The only example in the Middle East that can be numbered among this type is the twelve-sided chapel of the imposing fortress of Château-Pèlerin. Incidentally, this exceptional monument has provided the reference for those seeking in Gisors Castle a typical Templar construction oriented toward the twelve signs of the zodiac. The similarity between the zodiac and the chapel of Château-Pèlerin cannot be denied—but what does this prove? Were the Templars the only ones to possess knowledge of astrology? The entire Middle Ages was steeped in it, and the number of monuments built in relation to the houses of the zodiac or the position of the sun at certain times of the year are countless.

We do know that the original church of the Paris Temple was a rotunda with a dome supported by six columns. There is none similar in France but others like it can be found in England, London in particular. On the other hand, the Templar chapel of Laon—which is quite well preserved—has a fairly characteristic octagonal form. We are thus faced

---

1. E. Lambert, "L'Architecture des Templiers," *Bulletin monumental,* no. 112 (1954). See also the special issue of the review *Archeologia* (1969), as well as Régine Pernoud, *Les Templiers,* 34–46.

with two different types of architecture. The rotunda, obviously, is derived from the Holy Sepulcher of Jerusalem. As an architectural form it is incontestably charged with meaning: It is the image of the universe and also, from the esoteric point of view, is the very place where all cosmic energies combine, the equivalent of the cranium, where occur all the delicate transmutations of matter into mind. But this kind of edifice enjoyed only a very small diffusion in the Templar Order. It cannot be claimed that it is a Templar style, or even a style imposed by the Templars.

The same holds true for the polygonal churches that have nothing in common with the Holy Sepulcher. It was once thought possible to connect them to the model of the Temple of the Lord in Jerusalem, the famous Dome of the Rock, which is an octagon. Here again the symbolism is clear-cut: The number eight is traditionally connected to the idea of resurrection, which is why octagonal architecture is frequently found in the funeral chapels of cemeteries and, more generally, in all the sanctuaries built in memory of a saint or martyr. The Templars, for reasons that escape us, willingly adopted this type of architecture, but it cannot be said that it is specific to the order. If we were to take a census of the chapels built by the Templars, we would note that the rotunda and octagonal forms are nothing more than quite remarkable exceptions.

So what is the type of construction most common in the works of the Templar Order? A very simple rectangular form. If we were to accept the existence of a Templar style, we would discover that it is distinguished by its extreme simplicity or even sobriety bordering on the austere. It reminds us that at the time of its origin, the Temple was part of the Cistercian movement, and the Cistercian sanctuaries were characterized by an almost complete lack of embellishment and ornamentation.

Overall, the Templar chapels can be classified into two groups. The first group consists of rectangular chapels with a single nave, fifteen to twenty yards long by five to seven yards wide, and thick walls flanked by flat buttresses. The bays are narrow, generally grouped in threes, and the chevet is flat. The building is covered by a broken barrel vault with repeating cylindrical arches that determine the number of rows in the nave, most frequently three. It is clear that the number three was knowingly used, no doubt to indicate an idea of eternity—and not to represent the Holy Trinity, as has been claimed too often. The tripling of certain motifs is probably of remote Celtic origin and corresponds to a tradition that lived for a long time in the memories of builders and artists.

The type of chapel with a flat chevet was not widespread. It is most commonly found in central and southwest France and is the only type to be found in Gironde and Lot-et-Garonne, though it is also common in Charente-Maritime, in Poitou, in the Berry, and in northern Burgundy.

The second group consists of rectangular chapels with a chevet that terminates in an apse. This group seems to be the more common and can be found throughout France from Comminges to Brittany and from Navarre to Burgundy. The general structure of these chapels is absolutely identical to those with a flat chevet. It involves only one variation, and because there is no need to interpret the chevet by any other criterion than local style, it can be said that the demi-cupola apse often utilizes a portion of the available terrain.

But the sculpted decor of these chapels is absolutely rudimentary, whether the chevet is flat or forms an apse. If we are looking for symbolism, the details of the construction offer the best field of examination without requiring us to fall into delirious interpretation. All the oratories are oriented precisely in an east–west direction, rather than in the direction of Jerusalem, which is located to the southeast. In this they express a specifically Western orientation of Celtic origin. The east is in front, symbolizing birth, origins, and the primordial deity. The south is on the right and symbolizes light, the divine force in action, and life. Behind is the west, death, the Other World. On the left is the north, the negative side traditionally attributed to malefic forces. There is never any opening on the north side. This is no doubt primarily for material reasons: to provide protection against the cold or even to allow for the attachment of the sanctuary to other monastic buildings. But overlying this utility is a symbolic meaning, for even when there is no building attached to the north side, this wall is blind. It is obviously not a strictly Templar custom and can be found in many other sanctuaries.

There are always three bays on the east side, whether the chevet is flat or forms an apse. The central bay begins lower down and climbs higher than the other two. Might this be for the sake of harmony? There is only one opening on the west side, situated where the wall is leveled. One or two windows admit light into the nave from the south side. It seems that this basic outline is followed in the majority of chapels attributed to the Templars.

The exterior of the chapel is always quite simple. The entry portal, obviously located on the west, is formed by one or several arches in the middle, most often topped by an archivolt, with the entire construction resting on an abacus supported by small columns with molded bases. The archivolt is sometimes adorned with garlands or even a ribbon surcharged with diamond-shaped nail heads. In certain cases the capitals are decorated with foliage and crockets. But there are two motifs among these that are repeated and seem to be characteristic: sculptures depicting the Annunciation and two birds on either side of the cup from which both are drinking. This latter theme certainly appears to be of Templar inspiration and is reminiscent of the seal depicting two knights riding the same horse. Here again we find the compound group and traditional alchemical symbolism. It remains to be learned what meaning it had for the artists who worked for the Templars. It has often been seen, of course, as a depiction of the Grail. But there is hardly a convincing case to be made for this speculation. Every time a vase or a cup on a monument invites commentary, it is unfailingly connected to the Grail with no clear idea of just exactly what this illustrious Holy Grail was.

Some of the chapels contained paintings at one time, several of which still remain. The most famous are those of the Cressac Chapel (Charente), which depict armored knights fighting the Saracens. But these knights are regular Crusaders, not Templars, but in the background we can distinguish three Templars emerging from a city. These frescoes are undoubtedly the result of a generous donation from one seeking to immortalize his own feats. On the other hand, the frescoes of the San Bevignate of Perugia church in Italy seem clearly the work of the Templars, though it cannot be said that these paintings, nor the numerous remnants found elsewhere, were characteristic of a specifically

Templar art. Only the frequency of certain motifs indicates the Templar influence.

The theme of the Annunciation and that of the two birds have already been noted. But to these we can add the image of the two serpents. Countless depictions of the sun and moon have also been found, which suggests nothing original. There is also a cord motif, which brings to mind the denounced Templar gesture of placing a cord around the neck of a so-called idol before giving it to a new brother. Also common is the image of an abundance of dog roses, and the image of the lily, which seems to have enjoyed great favor. Generally speaking, though, there is nothing in the chapels that can be attributed specifically to the order, nothing truly remarkable that can lend credence to the belief in the existence of a particular Templar symbolism. As in architecture, the Templars used the same methods and symbolic figures used by the other monastic orders and initiatory soceties of their era for the transmission of certain coded messages.

There has been much written about the famous graffiti in the Coudray Tower of Chinon Castle as well as the symbols discovered in one of the wall towers of Domme (Dordogne). These images, which were never intended as art, offer interesting testimony because they were carved by imprisoned Templars. In Chinon the prisoners included Jacques de Molay and the top officials of the order as well as some brother servants, so the symbols do provide food for thought.

Found in the embrasures of the Coudray Tower, these graffiti include inscriptions, coats of arms, and different motifs whose symbolic value is very real, although their actual meaning is open to debate. The principal motifs are a cross surmounting both pierced and unpierced circles; Solomon's seal; spiral S shapes that are no doubt what is known as the *sol invictus,* the "unvanquished sun," symbol of the cyclical divine light that appears to die but then emerges from the darkness; a double character that resembles the Oriental yin-yang symbol; the three marks characteristic of the ancient brotherhood of builders; three interlaced circles that are pierced through the center; eight-rayed stars set in squares or shields known as carbuncles in heraldry; a symbol formed by two triangles meeting at their points; different styles of reversed crescents; and especially hearts that are radiating or are topped by bulges that may well be oversimplified depictions of flowers or flames. These hearts have attracted the lion's share of attention from specialists.

In fact the radiating heart is, in the Catholic religion, the emblem of the Sacred Heart, though at the time of the Templars, this worship had not yet been officially established. It seems, then, that it might be the symbol of the center of the Integral Being, of warmth and light in the Western tradition as well as the Islamic tradition, in which it signifies the fire of intelligence and love. We might ask if these radiating hearts are illustrations of the Templar's battle cry: "Long Live God, Holy Love!"

One such heart is topped by four oval leaves that might easily be taken for a flower. It is possible that this might simply be the stone worker's symbol, like those that can be seen in certain cathedrals of central Europe. But it could also be interpreted as a kind of Grail, or at least an object containing all the riches of the world and from which emerge plants representing life. In Brittany there is an image like this in the megalithic monument of Gavrinis (Morbihan), a kind of heart from which stems are sprouting. But this mysterious carving dates from at least 2500 B.C. It is true, however, that symbols are ageless and are constantly reused by different ideologies that follow one another. It should be noted that local legend in Gavrinis claims that Templars living on the nearby Île-aux-Moines sometimes visited the isle of Gavrinis, where they kept a house. Inside the tumulus mound there can be found three holes connected in such a way that we can place our hand through all of them at once. It is said that the Templars were held prisoner there and clasped hands through these holes.

On the right side of the monument of Gavrinis there is a very skillfully carved hand on the first stone. From the enchanting hand of prehistoric grottoes, to the hand of benediction, to the hand of glory found in German tradition, this sign signifies many magical or religious purposes. It may be a summons or a gesture of recognition, unless it is again a worker's signature. The question remains open. I'll add that this hand is near a double ax, an unusual but symbolic tool, the form of which can be found in the francisque.[2]

Other graffiti depict the Cross and other elements from the Passion. It is possible that a figure holding a lance recalls the Grail theme, perhaps the Grail Procession in which Perceval saw a young man carrying a lance spilling drops of blood. But couldn't it also be the spear of the centurion Longinus, who, according to tradition, stabbed Christ in the side? Here we find more origins of the Christian version of the quest for the Holy Grail. It's important to ask if the Templars, who were not intellectuals and professed to disdain profane distractions, had even heard of this profane Grail legend, which was, in fact, restricted to an aristocratic audience.

It is quite hard to form an opinion on the graffiti from Chinon. There can be no question of their origin, but they contribute no convincing evidence of a secret code of signs and images the Templars may have used. Truthfully, all these depictions couldn't possibly be any more orthodox.[3]

Those images found in the wall towers of Domme, where Templar brothers were also imprisoned for a fairly long period, offer much the same information. These graffiti have been carefully studied,[4] but no definitive conclusions may be drawn. Certain observations are vital, however: Only in Domme has the importance of the symbol of the cross to the Templars appeared so obvious. While the bare cross does not appear at all amid all the imagery of the Passion, it can be found above, with the sun and moon. This would be a very standard representation if the Virgin at the foot of the cross had not been replaced by a male figure who is not St. John, but who seems to be catching in a container a drop of blood from Christ's arm. We might consider him to be Joseph of Arimathea collecting Christ's blood in the Grail, according to the Christian version of the legend. But the graffito is far from clear, and furthermore, based on the very text of this legend, it was not from Christ's arm that Joseph

2. The double-bladed ax used by the Vichy government as its symbol. —*Trans.*

3. "Symbolique Templière," *Atlantis*, no. 216 (1963).

4. *Archeologia*, nos. 32, 33, and 38 (1970–1971).

collected the blood, but from his side speared by Longinus. None of this appears very convincing.

In at least one case a depiction of the Crucifixion shows the victim flanked by two other crosses that have been barely scratched onto the wall's surface, and which are interpreted as being those of the two thieves. However, it is curious to note that while the cross located behind the Virgin is an ordinary cross with pointed ends, that behind St. John includes two branches at an angle above the horizontal branch. These three crosses are, without question, exact copies of the Templar cross, which is often depicted.

In Domme, the crosses that are depicted alone are of different types. There is the pointed Latin cross, the lower portion of which is placed on a kind of knoll. Also seen are Greek crosses with branches of equal length, some pointed and some without points and some pointed and "stationed" together with Latin crosses having sharp ends and lower halves that come to a kind of three-pronged fork. These crosses, as well as the Crucifixion scenes, are classic depictions with hardly any alterations from those perfectly orthodox representations seen everywhere, even taking into account details that appear to be linked to the carvers' memories of what they read or heard.

What is odd about the Domme graffiti is how they cause the fundamental contradiction of the Templars to appear: On the one hand, the Templars denied Jesus and spat on the cross; on the other, they frequently drew crosses and Crucifixion scenes while imprisoned. Their drawings sometimes included inscriptions that seem to echo this contradiction: "This is my food and I believe in it," one has carved, speaking of the Eucharist; and another offers a kind of curse against the pope: "Clement, destroyer of the Temple." These read as both a protest to and a profession of faith in the Catholic doctrine. Ought we to conclude from them that the Templars incarcerated at Domme were not in on the Templar secret?

Alas, these representations, moving as they may be, provide us little information on a possible Templar symbology. It is always tempting to interpret a sign in one way or another, all the more so because symbols can hold multiple meanings depending on their context. But we find here the same contradiction that we find in other areas: The Templars seemed to have been made to say things they never could have thought. Though Philip the Fair's agents managed never to find a single baphomet in any of the Templar establishments, posterity has taken it upon itself to discover many—including the baphomet of Saint-Merri Church in Paris. We know this particular example is a sculpture dating from the restoration of the church, a stone carver's little joke. It is simply a devil figure, as is often found on medieval churches and cathedrals. But it does seem that for the last century or more a rich harvest has been made of these baphomets. Even the most minor gargoyle has been transformed into one. Even the most insignificant grimacing figure has been merged, without any proof, into the Templars' idol. Some seekers have even sought baphomets in nature, in places that were certainly sanctuaries at one time, but in a much earlier era. Some people have discoverd strange open-mouthed sculptures, and have claimed with certainty that they are baphomets. We must realize, however, that this representation of an open-mouthed deity—the screaming God or the god of eloquence—goes back to the times of the Gallo-Romans or the Gauls or even prehistoric peoples. If the Templars had truly practiced the bizarre worship of an equally bizarre idol resembling a bearded head, it would have been an image they found in folk tradition, where it likely served as merely a symbol. The severed head of Bran the Blessed survived for a long time in popular memory.

As we can see, none of this provides any argument in favor of a symbolism that is exclusively Templar or in favor of art that is particularly Templar. But this does not mean that the Templars did not play a role in the evolution of twelfth- and thirteenth-century architecture, art, and symbolism. They did, we will recall, have contact with the East, from which they returned with new ideas, new concepts, and sometimes new men. Assuming that among those whom they protected and who worked for them there were numerous architects, masons, and stone carvers, as well as many artisans and artists, there is no reason why the customs of the Christian West would not have been influenced. The

Templars first used the vocabulary of the Romanesque style that marked the era in which they began their existence. They next turned to Gothic art because it no doubt corresponded better to the needs of the time. Here some remarks are called for concerning the extraordinary blossoming of Gothic art.

The Templars were not, as is too often repeated, though with no proof, the inventors of the Gothic cathedral. Others took care of this for them. But it is an incontestable fact that they encouraged the construction and spread of the Gothic model, mainly through the expedient of the builder guilds connected to them. The Gothic sanctuary represented a complete break with the Romanesque model, not so much architecturally speaking—Gothic architects simply resolved with new technology (intersecting ribs on the vaults, flying buttresses) the problem of the stability of the walls—but with its reference to the new Gothic ideology.

The Romanesque church is a place of meditation, prayer, and concentration that folds back in upon itself. It permits the individual to blossom and allows for direct contact between the individual and the deity in a somber environment. In a word, the Romanesque edifice is an interior, individualist sanctuary exhibiting a mystery reinforced by architectural elements and plastic representations, inherited from the Gauls, that are clearly symbolic and essentially esoteric. Among these are the rotunda dome, the form and placement of the pillars, and the strange figuring of the capitals. Gothic art, in contrast, emphasizes light, soaring forms, and vastness. It is no longer an individual sanctuary but a collective temple where a community—visible and easily monitored, thanks to the light—gathers. There is no more mystery or secrecy—though the vibrant faith of the constructors of the cathedrals could, in fact, be unwitting obedience to a concealed intention to more easily dominate a crowd of faithful by gathering them together in a structured mass in which each individual can find his place in relationship to those around him. There is no more individual meditation here, and thus no more need for interior symbolism; the emphasis on the interior has been eliminated by the vast structure that overwhelms the individual, but may no longer thrill his soul. It may be noticed that the symbols and esoteric motifs of the Gothic cathedral have been pushed out of the interior of the building to find refuge outside—namely, on the porches. The esotericism of the Christian temple is now outside; distrusted, it has thus become profane. The Gothic cathedral belonged to a new world, a universal world certainly ruled more than ever before by God, but whose earthly—and fleshly—representative could well have been the embodiment of the famous Great Monarch that Philip the Fair dreamed of becoming.

From what we do know, the Templar Order pursued this goal of a universal world. By extending its vast web over the Western world, it aimed at nothing less than the establishment of that universal kingdom symbolized so perfectly by the gathering of the faithful in the Gothic cathedral, where they stand ready to listen to a sermon that will not suffer any contradiction. Here there is nothing individual or separate. Meditation and prayer are collective, as they are with the Cistercians, whose worthy sons the Templars were. And in the decor there is nothing either complicated or mysterious; such decoration might inspire *delectatio morosa*, or interpretations not in conformance with official doctrine.

Here is sufficient evidence to cast doubt on the possible existence of a Templar symbolism. It would have been totally contrary to their mission of "gathering in clarity," or at least gathering while leaving in ignorance those with no need to know. If there was any clerical treason, it is among the Templars that we should begin looking for it.

12

The Temple and the Grail

EVERY ERA SITUATES ITSELF in relation to a "time of origins," as Mircea Eliade labeled the dawn of humanity. But the epic, like the myths from which it gains narrative support, reactualizes ceaselessly, borrowing ideas from the past that are deemed opportune to bring back from the shadows of memory. The history of the Templars that is known, authentic, and not open to debate possesses obvious similarities to an epic: the presence of knightly combat, a noble ideal to defend, the struggle between good and evil, the intervention of mysterious forces, and the impassioned quest for a mysterious object, whether it be a treasure, a secret saved from the Flood, or a magical formula that, when used correctly, is capable of transforming the world. Like the fabled King Arthur, who was no king but a simple leader of knights; like Charlemagne, who did not have a flowing beard; like Alexander the Great, who, during the entire Middle Ages, was regarded as a High initiate, the Templars have crossed out of history to enter into the tumultuous cycle of myth.

Myth, however, should not be considered as simple invention. Myth is a reality that is as powerful as any historical event because it is immanent and can materialize ceaselessly in the most varied forms. It is an unvariable and unvarying mental structure that forms part of humanity's legacy. When it incarnates, it necessarily does so in comprehensible and tangible realities for the era in which it reappears. No one today would deny that it was by virtue of the myth reactualized in the legend of the *Iliad* that a German archaeologist was able to rediscover the authentic remains of Troy. Yet historians of previous times mocked the childishness found in the mythological tales and countless legends of humanity. But we must tread cautiously in this domain. We should especially not forget that history as it is taught, with its incontestable bits of information, transports a number of myths that are unfathomable at first hearing, and that historical figures are often, even against their will, the incarnations of myths that are no longer remembered but continue to stir in the shadows of human consciousness.

Everyone has heard of the golden apples from the Garden of the Hesperides. We know that Hercules won these golden apples from the daughters of Atlas, whose Garden of the Hesperides (clearly indicating that it was west of the known world) was defended by a mighty dragon and the even mightier giant Anteus. The names of Atlas and Anteus give reason to believe there is a connection between this place and the land of Atlantis as recounted by Plato. The same kinds of connections can be made from the golden fleece. It was won by Jason—with the help of the sorceress Medea—from the strange folk living in the Caucasus, the same site where legend says Prometheus was chained for having stolen fire from heaven to give to humanity. What could be hidden behind this?

The Templars, widely known for their heroic feats as well as their mysteries, inspired the hatching of a veritable legend spread by both historians and dreamers over the course of the centuries. Both groups combine in a "dark and profound union." It is not surprising, then, to find that the Temple has been integrated into the myth from the era of its flowering, if only into the Grail legend. Of course, there is no need to waste any time determining whether or not the Templars were victims of metaphysical daydreams. It is not they who hold the responsibility for the integration of their order into one of the most enigmatic traditional tales known to humanity. But the fact that they have been thus connected, and that this connection was established at a time when the order still existed, should give us food for thought.

To tell the truth, the Templars appear in only one of the many versions of the Grail legend—and as secondary rather than central figures.[1] This is the German version by Wolfram von Eschenbach, an early-thirteenth-century Bavarian writer. We might immediately observe that in this context it would be more likely to find the presence of the Teutonic Knights rather than the Templars. But for Wolfram von Eschenbach, the Templars are the knights who, with the mysterious Anfortas, the Fisher King, are charged with guarding the Holy Grail in a castle bearing the name Montsalvaesche, meaning "Mount Salvation," or, more likely, Savage Mountain.

Let us go back to the text itself, specifically to the chapter in which Parzival (Perceval) is the guest of the hermit Trevrizent, who turns out to be his maternal uncle. Trevrizent explains the mysteries of the Grail to the young hero:

> This is something I know well. Valiant knights dwell at the Castle of Montsalvaesche, where the Grail is kept. These are the Templars who often ride to far lands in quest of adventure. Whether they win glory or find humiliation in their battles, they accept it with a tranquil heart as expiation of their sins. In this castle resides a band of proud warriors. I would like to tell you what they live on. Everything they eat comes from a precious stone whose essence is complete purity. If you do not know what it is, I will tell you: It is called the *lapsit exillis*.[2] It is by virtue of this stone that the phoenix can be consumed by fire and burnt to ashes yet be reborn from these ashes.

---

1. I have gathered together some documentation concerning the different and sometimes conflicting versions of the Grail legend in a chapter of *Montségur et l'énigme cathare* (Paris: Pygmalion, 1986), 267–72. Everything I say there about the Cathars and their connection with the Grail legend is equally valid for the Templars, at least as information. Concerning the overall topic of the Grail legend, I have made a complete study based on all the available sources in order to demonstrate the specific features of each version, which obey a personal motivation or interpretation through a predetermined context. See J. Markale, *The Grail* (Rochester, Vt.: Inner Traditions, 1999).

2. A term mistranslated by Wolfram that has since given rise to numerous interpretations. The explanation that seems to be the best is *lapsis e coelis,* meaning "stone (fallen) from the sky," which hearkens back to the tradition of the Ka'aba in Mecca. This is the only version of the legend in which the Grail is a stone. In the others the Grail is more often a cup, a bowl, a chalice, or, in the Welsh version, a platter holding a man's head bathed in blood.

It is by virtue of this stone that the phoenix molts to reappear in all its glory, as beautiful as before. There is no man so ill who, brought into the presence of this stone, will not be assured of escaping death for an entire week following the day on which he saw it. He who sees it ceases to age. This stone gives a man such vigor that his skin and bones immediately regain their youth. Its other name is the Grail.[3]

We can immediately notice that the mysterious object, whatever its origins, that gives nourishment, strength, and health to the Templars charged with guarding it is somewhat comparable to the head the Templars were accused of worshiping and which, according to certain testimonies, brought them prosperity and good harvests. Could the famous baphomet then be identified as the Grail? At first glance, yes—but let's not forget that the baphomet does not exist as an actual material object. It is purely symbolic and would appear only within the framework of a liturgical fiction whose content has been lost to us and that the majority of the Templars did not understand. Intimidation took care of the rest: The accused described in good faith a head that had never been presented to them except within the form of what was a well-articulated narrative that, if discovered, would certainly go far in revealing the solution to the mystery. But this hardly matters. The fact is that there is a clear analogy between the head of the Templars and the Grail described by Wolfram, especially if we look to the Welsh version of the legend, in which the Grail is a head bathed in blood and carried on a platter.

But this does not imply that the Templars were personally responsible for this similarity. We must find out why Wolfram von Eschenbach believed he himself was authorized to establish such a clear, precise link between the Templars, who in his time still enjoyed an excellent reputation and had not been accused of any misdeed, and the Grail tradition, a tradition of Celtic origin that the German writer revised and corrected with a purposely esoteric slant. If we are to believe Wolfram, this Grail

---

3. *Parzival*, vol. 2, translated by Ernest Tonnelat (Paris: Aubier-Montaigne, 1934), 36–37.

was utterly orthodox, and consequently the Templars could not be suspected of heresy:

> On this day [the Grail] receives from on high that which gives it its greatest virtue. Today is Good Friday. This is the day one can see a white dove soar down from the sky. It carries a small white host and places it on the stone. Radiantly white, the dove resumes its soaring flight back into heaven. Every Good Friday it brings, as I have told you, the sacred object that gives the stone the virtue of providing the best drink and the best dishes of any whose aroma has been spread in this world. Paradise has nothing more delicious. I am speaking here of fruits produced by the earth. Furthermore, the stone gives its guardians game of all sorts: animals that breathe air and can be seen flying or running, or even fish who swim through the waters. This is the emolument that, thanks to its secret virtues, the Grail provides its knightly brotherhood.[4]

We find ourselves again faced with the perpetual contradiction of the Templars. They are nourished, symbolically speaking, by the Eucharist. But how can this be reconciled with the non-recognition of a Jesus God, which seems to have been proved by the ritual of denial? Certainly this text shows that the Templars had a reputation for eating and drinking well, but that does not resolve the contradiction. Evidently, according to Wolfram von Eschenbach, these were strictly orthodox knights who declared their faith in the physical presence of Jesus and even made it the pivot around which their life was organized. They would be nothing without that dove who brings the host to the stone on Good Friday, the day of the Crucifixion, a day that, however, they appeared to reject. The image of the dove carrying the host hearkens, of course, to the well-known tradition of the vial containing the sacred oil that was carried to Reims by a mysterious dove, symbol of the Holy Ghost.

Might these be elements from a ritual concerning the sacred nature

---

4. Ibid., 37.

of kings? This has been suggested quite often with regard to the Grail quest. In many respects, the search for the sacred object through a series of initiatory ordeals and the enthronement of the Grail hero are the manifest proof of a ceremony concerning royalty. Its origin is easily recognized in different myths from a variety of traditions. The Celtic ritual can be deduced from what we know of it through Irish texts: It includes the presence of a magic stone, the Stone of Tara, which shouts when someone who will be named king sits upon it. This is the famous Fal Stone, a phallic stone if ever there was one, which was allegedly transported to Scotland, where it became the Stone of Scone and served at the coronation of Scottish sovereigns before being incorporated into the enthronement ceremonies of British sovereigns.

The form the object takes hardly matters—it may be a stone, a vessel, or a head. What interests us is the presence of the Templars in this legend. Where did they come from? Surely their recruitment did not at all follow the standard procedures of the Temple. Wolfram recounts this strange story:

> As for this who are summoned to the presence of the Grail, I would like to tell you how they may be recognized. On the edge of the stone a mysterious inscription will appear that says the name of those who—young men or maidens—are designated to make this blessed journey. The removal of this inscription does not require it be scratched out because it vanishes before the very eyes of those who see it as soon as they have read the name. All the grown men to be seen in this castle came there as children. Happy the mother who has given birth to a child destined to serve the Grail! Poor and rich rejoice alike when they are told they must send their child to join this holy band. The elect are sought after in the most diverse countries. They are then and forever more protected from sinful thoughts whence shame is born, and they receive from heaven a beautiful reward: When their life on earth has ended, they will enjoy supreme bliss above.[5]

---

5. Ibid., 37–38.

There is something quite odd about all of this: What Wolfram is telling us concerns the Grail guardians, who are Knights Templar. But women are included among them, as are boys and girls, who are received in their band as children. This appears contrary to Templar custom, despite the testimony of Brother Ponsard de Gisy, preceptor of the House of Payns, on November 27, 1309.

> Item, the masters who create the brothers and sisters of the Temple obtain from the aforementioned sisters promises of obedience, chastity, and poverty and the aforementioned masters promise them faith and loyalty as to their sisters . . . Item, when the aforementioned sisters entered the order, the aforementioned masters took their virginity and that of the other sisters who were of a certain age and who thought to be entering the order for the salvation of their soul. The masters must have had their way with them by force, and the aforementioned sisters had children and the aforementioned masters made their children brothers of the order.

It is true that we have seen better than this in certain medieval and Renaissance convents. There are numerous, varied, and overwhelming testimonies to this effect and from Rabelais we can see that it was not always mere slander. Ponsard de Gisy's deposition may be considered more than suspect because it was obtained through torture. However, because there is never smoke without fire, we may ask how far his confession was from an accurate description of the abuses observed in certain Templar establishments.

That said, the Order of the Temple was never open to women. It is for that fact that the Templars had the reputation of practicing homosexuality. However, the Temple sometimes included women in its activity. If, for instance, a widow who was alone and childless wished to give herself to the Temple, she was most often accepted, but as a *donat*, meaning an associated outside member who did not take part in monastic life. An example of this was a noblewoman from Roussillon named Azaïs, who made a gift of her fief to the order and promised to serve the Templars exactly as did countless artisans, farmers, and workers of that time. Some documents mention sisters of the order, but when the context is examined, they are seen merely to be women who have taken monastic vows before a bishop associated with the Temple. There is absolutely nothing to be found that contradicts the absolute prohibition of Templar brothers from associating with women. Nonetheless, the details recounted by Wolfram von Eschenbach remain quite disturbing, and all the more so because the entire tale of Parzival turns around a shameful wound received by King Anfortas, guilty of having loved a woman not worthy of him, and is bathed in a bizarre atmosphere of gaily blended mysticism and sexuality.

But what is important in this story is the mysterious and definitely magical way in which the new guardians of the Grail are recruited. It seems that these Templars are members of a particularly closed and extremely secret society. It is not a caste, which would presume that membership was based on birth, or a college, which assumes selection through co-optation, or even a brotherhood, which assumes, as with the Templars, admission on merits determined by the other members of the society. The choice is made here in totally magical fashion and depends in no way upon the Grail guardians themselves. Wolfram's Templars are an elect selected by an unknown criterion and destined to fulfill equally mysterious missions. It is purely and simply what is called an *elite corps*. This idea, transparent through Wolfram's entire narrative, is amplified in Wagner's opera *Parzifal*. It is not surprising, then, that *Parzifal* was Adolf Hitler's favorite work and that he planned to have it performed on the day of the Third Reich's final victory. The connotations of Wolfram's Templars are quite alarming, because they cannot help but bring to mind certain specialized corps that were in great favor during the Nazi period. We cannot help thinking, as well, of secret societies like Thule, which preceded the ascent of Nazism and provided its ideological and mythological framework.

The question that arises can be stated thus: Was Wolfram consciously aware of what he was doing when he presented the Grail guardians, who are Templars, as members of an extremely closed and secret elite corps?

This is an important question because it can allow an explanation for the sensibility of the historic Templars to emerge. If the answer is yes, it implies that Wolfram knew the Temple constituted a secret society with precise plans for world domination. But before we attempt to determine the answer, it would be a good idea to refer to other passages from Wolfram's work:

> There are angels who did not wish to take part when the struggle began between Lucifer and the Holy Trinity. All of these good and noble angels were constrained by God to come down to earth and assume guardianship of the stone. And the stone remained pure. I do not know if God forgave these angels, or if He damned them. If His justice allowed it, then He summoned them back to His side. Since that time the stone has been guarded by those appointed by God Himself and to whom He has sent one of His angels.[6]

The theme here is notably Cathar.[7] If we understand correctly, the Templars, who are chosen by God to guard the Grail, are the equivalent of angels. Here is pure elitism, not to mention Calvinism before the fact. God makes the decision—a perfectly orthodox Christian expression, but with a singular nuance: God has become an elitist, choosing only those who seem pure enough to protect the purity of the stone. There is an idea of the conservation of racial purity in this story. But that is not all:

> Within this castle dwells a noble brotherhood. Its members, through valiant force of arms, have warded off men from all lands who approach the Grail, save those whom the inscription at Montsalvaesche has designated as being invited to join this Holy Company.[8]

In this we can see not only elitism but also the removal, if not out-

6. Ibid., 38.

7. Jean Markale, *Montségur et l'énigme cathare,* 265–88.

8. *Parzival,* translated by Ernest Tonnelat, 39.

right elimination, of all those who have not been designated to take part in the Feast of the Grail yet seek to do so. In one of Wolfram's much lesser known texts, a poem entitled *Titurel,* which relates the history of the ancestors of Anfortas, thus also Parzival, we may find some extremely interesting details. It is still the Templars who are included, but here they are more than ever convinced of their own superiority:

> The entire Grail Company consists of an elect who are fate's dar-lings in this world and the next, to be always counted among those who have won undying glory. Whence that seed was carried out of the land of the Grail, it was made fruitful and the scourge of dis-honor to he who reaped it.[9]

Wolfram's ideas are extended in a very long poem written by a certain Albrecht, author of a *New Titurel,* in which Montsalvaesche is no longer a fortress but the Temple of the Grail, where strange ceremonies take place presided over by the Templars. Their "brotherly" aspect is stressed even more strongly than ever here, grouped as they are in an indestructible community that is the sole keeper of the unique message that will inevitably one day dominate the world and rid it of sin.

It seems beyond the shadow of a doubt that Wolfram (and those who followed him on this path) consciously identifies the Grail guardians as Templars. But he is not satisfied with portraying them as a community of soldier-monks. He makes them into a secret hermetic society with its own rituals, a necessary initiation, and, especially, a goal of world domination. And the reason for this conquest of the world? It can be found in the *New Titurel:* the extermination of sin. The goal is a noble one. But in looking at it again, it is not so far from the famous statement "Kill them all! God will know his own!"[10]

---

9. Markale, *The Grail,* 128–60.

10. Simon de Montfort, leader of the Crusade against the Albigensians, said this when asked by the troops under his command how they could distinguish the "innocent" townsfolk of Béziers from the Cathars. —*Trans.*

Did Wolfram know the true secret of the Templars? Everything seems to be pointing that way. Wolfram was aware of quite a bit and was privy to a marginal tradition that was beginning to express itself through the means of a certain illuminism for which Bavaria was the precise center. Germany at the beginning of the thirteenth century was, in fact, a crucible for a number of apparently contradictory influences, and from this emerged a spirituality that was as far from orthodox as was Cistercian mysticism. Minnesingers' poetry was the prelude to a literature that went beyond the strictly courtly stage to that of hermeticism. The profile of Jacob Bohème was already looming on the horizon and a completely heretical tendency of thought was taking shape in apparently orthodox works. A taste for mysterious rituals and initiations was developing. The number of alchemists was growing. The peculiar science of traditional alchemy was not only the quest for methods of transforming lead into gold, but also a personal asceticism that had as much bearing on the mind as on matter and which sought to discover the great secrets that govern the world. Knowledge of these secrets would enable domination of the world through mastery over religion, seizure of political and economic power, and the exclusive use of science.

Of course, such experimentation and ascetic tendencies were reserved for the intellectual and spiritual elite—you couldn't have one without the other during that time when the profane was still not distinguished from the sacred. Ordinary mortals were totally excluded. This explains the preference for secrecy that characterized such undertakings, and the birth of what is known as esotericism as the deliberate intention to transmit only coded messages reserved for those who know how to read between the lines. This esotericism infiltrated everywhere, transferring new meanings onto symbols from the past. Wolfram von Eschenbach evolved in the midst of all this intellectual ferment that was drawing farther and farther away from an officially sanctioned model. It was in this environment that he deliberately hung the Templars to the Grail theme.

We know that in *Parzival,* the Grail theme is far removed from the Celtic model still visible in Chrétien de Troyes' work and still completely intact in the Welsh version. For the German author the theme has taken a significant detour and been enriched by numeorous elements that are not only Germanic but also borrowed from the East, from both the Muslim and the Indo-Buddhist traditions.[11] It is for this reason that we can say that Wolfram provided a Germano-Iranian version of the legend.

It remains no less true that the Grail occupies a very secondary place in *Parzival*. It seems that the Templars, keepers of a secret tradition, are the most important characters, or are at least those to whom Wolfram wished to draw attention. The initiatory aspect of the quest seems to prevail over its mystical aspect. In fact, it is not through a long and perilous asceticism that one attains Montsalvaesche and moreover enters it, but rather because one has been mysteriously designated in advance by the letters that appear on the stone fallen from the heavens. Becoming a Grail guardian is equal to becoming not only a monk or a priest but a warrior as well. Was Wolfram seeking to reconcile the spiritual man with the physical man? Without a doubt, and this is completely in the spirit of Bernard of Clairvaux, although it goes singularly beyond the personal asceticism preached by the Cistercian monk. Kundry, the strange sorceress with numerous guises and conflicting faces, says to Parzival: "You have won peace of soul and the joy of the flesh in a faithful desire." This is an allusion to the hero's faithfulness to his wife, Condwiramur. But what is the price to be paid for achieving this harmony of the two fundamental tendencies of the human being who has his head fixed on heaven but his two feet on the ground? This is where everything becomes ambiguous.

Parzival, who is the elect par excellence, the one who has been so long and anxiously awaited, has succeeded in rediscovering the road to Montsalvaesche, though it is Kundry who sought him out and led him along many tumultuous paths because Parzival's name was inscribed upon the stone. Parzival cures his uncle, King Anfortas, of his humiliating wound simply by asking: "Uncle, from what are you suffering?" Parzival is a miracle-working king whose thaumaturgy lifts him onto the throne of the Grail. He establishes his power at Montsalvaesche. He sends his brother Fairefils to the East. He rules in secrecy over an ideal kingdom as

11. Markale, *The Grail*, 151–83.

the priest-king whose authority is twofold, a synthesis of the two functions embodied in India by Mithra and Varuna. He does not need to share his power with a priest—or a druid or a Brahman—because he is himself a priest. But is he truly a priest of God? It seems he is instead a priest of a bizarre and somewhat heterodox cult, that of the Grail, for the Grail, even with the word *holy* attached to it, remains a magic and symbolic object.

King Parzival has a son, the boy whom tradition names Lohengrin, and who would become Lorrain Garin in the chansons de geste. In any case he is the Swan Knight who weds the duchess of Brabant on the condition the duchess never asks him his name: "A knight led by a swan was sent to her from Montsalvaesche. This was the knight that God had destined for her."[12] We know the rest of this story, which Wagner—again—magnificently set to music. The duchess asks him who he is: "Then his friend the swan brought forth a beautiful yet flimsy craft. The knight left in parting some precious relics that he had owned: a sword, a horn, and a ring."[13] But he also leaves the duchess some handsome children, who by themselves were the founders of a lineage.

Was it common knowlege that the conqueror of Jerusalem, Godefroy de Bouillon, claimed descent from Lohengrin and thus from Parzival, king of the Grail? Some claim that Godefroy de Bouillon was the founder of the so-called Order of Sion, which in turn is claimed to have inspired the founding of the Knights Templar. We always seem to find ourselves back at the beginning, even if this beginning is surrounded by the tenacious fog of legend. There is good reason, however, to ask if it is truly a legend, or why it is that someone cleverly connected a number of legends. Wolfram von Eschenbach appears to have been definitively informed in this regard, which would be why he placed the Templars at Montsalvaesche to guard the Grail. This would be an argument—the only argument, but a very significant one—in favor of the existence of the Priory of Sion, whatever its actual name may have been.

---

12. *Parzival*, 39.

13. *Parzival*, 240.

The Templars would have been created, then, to guard the Grail. But we must know what twelfth- and thirteenth-century authors, including Wolfram, meant by Grail. It does not seem that the Grail was truly considered to be an object before its Cistercian recuperation, drawn from the Gospel of Nicodemus, in which the mysterious vessel was filled with the blood of Jesus, who died on the Cross. It was hoped that this manifestation would transform it into an instrument of propaganda in favor of the worship of the Precious Blood. The different forms the Grail has taken testifies to the fact that it was considered to be only a symbol.

In the majority of texts related to the Arthurian tradition, the Grail is designated as the Holy Grail. In the manuscripts this is usually transcribed as Sangreal or Sangral. Here we find a subtlety that is quite in keeping with the tone of medieval authors, ever ready to make plays on words in the interest of transmitting a message in innocuous terms. Wolfram, for instance, who always entrenches himself behind the authority of a certain Kyôt or Guyot of Provence, is making fun of his readers. His Kyôt or Guyot does not exist. It is a simple play on words using the old French verb *guiller,* meaning "to deceive." But at that time it was considered good form to take a stand behind an informant who held the true version of a legend, and sometimes to do so using the tricks of words with double meaning. If we split Sangreal in the standard fashion, we end up with San-Gréal, or Saint Graal [Holy Grail]. But if we break it up as Sang-Réal, moving the point of division by one letter completely changes the meaning and it becomes Sang Royal [royal blood]. But what is this royal blood?

In all the tales of the Arthurian epic in which Arthur is the pivot of the ideal society, the hero of the Grail Quest, whether Parzival, Perceval, Lancelot of the Lake, or his son Galahad, is part of a royal lineage, an initiatory lineage, that sometimes goes back to David. It is necessary that the Grail King, who is awaited so impatiently to restore fertility to the slumbering kingdom of the Waste Land, be the issue of this initiatory royal blood.[14]

---

14. I have elaborated on this point in *Montségur et l'énigme carthare,* 289–302 (the chapter on the royal blood).

The task involves not only healing the wounded Fisher King, but also—and especially—restoring life to the kingdom whose lands are stricken with sterility. This symbol appears quite clearly. The Templars have been charged (according to Wolfram) with the responsibility of watching over the purity of the Grail (the royal blood), even if this requires the systematic elimination of those who wish to approach this royal blood without having been chosen. When these Templars have found the right person to be their king, the kingdom will be regenerated (sin will be abolished from it). This may remind us of certain fairly recent events involving black militias blindly obeying their predestined leader, purifying the world in blood and fire in the hope of seeing a new world ruled by a Great Monarch.

Such a comparison may be shocking to some, but it was Wolfram who put it into words and the ideologues of Nationalist Socialism were not mistaken about its meaning. Parzival, for them, was the mythological archetype of their activity. Wolfram knew full well who the Templars really were.

Philip the Fair himself, in seeking to bear the title bellator rex, wished to become the Grail King, the keeper of the royal blood that he hoped to pass down to his descendants. Unfortunately, the Templars did not want him as their king. He was probably not the one they were expecting and his name had not been inscribed upon the stone. At this point Philip the Fair, who also knew full well who the Templars were, set everything in motion to destroy them because he could not allow such a formidable company to choose another as king of the Grail and turn against him. It was a question of life or death. Philip the Fair won, and the Templars lost. Here myth becomes one with history.

Is this an exaggeration? Let's examine the web spun by the Templars over Europe and especially France. What was its purpose? The Templar Order is the culmination of the West's civilizing lineage, and this outcome had been prepared well in advance. The order's mission was in the West; the defense of the Holy Land was merely a means to that end—a means of knightly probation and for gaining power because the Templars' publicity was centered on this defensive role. The donations the order received were certainly for this defense and it is unlikely they would have received any if their true role in the West was revealed.[15] The ritual of denial can now be seen for what it is: a fundamental belief in a Christ-King who no longer has anything in common with the vague image of a crucified man. But as in any secret society with an initiatory structure, only certain brothers knew the doctrine behind this ritual. The others, obscure men without rank, simply followed orders after taking their oath of obedience. They spat on the cross and marched off to fight and die in battle. This did not hinder in any way their belief in God. But they were being used to prepare a very earthly kingdom for a time following the cure of the old wounded king, when it would regenerate and grow green again, as it was in the beginning when Earth was still virginal.

Again we turn to the words of Wolfram von Eschenbach:

> A happy fate was often offered the knights of the Grail: They give succor to others and are themselves aided by destiny. They welcome to their castle young children of noble birth and beautiful face. At times a kingdom may find itself without a leader; if the people of this domain are submissive to God and He wishes them to take a king selected from the Grail company, they will honor His wish. The people must respect the king who has been chosen in this manner for he is protected by the blessing of God. It is in secret that God sends out His elect.[16]

It is unquestionably through a legendary tale, and thanks to Wolfram von Eschenbach, that we can seek and gain a better understanding of history. This is probably why so much passion has been expended searching through obscure underground corridors: There is the hope of discovering a myth of much greater reality than any authenticated document.

---

15. Louis Charpentier, *Les Mystères Templiers* (Paris: R. Laffont, 1967), 74.

16. *Parzival*, 57.

13

The Temple in Ruins

WITH HIS PAPAL BULL of March 22, 1312, Pope Clement V abolished the Order of the Templars. But this was not an act of judgment as much as it was simply an act of authority, the decision of an authority to dissolve an organization that, when all is said and done, was only subordinate to it. This dissolution, however, in no way concerned the fate of the members of that order. From the moment when the order ceased to exist, they became no more than isolated individuals, each personally responsible for his actions. With his papal bull of May 6, 1312, Clement V delivered into the hands of secular justice those Templars who had been found guilty or who, having confessed their guilt, had fallen back into error. Those found innocent would receive a pension and be given admission into the monastic order of their choice. This apparently quite liberal arrangement was subject to the pleasure of the king of France and pertained to only subaltern members of the Temple. The others ended up in prison or on the stake.

It had already become necessary to resolve the delicate problem of Templar property. Certainly everything, at least what was in French territory, had already been seized by agents of the king, but only temporarily. Clement V had claimed this property for the Church in order to use it for the Holy Land, but the king of France—and other sovereigns— preferred to take on the administration of the property himself in order to personally profit from it. There was a clear declaration to this effect shortly before the papal decision concerning the devolution of Templar properties and after discussions took place in the back rooms of the Vienna Council and throughout the four corners of Europe. All involved were looking to enrich themselves personally in a shameless scramble for this wealth.

The pope felt the simplest solution was to turn over all Templar property to the Hospitaller Order. Because the Hospitallers and Templars were similarly structured and were often neighbors, the transmission would be easy, and because the Hospitallers' objectives were quite close to the those of the Templars, this appeared to be the fairest solution. During the entire time the affair had dragged on, the Hospitallers were careful to avoid taking a stand either for or against the Templars. They were eager not to draw too much attention to themselves, being fully aware that what had happened to the Templars could also happen to them.

But the Western sovereigns were little disposed to the distribution of the Templars' property to the Hospitallers. Some wished to maintain ownership of the property they were now administering, while others distrusted the Hospitallers. Still others argued in favor of the creation of a new order. Nobody was in agreement and the pope found himself in the minority at the council, for the majority of cardinals deemed that the Templars' guilt had not been established convincingly.

It was Enguerrand de Marigny, another minion of Philip the Fair, who found a way through this roadblock. After many fruitless discussions, he eventually convinced the king to accept a compromise with the pope. On May 2, 1312, Clement V issued the bull *Ad providam*, awarding the Templar properties to the Hospitallers, with those in Spain and Portugal held in reserve. In the kingdom of Valencia, the Templar properties, combined with those of the Hospitallers, would be distributed to a new order founded in Aragon, the Order of Montesa; and in Portugal they would go to the new Order of Christ, made up almost exclusively of former Templars. In Castille, however, the greater part of Templar property had already been appropriated.

The Hospitallers of St. John of Jerusalem therefore recouped the lion's share of the domains and goods of their rivals. But they did not do much with it and the Hospitaller Order, which would later become the Order of the Knights of Malta, was in a state of collapse. We have to conclude that the time was no longer propitious for orders of soldier-monks who no longer had the Crusades to justify their existence. Following the whole affair, the Templars generally could be divided into three groups: those who were condemned, those who were found guilty but reconciled with the Church, and those who were found innocent. Obviously left out of this equation are the Templars who were fortunate enough to escape the dragnet, both those who fled abroad and those who contrived to be overlooked. What became of them? This is a difficult question to answer because, in principle, they did everything in their power to avoid ever becoming a subject of discussion.

It is these Templars who vanished clandestinely who have especially excited the imaginations of chroniclers, historians, and contemporary authors, particularly from the eighteenth century to the present. In fact, it is thanks to these authors that the claim can be made that "the Templars are among us." It still remains to be seen what condition they might be in, for like it or not, the Temple is in ruins on the top of the cliff.[1]

It was essentially in the milieu of eighteenth-century Freemasonry that the tradition of the occult permanence of the Temple began to spread. The origin of this tradition can be traced back to the knight Ramsey, an English Catholic living in France who—it is not known on what real basis—wished to establish a connection between Freemasonry and the Crusades. A postulate serves as the starting point of this story: The Masons—in other words, brotherhoods of builders, who were protected if not animated by the Templars—would have had access to secret documents (of course, rediscovered in Jerusalem) that revealed the ancient wisdom of the builders of the Temple of Solomon. Then, around 1760, certain German lodges, at odds with the egalitarianism and rationalism of operative Masonry, introduced into speculative Masonry a hierarchy, grades, and, most important, secrecy. These lodges appealed to history

---

1. From a poem by Leconte de Lisle that has nothing to do with the Templars.

for justification of their actions and grafted this speculative Masonry onto the Temple, regarded as the holder of great secrets from the past.

This is all speculation, of course, but it does not prevent contemporary Masonic brothers, during certain ceremonies, from rendering homage to Jacques de Molay and cursing Philip the Fair and his successors. There is no question that the alleged link between the Temple and Freemasonry poses some delicate problems, but this is not the proper forum in which to examine them. The affiliation appears much more symbolic than real and in this particular case is not historically open for debate.

We know that French Freemasonry is an offshoot of Scottish Freemasonry. Independent of the secret societies that toiled in the shadows of the seventeenth century for the restoration of the Stuart monarchy, the first lodge, founded in Paris in 1726, was established under the patronage of St. Thomas of Canterbury (Thomas à Becket). Following many ruptures and expulsions, this lodge became the Grand Orient of France. In 1756, Baron de Hund created a dissidence in the Scottish Rite and established the "rectified Scottish Rite" or "strict observance." This movement found fertile soil, especially in Germany, and influenced people like Mozart, Lessing, and Goethe. Baron de Hund, seeking justification for his dissidence, restyled an ancient tradition to contemporary tastes. This tradition is obviously one that cannot be verified, but it insisted on the permanence of the Templar Order. In fact, it avowed that a certain number of Templars who managed to evade Philip the Fair's police net found refuge in Germany, Spain, and Great Britain. This probably was true, as far as it goes. But it also served as the basis on which was grafted this story of the Templars' history after their demise.

Apparently, two hundred thirty-seven Templars, including chaplains, knights, and artisans, took refuge in the powerful commandery of London. Among them was an alchemist described as an authentic keeper of the great secrets of the royal art, a man named Guidon de Montanor. He took on as his favorite disciple and, in some ways, spiritual son another escaped Templar, Gaston de la Pierre Phoebus. Several months later, fearing the maneuvers of England's king, Edward II, the majority of emigrant Templars left London and sought refuge in Scotland, where they could depend on the loyalty of King Robert the Bruce. They established themselves on the Isle of Mull, where they found several French Templars already incorporated into the Scottish *ost*. Having heard of the death of Jacques de Molay, these Templars, in accordance with their Rule, elected as successor to the post of grand master a certain Pierre d'Aumont. Meanwhile, Gaston de la Pierre Phoebus, encouraged by Guidon de Montanor and protected by the king, created a college of alchemists of the Templar tradition to whom he communicated the secrets and mysteries of the order.

Then, because they were all appalled by the attitude of Pope Clement V, they decided to leave the Roman Catholic Church and establish their own, a truly evangelical church that was keeper of the wisdom and traditions of the Templars. As a symbol they adopted the *pelican in his mercy,* a heraldic and Rosicrucian term that evokes a pelican in its nest, wings spread, feeding six of its young on its own flesh and blood. This symbol was subsequently adopted by the Masonic Order of the Knights of the Rose + Cross and the Black Eagle. This was how a sacred college was erected, the heirs of which can still be found in Scotland.

However, in 1316, when Cardinal Jacques d'Euse, an enthusiast for alchemy and the hermetic sciences, became pope under the name of John XXII, Gaston de la Pierre Phoebus and twenty-seven of his companions decided to make a discreet journey back to France. Their first stop was Avignon, where John XXII gave Gaston de la Pierre Phoebus an audience and promised him his protection. He gave him a mission to return to Scotland and bring back to Avignon the elite of Robert the Bruce's brothers in arms.

But because the roads were infested with brigands, before leaving on this dangerous journey Gaston de la Pierre Phoebus took the precaution of confiding the essential secrets of his knowledge to a prior in the Hospitallers of St. John, a former Templar who lived at Pont-Saint-Esprit. Well for him that he did so, for he and thirteen of his companions perished in an ambush not far from Mans. Only five of his band survived and made it back to Scotland. They returned to Avignon with a company led by Jacques de Via, who was the nephew of Pope John XXII.

The prior of Pont-Saint-Esprit had, over time, fashioned a new Templar Rule. The sole and last remaining keeper of the secrets of the Temple, he passed them on to those he deemed worthy of receiving them—to Jacques de Via, in particular. A college of thirty-three sages was elected, which placed at its head Jacques de Via, of authentic succession from Gaston de la Pierre Phoebus. A Templar church developed but remained secret, which did not prevent the poisoning murder of Jacques de Via on May 6, 1317. His successors called themselves the elder brothers of the Rose + Cross, and the group is claimed to exist down to this day.

This story reveals a great deal about the impact of the Templars upon the intellectual and spiritual life of the West. This mysterious order composed of warriors as well as sages could not disappear without a trace. In every disaster there is at least one survivor to tell what actually happened. No, not every single Templar could die. And no matter if there are some inconsistencies in this narrative—namely, that on the date of the founding of the order in June 1312, with the election of a new grand master, Jacques de Molay was not yet dead. And what part does alchemy play in all of this? It would seem that the Templars should primarily have been combatants, administrators, and financiers, and not philosophers spending their lives in their libraries or laboratories.

But there is another story that is parallel to this one. Do not forget that in Scotland the Templars elected as their grand master Jacques d'Aumont. It is from him that branches of what we could call today the neo-Templars claim descent. Their story deserves a hearing.

When Jacques de Molay realized that no hope remained for either him or the Templar Order, his sole thought was of preserving, propagating, and perpetuating the Templars' knowledge and fundamental principles, which reached deep into the remote past. It is claimed that several days before his execution, he revealed certain secrets to his nephew, the count of Beaujeu, and ordered him to go down into the tomb of the former grand masters and take from beneath one of the coffins a triangular-shaped crystal jewel box. The count of Beaujeu obeyed and returned to Jacques de Molay with the box. Molay, satisfied with the successful passing of the test he had imposed upon his nephew, then made a total confession to him, revealing all the mysteries, and then had him swear an oath that he would do everything possible, until the end of time, to revive the order. Molay then entrusted the count with the jewel box, which contained a relic given to the order by King Baudoin of Jerusalem—nothing less than the index finger from the right hand of St. John the Baptist. Last, he gave him three keys that would allow him to open a chest hidden in the tomb of Molay's predecessor.

Following the death of Jacques de Molay, Beaujeu made contact with nine Templars who had escaped this ordeal and with them went down into the mausoleum. There they took the chest and emptied two hollow pillars that had been filled with great treasures. They then sought to place this precious hoard in safe storage in what we are told was Cyprus, but why not Gisors?

Beaujeu was unanimously elected grand master by his companions. But better to conceal the order he was restoring, he instituted new ceremonies that he disguised under cover of the Temple of Solomon. Beaujeu's successor was Jacques d'Aumont, who founded a lineage of grand masters that persists even into this time. But great care is taken not to disclose the actual identity of the grand master. It is is a mystery. Yet another one.[2]

It was during the First Empire and before a large audience that an Order of the Temple officially reemerged, one that did not make secrecy its cornerstone. The individual behind this reappearance was Bernard-Raymond Fabré-Palaprat, born in Cordes in 1773. He was most likely a doctor, but he is more easily classified as a charlatan. One fine day he abruptly declared himself Jacques de Molay's successor and transformed the club over which he presided into a Templar sect of which he, obviously, was the grand master.

He justified his claims by displaying a treasure consisting of Jacques de Molay's helmet and several bones that were supposedly collected from the ashes of Molay's execution. Furthermore, he had a document created in Gothic letters that denoted the succession of all the grand masters of

2. For more on all these traditions, see *Atlantis*, nos. 215, 216, and 217.

the temple from the time of Jesus Christ. Moreover, after the Regency he used an authentic Masonic affiliation, which gave an appearance of veracity to this document, which his contemporaries studied seriously for several years before categorically rejecting it.

Of course, this new Templar Order received donations and even sold titles of nobility—or what were claimed to be such titles—to naïve souls with a desire to regild their family coats of arms. It also sold insignias, decorations, and ceremonial vestments, from which the grand master profited handily. Its success was enormous.

Napoleon himself fell into the snare. Fascinated by the Templars' history, he encouraged Fabré-Palaprat in his undertakings and lent him his personal guard for a solemn ceremony that took place on March 28, 1808, at the Saint-Paul- Saint-Louis Church of Paris in memory of Jacques de Molay. The Mass was celebrated by Father Clouet, chaplain of Notre-Dame, who in his sermon extolled the piety and military virtues of the Templars, defenders of the Holy Land. The church was filled with everybody who was anybody in Paris during that era.

This new Temple outlived the Empire. In 1833 Fabré-Palaprat organized a large ceremony in the Court of Miracles. There was a long period of prayers for the sovereign (who as the son of a regicide was therefore of a line that had avenged Jacques de Molay), and apparently scantily clad canonesses collected donations, an essential element for this kind of ritual. This was the apotheosis of Fabré-Palaprat, who was then beginning to exhibit signs of mental derangement. He died in 1838 and his successor was an Englishman, a certain Admiral Smith. Shortly before his death, Fabré-Palaprat had taken as his ecclesiastical primate one Father Chatel. A rift had developed between them and the two men charged each other with being a charlatan and an imposter. Father Chatel ended his days as a grocer, but he did find time enough to establish his own church, which, it appears, still exists.

As for Admiral Smith, he died in 1840 after having fulfilled his Templar duty in Algeria, where he fought alongside the French against the infidels. His succession provided the opportunity for a number of rifts and scandals and this new Templar Order died amid total indifference. But there are those who whisper that it found a way to be reborn from its own ashes.

Throughout the world there are a countless number of groups claiming direct descent from the Templars and to be the authentic representatives of that tradition. For the most part these "orders" are perfectly well known and perfectly official. We find the same phenomenon here as with the druids; there have never before been so many neo-druids as there are today. Do the members of these Templar "orders," who generally come from the upper class, remember that their remote predecessors "never combed their hair, rarely bathed, and preferred to appear with their hair in disarray, their face streaked with dirt and burned black by the sun"? If there really are any authentic Templars in our day, they have taken steps to remain unnoticed.[3]

The Temple is in ruins. Philip the Fair and Pope Clement V have been accused of being responsible for that destruction. This is no doubt true, but only on the surface. The Temple had to have carried the seeds of its own destruction within. At the beginning of the fourteenth century it had become a social and economic institution that no longer conformed to its founding ideals. The Holy Land had been definitively lost for the Chris-

---

3. In any case, the Templar spirit remains—not to mention the Society of Jesus, which, from the sixteenth century onward, has spread across the globe, forming an extremely powerful network that answers only to the papacy (one has spoken of a Black International). However, we can establish comparisons with contemporary organizations that do not invoke at all the sponsorship of the Temple. It is impossible not to think of this worldwide organization that still makes the news today. Its basic premise is mystical: It involves the creation on earth of a veritable kingdom of God through resolute combat against materialism and through guiding the human community to live in the Spirit. The means used are quite close to those of the Templars. First, those who belong to the sect are firm in their convictions and work for the greater good of the community. What difference is there between them and monks? But this allows them to have a steady supply of cheap manual labor. This sect receives donations and makes them flourish. It administers them so well that it owns possibly the fifth or sixth largest fortune in the world. It owns domains, lands, industrial operations (where those who receive their charity work), fleets, shares in global businesses, newspaper groups and other media outlets. This enterprise is like an octopus that is diversified and active throughout the entire world. Its setup is reminiscent of the Templars' web. And like the Templars, it has its "infidels" to fight, in this instance the Marxists, or those who are labeled as such. It is for this struggle that it receives donations, as did the Templars, to ensure the victory of Christianity over the enemies of the faith. And in certain countries where it is solidly established, such as the United States and some nations of Latin America, it has a profound political influence. All of this presents remarkable similarities with the Templars.

tians and Ramon Lulle's flights of fancy concerning the Christian conversion of the Muslims had little chance of being realized, even if Philip the Fair had succeeded in being elected grand master of the new order he wished to create out of the Temple, the essential pivot of this embryonic power.

In reality, the destruction of the Templars marked the end of a world that still held illusions about possible cooperation between civil and religious power. The myth of Mithra and Varuna, the druid-king pair, the legend of King Arthur and the magician Merlin, the emperor and the pope—all formed part of an ancient traditional design. And the Templars were representatives of this design. The Templars, in fact, "by their dual nature as monks and knights, embodied an important aspect of spiritual authority, differing from the papacy but one the papacy fully accepted and which, in the thinking of their founder, St. Bernard, should, precisely through its original character deriving both from the 'brahman' and 'kshatriya' classes, ensure the maintenance of the harmonious balance of secular society in the traditional orthodox perspective."[4] But the Temple may have had secret intentions. There is always a profound gap between stated intentions and their realization.

If it was just that simple, if the Templars had no other mission than protecting pilgrims to the Holy Land, if they had only been victims of arbitrary authority, if Philip the Fair had not been an odious tyrant capable of the worst crimes to fill the coffers of the kingdom, where would the mystery be that the Templars pose to each of us?

Were the Templars poor martyrs of the Christian faith facing a base king and a wicked pope? Let's not be so naïve. Once we have seen the entire Templar dossier, including the mythological elements, it is impossible to believe in their innocence. They denied Jesus and spat upon the cross. Were they forced to do so? Yes, but they did it. And exactly who was it that forced these poor Templars to perform these hardly orthodox actions? By all evidence the Order of the Temple was dual in nature, but not only, as is commonly said, in being a synthesis of those who pray and those who fight. It was dual because of the secrecy surrounding it, a

---

4. Jean Hani, *La Royauté sacré* (Paris: Trédaniel, 1984), 260.

secrecy that must have been concealing something. The Temple was a dark order. Or rather, there was a dark Temple to which the other order submitted blindly. Let's listen to the words of Wolfram von Eschenbach, who knew the whole story: "Since that time the stone has been guarded by those God himself has chosen." And when a kingdom is without a king, a man of the Grail—in other words, a Templar is sent there: "and the people must respect the king who has been chosen in this manner." And finally, "It is in secret that God sends out his elect." The distinguishing feature of a dark order is to make people believe that it does not exist. The Jerusalem the Templars allegedly defended has no more spatial or temporal reality than the Montsalvaesche of Grail legend.

This is where the secret of the Templars lies. Despite torture and physical cruelty, those who knew did not speak of it. But what they did not say was inadmissible and incomprehensible to those who sought to make them speak and, in the final analysis, would have been found totally unbearable. Like the true Christian message that has been carefully and systematically eliminated from the Gospels, not all truths are good to hear. Clement V knew this full well, which is why he sought to avoid any judgment of the Templars by claiming power of authority, a sacred act to which he had full right.

The question is no longer about knowing who was innocent or guilty in this whole affair that has moved far beyond the simple historical context in which some have sought to cage it. The question belongs to an entirely different domain, that of the mysticism of St. Bernard and that of the Holy Grail legend. There should be no surprise that it touches on a disturbing element because on this higher plane there is neither good nor evil, neither black nor white.

The question is threefold: What exactly did the Templars know? What was the secret they died to protect? It was an inadmissible secret, at least in their time—is it still so today? The secret of the Templars lies in the ruins of the Temple. The ruins of the Temple are now everywhere and nowhere. Perhaps the secret lies sleeping in the underground corridors of Gisors, protected by tons of rubble and a layer of concrete. The main thing is to know what we are looking for.

Index